Peter Chippindale was a staff reporter on the *Guardian* for seven years, and spent two years as a reporter for London Weekend Television. He has freelanced extensively for a number of publications and is the author of five other books. He is married and lives in Islington.

Chris Horrie is an award-winning magazine journalist and has contributed to a large number of magazines, newspapers and television programmes. This is his first book. He lives in Hackney.

DISASTER!
The rise and fall of
News on Sunday

Anatomy of a business failure

Peter Chippindale and Chris Horrie

SPHERE BOOKS LIMITED

SPHERE BOOKS LTD

Published by the Penguin Group
27 Wrights Lane, London w8 5tz, England
Viking Penguin Inc., 40 West 23rd Street, New York, New York 10010, USA
Penguin Books Australia Ltd, Ringwood, Victoria, Australia
Penguin Books Canada Ltd, 2801 John Street, Markham, Ontario, Canada l3r 1b4
Penguin Books (NZ) Ltd, 182–190 Wairau Road, Auckland 10, New Zealand

Penguin Books Ltd, Registered Offices: Harmondsworth, Middlesex, England

First published by Sphere Books Ltd 1988

Made and printed in Great Britain by
Richard Clay Ltd, Bungay, Suffolk
Filmset in Monophoto Bembo

It is Sunday afternoon, preferably before the war. The wife is already asleep in the armchair, and the children have been sent out for a nice long walk. You put your feet up on the sofa, settle your spectacles on your nose, and open the News of the World. *Roast beef and Yorkshire, or roast pork and apple sauce, followed up by suet pudding and driven home, as it were, by a cup of mahogany-brown tea, have put you in just the right mood. Your pipe is drawing sweetly, the sofa cushions are soft underneath you, the fire is well alight, the air is warm and stagnant. In these blissful circumstances, what is it that you want to read about?*

Naturally, about a murder . . .

George Orwell, *Tribune*, 15 February 1946

Publisher's note

This book is the history of News on Sunday Publishing plc, which was established to produce the original *News on Sunday*.

The company went into voluntary receivership on 16 June 1987. *News on Sunday* published after that date was a wholly separate newspaper published by Growfar, which purchased the title and the assets from the Receiver.

Acknowledgements

The authors would like to thank the many people both within and outside *News on Sunday* who agreed to be interviewed, sometimes at great length, or otherwise made information available to us. Thanks are especially due to John Pilger, Keith Sutton, Gerry Taylor, Clive Thornton, Owen Oyston, Brian Whitaker, Alan Hayling, Chris Walsh, Hilary Wainwright, Nick Horsley, Anthony Everett, Christine Jackson, Mike Taylor, Brian Astley and John Bartle. Several other people talked to us on an 'off the record' basis.

Useful insights were also provided by Jill Armstrong, Cynthia Cockburn, Liz Cooper, Polly Pattullo, John Palmer, Carlos Guarita, Carmel Bedford, Mike Power, Bill Packford, Melanie McFadyean, Mike Rohan, John Hoyland, Henry Stewart, Roy Barber, Eugenie Verney, Kerry Marcus, Pat Edlin, Colin Jacobson, Rick Anderson, David Pallister, Alison Macdonald, Jon Bowman, Terry Thomas, Julian Allitt and Margaret Rooke. Our special thanks go to David Leigh for his encouragement and support.

The biggest thank-you of all goes to Sally and Rosie, who read parts of the manuscript and patiently put up with the strains imposed by authors writing to a very tight deadline.

NEWS
ON SUNDAY

EDITORIAL CHARTER

News on Sunday's Editorial Charter has been drawn up by the paper's founders to set out the main editorial principles on which the paper is based. It is not intended to tie the editor's hands, but to set out in broad terms what the paper stands for and what it does not. A Founders' Trust has been set up with special rights to help ensure that the paper will continue to abide by the principles set out in the charter.

1. NEWS ON SUNDAY is a socialist publication. The open democratic nature of its socialism is spelt out in the principles outlined in the Charter.

2. NEWS ON SUNDAY is and will remain independent of all political parties and institutions. Its attitude to any political party will be guided by the extent to which its policies and practices accord with the general aims of *News on Sunday* as outlined in the Charter.

3. NEWS ON SUNDAY recognises that Britain is a society based on the unequal ownership of wealth, prosperity and power, and will seek to inform the readers of such inequalities, their causes and effects.

4. NEWS ON SUNDAY believes that everybody has the right to basic necessities – such as housing, education and health care – in the form of public services and a minimum income sufficient to maintain a decent standard of living.

5. NEWS ON SUNDAY is opposed to all forms of sexism, racism and all discrimination which denies the capabilities and potential of the individual.

   News on Sunday will express its commitment to anti-racism and anti-sexism both in its employment practices and in its news and feature coverage. It will reflect the multi-cultural composition of British society.

   As an employer *News on Sunday* is committed to providing genuine equality of opportunity. It will adopt the Equal Opportunities Statement from GLEB and will adhere to the Campaign for Press and Broadcasting Freedom's Code of Conduct on Sexism, the NUJ's guidelines on race and reporting on racist organisations, the NUJ's Equality Council guidelines on the coverage of homosexuality.

6. NEWS ON SUNDAY will support workers and their trade unions when they take industrial action, except in so far as action is in direct conflict with the principles in the Charter, and will seek to increase understanding of the origin and background of such conflicts.

7. NEWS ON SUNDAY will be internationalist in outlook. It will aim to increase understanding of all people and their cultures, particularly those striving for participatory democracy. The paper will support groups of people seeking to gain more control over their own lives. It will align itself with those whose beliefs are close to the beliefs expressed in the Charter.

   News on Sunday will oppose the division of the world into power blocks.

   News on Sunday will support the right to self-determination of all peoples. It will oppose interference by foreign states in the affairs of a country. The paper will support people fighting to free their country from foreign occupation, from racist regimes or from any form of dictatorship. *News on Sunday* will seek to increase understanding of the history and causes of such conflicts.

8. NEWS ON SUNDAY believes that the root cause of the present troubles in Ireland is the British presence in that country and the first step towards a solution can only be started once that presence is removed.

9. NEWS ON SUNDAY supports the civil liberties embodied in the NCCL Charter 1985. It will oppose moves towards increased police and military power and will support moves towards greater democratic control and accountability of state forces and freedom of information.

10. NEWS ON SUNDAY recognises the dangers of damaging the ecological balance of the world. The paper will advocate the conservation of natural resources, habitats and species and will support appropriate campaigns and movements.

11. NEWS ON SUNDAY opposes the imposition of suffering on animals in pursuit of profit or pleasure. Where such suffering is integral to medical research, *News on Sunday* will actively encourage alternative methods of research.

12. NEWS ON SUNDAY supports the demand for the worldwide abolition of nuclear, chemical and biological weapons. The paper believes that the unilateral abandonment by Britain of nuclear weapons, bases and alliances is a vital step towards this eventual goal.

Typeset and Printed by Calvert's Press (TU) Workers' Co-operative 01-729 1474

Preface

News on Sunday was an unmitigated business disaster by any standards. An investment of £6.5 million produced three poor editions of a Sunday tabloid newspaper before the company was effectively bankrupt. Each copy of the paper that was sold cost the shareholders £5.38 – more than the price of this book.

The paper was unusually financed, with the majority of the investment coming from the general funds of various trade unions and the pension funds of local authorities throughout the country. This meant that much of the cost was borne by workers and old people; but at the same time the blip which it caused on the financial graphs of the mammoth funds was barely noticeable. It wasn't the financial disaster, but the political one, which really counted. *News on Sunday* came at a time when the left in Britain had set itself the task of either reorganizing and modernizing for the 1980s and 1990s, or dying. The paper was supposed to give the left a new lease of life. Instead it turned out to be another nail in its coffin.

The authors do not seek to attack any of the attitudes and policies of the new left politics which the paper represented. They personally share many of them. But this is not a book about theory, it is a book about practice, and we hope it goes some way towards explaining to those who invested money, time or faith in the project what went wrong. We do not pretend that this is the definitive history of *News on Sunday*. There is talk of an official version to emerge from the smouldering ruins of the paper's labyrinthine committee structure in years to come. If – or when – it does, we look to it to set us straight if we have erred in any way in interpreting the extraordinary events in the paper's short and stormy life.

We cannot be entirely objective, as we both worked for the paper in senior editorial positions. Coincidentally we joined at the same time, ten weeks before launch, both 'headhunted' at short notice.

Chippindale joined in London as Special Projects Editor and Horrie in Manchester as Editor of the colour section. In addition Chippindale was briefly Assistant Editor (News) in Manchester and a worker-director on the Board after launch.

Since the paper collapsed a stream of 'it wasn't my fault' pieces have appeared in the press, each blaming other parts of the organization for the failure. We have already been accused of having our own axe to grind.

If so, this is it.

Peter Chippindale, Chris Horrie
Islington, September 1987

Contents

Chronology

1985 and before

1978. Lowe has Great Idea in aeroplane (legend).

March 1984. Lowe and Walsh get £750 grant from GLC for pre-feasibility study. Clive Thornton and John Pilger advise the project.

March 1985. Greater London Enterprise Board and trade unions provide £80,000 for full feasibility study.

18 October 1985. Dummy newspaper produced by Hayling, then an officer of the GLC industry and employment branch. Pilger supervises editorial.

November 1985. RSGB market research indicating sales between 750,000 and 1.2 million for paper pitched between *Sunday Mirror* and *Mail on Sunday*.

1986

January. Feasibility study finished. Thornton resigns. Nicholas Horsley of Northern Foods agrees to become Chair.

13 February. Jeboda formed.

31 March. GLC abolished. Hayling becomes chief executive. Pilger joins Board of Directors.

9 July. Share sale opens. Issue sponsored by Guinness Mahon.

12 August. News on Sunday Publishing plc capitalized at £6.5 million in £1 shares. Owen Oyston joins Board of Directors after last-minute purchase of £100,000 worth of shares.

1 September. Gerry Taylor appointed principal adviser to the Board.

4 September. Keith Sutton appointed editor, John Pilger editor in chief. Pilger leaves shortly afterwards to go to Australia.

16 September. Bartle, Bogle, Hegarty (BBH) appointed advertising agency.

2 November. Pilger and Sutton row at Kennedy Hotel on Pilger's return.

7 December. Sutton's first dummy edition.

16 December. Pilger walks out.

1987

2 January. Pilger article in *New Statesman*. Hayling appointed editorial director. Gerry Taylor appointed chief executive.

24 January. Taylor resigns as chief executive, but stays as adviser.

26 January. Taylor outlines 'Plan B'. Break-even circulation upped to nearly 1 million.

5 February. Manchester office officially opened.

24 February. Hayling rejects NO TITS, BUT A LOT OF BALLS slogan produced by BBH.

7 March. First 'live' dummy features Zeebrugge ferry disaster.

17 March. BBH resign.

1 April. Hayling resigns as editorial director and takes charge of London office. Goes to health farm.

8 April. Hayling returns. Last-ditch effort to have Sutton sacked.

26 April. Launch issue published. 1.5 million copies printed. Total sales 518,300.

28 April. Horsley goes to see Oyston at Claughton Hall, tells him it is all over.

7 May. *Financial Times* reports cash crisis.

11 May. General election announced.

12 May. Oyston and Transport and General Workers' Union pledge

subordinated loans to 'fighting fund' to keep paper going during election campaign.

17 May. SPANKER PROCTOR edition of the newspaper starts election coverage.

28 May. Oyston appoints Roy Barber interim chief executive and David Jones editorial director after Founders have given up right to veto firing of editor.

1 June. Marketing department sacked by Barber.

3 June. Sutton sacked.

11 June. General election.

12 June. Oyston demands surrender of Golden Share. Founders refuse.

14 June. Eighth and last issue of original *News on Sunday*. Sales 202,000.

16 June. News on Sunday Publishing plc goes into voluntary receivership.

18 June. Oyston's company Growfar agrees with Receiver to produce paper under licence. Growfar begins negotiations to buy *News on Sunday*'s assets and become the publisher.

23 June. Total staff of 181 of old company dismissed. New staff of 72 hired by Growfar from old employees.

8 September. News on Sunday Publishing plc put into liquidation. Creditors told payment will be at least 90p in the pound.

20 November. Paper closed by Oyston after circulation drops to 115,000. Oyston puts losses at 'at least £2 million'.

1 · The Fragments

Big Flame

According to the legend, the story of *News on Sunday* began in 1978 with twenty-four-year-old Ben Lowe gazing moodily out of the aircraft window on a flight back from Canada to England. He was not looking forward to his return. His last two years had been spent taking a master's degree in political science at Queen's University, Kingston. Now time had run out and he was about to be plunged back into the horrible reality of his own miserable country, and particularly its miserable politics. Sighing, he leafed through the English newspapers, the first he had really looked at for months. The usual filth. Biased rubbish, distortions, Tory propaganda, consumer pap, trivia, silly stories – they hadn't changed. If anything, they'd got worse. How could people buy this stuff? No wonder they were getting a raw deal.

As he sipped his drink his mood grew darker. Something should be done about it. People should be given a chance to read a proper newspaper – one that was decent, honourable and humane. One that reflected his belief in full-blooded socialism, a belief he was sure so many of them shared. It was their right.

His thoughts drifted to his own future, which at that time was uncertain. What was he going to do when he was back? Put up with it all like everybody else, he supposed glumly. Moan about it and do nothing like all of them. Then, floating at 30,000 feet above the icebergs of the North Atlantic, he was struck by the Great Idea. He, Ben Lowe, would start the newspaper of the new dawn, the paper that would restore faith in the discredited medium, the paper that would be not just a paper, but far more. Dare he think it – the paper that would be the basis for a new political movement that would sweep the country. The paper for the people.

If you ask Ben Lowe if this account of events is true, he smiles self-deprecatingly and says shyly: 'Not quite.' But then Ben Lowe is not the stuff of which legends are made. And he is quite adamant about one thing – the paper was his idea, whatever anybody else involved with *News on Sunday* may claim.

Lowe had not gone to Canada for just academic reasons. Part of his decision to study abroad had been a personal protest against the ditching of full-blooded socialism by Harold Wilson's Labour government. Like all left-wingers, Lowe loathed Wilson, who had been elected in 1974 on the back of the wave of industrial militancy which culminated in the miners' strike of that year. But instead of getting on with the revolution, which Lowe believed was Wilson's historic duty, Harold had immediately 'sold out' to the capitalists by adopting right-wing policies approved by NATO and the International Monetary Fund. By the time Lowe settled down back in London, Wilson had bowed out and handed the mantle of Leader of the Labour Party and Guardian of British Socialism to James Callaghan, the right-wing Labour MP for Cardiff. Lowe watched, his lip curling, as avuncular 'Farmer Jim' took Wilson's mastery of the new political art of the television interview to fresh heights of reassuring vacuousness.

Lowe blamed the newspapers and television for transforming the storm clouds of revolution he had sensed as an undergraduate at Sussex University into this thin drizzle of social democracy. The media were going to enormous lengths to lure 'the people' away from their revolutionary destiny into the gaudy sideshows of consumerism. But his contact with the 'real people' had, to be honest, been limited. He was a baby-faced product of the concerned middle classes, born in Derby and whisked off to the Home Counties at an early age. He was very bright, and sailed through the Royal Grammar School at High Wycombe to Sussex University, where he arrived in 1972 to read Languages.

Although interested in politics, Lowe had little in common with the industrial militants who dominated the political stage in the early 1970s. His style was that of the laid-back, softly spoken, pro-feminist new man, a long way from the aggressive, blustering, male chauvinist approach of most trade-union militants. Their vision rarely seemed to extend beyond the size of their pay packets or of the tits in the vile papers they read. Lowe still believed 'the workers', with their industrial muscle, were the key to the British revolution. But he was sniffily dismayed at their delight in consumerism and sheep-like attitude to the reactionary rubbish in the papers. He was proud that he, and others like him, had not fallen for the con-trick.

Lowe's interests extended to a wide range of issues – sexual politics, the environment, nuclear disarmament, anti-racism – all of which had emerged from the 1960s hippy and student-based protest movements. Although his conservative clothing and mild manners didn't show it, he was becoming a 'Right-On', and he would support anything on the new agenda. This gave him an endless shopping list of radical causes which had no apparent connection, but were bound together by the radical-chic lifestyle of their supporters. His quiet rage about the papers, and the idiots who paid good money for them, grew more intense as he began to grind away in a job as a research assistant at the *Financial Times*. He read the whole range of papers on most days, and was appalled by their cynical and gleeful exploitation of Callaghan's faltering stand against what was labelled 'mindless militancy' at Labour's grass roots. The coverage seemed to be for the exclusive benefit of the Tory Party. If causes dear to his heart, such as feminism, even figured at all in the mass-circulation papers, it was to serve as the butt for an endless stream of cheap jokes.

The only paper which stood out against the tide was the Communist Party's *Morning Star*. But its only function seemed to be promoting the image of its Soviet paymasters and flattering its dwindling readership of old age pensioners and trade-union officials. For once Right-On people like Lowe were in total agreement with the rest of the population – the *Morning Star* was a write-off, its credibility rating below zero. Then there were the dozens of papers produced by the various Trotskyite sects, the largest of which, in circulation terms, were *Socialist Worker* and *Socialist Challenge*. If there was a strike or industrial dispute *Socialist Worker* and *Socialist Challenge* sellers would rush to the gates to lecture workers on how they would lose their 'struggle' if they stopped short of Permanent World Revolution. Their newspapers existed solely to point this out, and were designed to lead readers to the inescapable conclusion that what was needed was a new political party, free from the sell-outs of the Labour Party and the trade-union leaders. To do this, unfortunately, meant filling the pages of their papers with the depressing and unfathomable minutiae of far-left politics.

On the other hand, some of these papers had real flair. *Socialist Worker*, edited by Paul Foot, was a passable imitation of the *Daily Mirror*, and the International Marxist Group's *Socialist Challenge* was edited by the imaginative and talented former student revolutionary leader Tariq Ali, who was 100 per cent Right-On. Their individual circulations were tiny. But, Lowe wondered, what if they pooled their resources and produced a paper jointly? If they abandoned factory-gate sales for proper commercial distribution through newsagents, the combined circulations might add up to something worthwhile. Lowe, who loves playing with figures, did some research and estimated sales could reach as many as 400,000 – more than the *FT* where he worked, and a respectable figure at the quality end of Fleet Street.

The trouble was that there was no chance of getting the sects to co-operate. Their hatred for each other was even greater than for the capitalist enemy, and they were constantly locked in internecine warfare in which they accused each other of a battery of heinous crimes. The charge sheet varied. It could be 'neo-Stalinism' (refusing to say Russia was a capitalist country); 'Pabloite revisionism' (deciding to join the Labour Party secretly); 'tailism' (waiting for trade unions to organize strikes rather than getting on with it yourself); 'liquidationism' (dissolving the sect into a larger movement, hoping that its ideas will catch on); 'parliamentary cretinism' (advising people to vote Labour); 'stageism' (not demanding everything at once); or even 'centreism' (expressing a liking for Tony Benn).

Lowe knew the sects and the papers they churned out were going nowhere. They were stuck in the ghetto. Now, as he started making notes to put the Great Idea into more concrete form, he proposed a paper that would be only 'quasi-revolutionary' and therefore have a wider appeal, and 'non-sectarian', so it was not be in hock to one particular sect or group. Lowe had the seed of a good idea, and there was some encouragement. A new approach was being mooted in the heaving undergrowth of ultra-left literature. People were tiring of old-style 'workerist' ultra-left politics and standing at factory gates being laughed at by the very workers they were supposed to be leading to the new Jerusalem. Attention was switching to continental groups such as the Italian 'autonomists', who rejected the fruitless and mind-numbing discipline and line-toeing demanded by the other builders of the New Revolution. Right-Ons like everything about Italy, where even the Fascists are nattily dressed. The autonomists proposed networks of similarly minded Right-On people, separately involved in all manner of 'struggles'. They had a revolutionary theory that the combined effect of all these 'struggles' would be to needle and irritate the capitalist system until it finally collapsed in an exhausted heap and died. Various papers and magazines were beginning to thrive in this new atmosphere. *Spare Rib* was already well established, and was joined for a period by the *Leveller*, another collective magazine, and the *East End News*, which produced the first attempt to appeal to 'the masses' of East London by dressing up Right-On concerns in chirpy Chas'n'Dave-style modernized Cockney.

And the new Italian thinking was beginning to affect the sects themselves. To any outsiders curious enough to look – and there weren't many – the Liverpool-centred party-cum-discussion group Big Flame seemed identical to any other of the tiny Trotskyite grouplets. But although it had the standard minute membership and tatty newspaper hawked erratically round student unions, shopping precincts and Tube stations, Big Flame was different. It had absorbed the autonomist Right-On thinking and described itself not as a political party as such, but as 'The Revolutionary Socialist Organization'.

Big Flame was based on the Italian revolutionary group *Lutte Continua* (the struggle goes on), which sought to combine the autonomist belief in a loose network of Right-On groups with a separate political party which would guide them all. It was a neat idea, and one which placed it half way between the rigid disipline of the Trotskyites and the hopeless chaos of the Anarchists (or Libertarians, as they preferred to call themselves) on the ultra-left spectrum.

And Big Flame had a reputation for humanity compared with other ultra-left sects with their habit of expelling people *en masse* in a hail of jargon-ridden abuse, and demanding Moonie-type self-criticism from slackers who failed to meet newspaper sales quotas. To join you had to say you believed in all the usual stuff about the Working Class leading the Revolution, but a general interest in being nice to people was all that was really required. It was a sort of revolutionary version of the Lions Club. The nearest equivalent at the time was Peter Hain's Young Liberals. People who knocked about the revolutionary left at the time still remember Big Flame fondly as a fundamentally nice organization.

It started life in Liverpool in 1971 and took its name from a television drama-documentary on the declining port's dockers, who were constantly being 'sold out' by the local trade-union branches. The aim was to attract intelligent revolutionaries disgusted by the ramshackle right-wing local Labour Party and the once influential Communist Party.

As with all ultra-left groups, its members' political lives were overshadowed by the dreadful possibility of a sell-out – the biggest danger in ultra-left politics, and always on the cards. Leon Trotsky had said that a socialist revolution in Britain was being prevented by one thing alone – the habit of the leaders of the Labour Party and trade unions to compromise with the ruling class by becoming part of the system. The biggest example had been the General Strike of 1926 when a settlement was negotiated with Churchill. It had happened time and time again, and the Trotskyist answer was 'democratic centralism', an authoritarian form of discipline by which anybody suspected of a sell-out was expelled, keeping the organization pure. The anarchist solution was more imaginative – neatly avoiding the possibility of sell-out by having no leaders at all.

The sell-out concept was inherited by all Right-On people, and became a central part of their thinking. But most thought the anarchist 'no leaders' approach was silly. Leaders were to be tolerated as long as they were not permanent, and as long as they were held constantly 'accountable'. Right-On movements such as the feminists and the peace campaigners evolved complicated systems to ensure this happened. Spokespeople or representatives had constantly to justify their activities and statements to committees, which in turn would have to report back to steering groups and working parties elected by conferences and regional groups. No person in a position of power was ever to be trusted, especially if he or she was on your side. It was realized that 'accountability' often resulted in organizational muddle and indecisiveness, and sometimes in sheer paralysis. But this was a small price to pay for insurance against a leadership sell-out. And the approach was said to have a huge plus-point as well. Working on the principle that each person's experience is equally valuable, it then follows that if ten people ponder a decision, it will be ten times better.

Big Flame followed these principles and was therefore kept loosely structured. The organization's broad philosophy and open-endedness allowed people to arrive carrying all manner of political baggage. Henry Stewart, later to juggle many millions as *News on Sunday*'s financial wizard, was a Big Flame Maoist who helped start operations in the north-east of England. Others were Big Flame Feminists, Big Flame Pacifists or Big Flame Single-issue Campaigners. Ben Lowe found the organization the perfect place for helping develop his idea of a 'non-sectarian' national newspaper, so he joined as well.

Big Flame didn't have permanent leaders, but it did have superstars. One was Alan Hayling, who was later to play a central role in the story of *News on Sunday*. Hayling is a man of considerable and obvious intelligence, with dishy looks and great charm which made him a favourite with some of the women comrades. He cut a dashing figure at the many conferences he addressed, raising his hand from time to time to stroke his dark curly locks as he poured out pure reason in soft well-modulated tones with a sincerity that was almost painful.

Hayling's left-wing politics were to a large extent the result of his background. His Jewish mother had narrowly escaped from Romania in the 1930s when the local Iron Shirt goon squad began slaughtering Jews with a barbarity which sickened even their Nazi German allies. She had fled to England as a refugee, and married his father, who was a teacher. The family lived in London, where Hayling was born in 1949. When he was twelve, his father found a better post in Liverpool, and the family moved up north.

Hayling was a brilliant pupil at school and was soon marked down as Oxbridge material. After a year spent in Uganda as a volunteer science teacher he passed the Cambridge entrance exam with ease and graduated with a double first in natural sciences in 1969. The world was at his feet.

Between long stints in the physics labs, Hayling had dabbled in student journalism and decided to make his career in the media. But instead of working on *Varsity*, the established undergraduate paper, he was already determined to be different. He and others set up a rival 'underground' publication, the *Shilling Paper*, which, though a great success on its own terms, was useless as a credential for getting straight on to a Fleet Street paper such as the *Sunday Times*.

So Hayling, not interested in a normal local paper apprenticeship, tried television. He was instantly offered traineeships by Granada in Manchester and the BBC in London. He chose the BBC and was given a post in the Science Unit, where he was put straight on to making radio programmes. His progress was predictably rapid, and after eighteen months he made the move to television, even though it was only as an assistant on *Pets and Vets*, an animal welfare show. He quickly crossed to the peak-time *Burke Report*, and from there landed a plum assistant producer's job on the pop-science flagship *Tomorrow's World*. Again he showed enormous potential, at once getting a feel for the audience and realizing people were interested in gimmicks and gadgets rather than dull, but more enlightening, scientific theory with pictures of boffins pottering about in laboratories. But by now he was getting bored with the relative backwater of the Science Unit and wanted to go to News and Current Affairs, which was not only more glamorous, but offered a more direct opportunity to put his political ideals to good use.

His chance came with an offer of work on *Children in Crossfire*, a documentary about the psychological impact of terrorism and army occupation on the children of Northern Ireland. But he immediately disagreed with the producer about the politics of the show, and was sent back to the Science Unit. His transfer to current affairs was blocked – the result, he still believes, of direct political discrimination. Increasingly frustrated, he walked out in 1974 to help found Newsreel, an independent collective making films for the Labour movement.

Although Newsreel made some startlingly good documentaries, shortage of funds was a constant problem. But at least Hayling was free to follow the dictates of his large and sometimes cumbersome political conscience. In 1976, just as he was planning to produce a film about the motor industry, Newsreel hit one of its frequent cash crises. To combine research for the film with earning money, he took a job at Ford's Langley plant near Heathrow as a production-line worker in the body trim shop.

He found that he liked it. Not the work, which was back-breaking and tedious – he specialized in bolting on bumpers and screwing down steering wheels on trucks – but the mostly Asian workforce whose respect and confidence he soon won as a shop-floor activist. He stayed for seven years, at first steering clear of the official trade-union structure which, as a Big Flamer, he regarded as a huge sell-out. Instead he concentrated on the unofficial Ford Workers' Combine, which bypassed the official union structure dominated by the Transport and General Workers' Union. The Combine linked far-left activists and militants in Ford plants right across the country and, in theory, throughout the world.

In the early Liverpool days of Big Flame the comrades had been obsessed with the potential of Ford workers as leaders of the British revolution, and had put great effort into organizing and recruiting at the local Halewood plant. And although 'workerism' was on the wane by the time Hayling turned up on the Langley personnel officer's doorstep, he earned many brownie points among the comrades by becoming a 'genuine' member of the proletariat. By day Hayling would help organize the workers at Langley, and in the evenings he would throw himself into pressure-group work. He helped set up the Troops Out movement which campaigned for withdrawal of the British army from Northern Ireland. He became a close friend of Sheila Rowbotham, the feminist historian who, together with feminist economist Hilary Wainwright and Big Flamer Lynne Segal, wrote a book which was of enormous importance for the far left in the early 1980s – *Beyond the Fragments*.

The theory behind *Beyond the Fragments* was simple. The confident mood of the left in the 1960s had been part of a sudden wider upsurge in creativity concentrated on the arts, pop music, fashion, 'lifestyle' and sexual attitudes. But activists on the new Right-On 'lifestyle' issues, such as sexual and racial equality and low-level economic development and ecology, had splintered into hundreds of fragmented pressure groups, local campaigns and tiny far-left political 'parties' and discussion groups. Many saw themselves as being above the grubby world of traditional politics and the professions, but often felt they could be like Richard Branson, the one-time hippy and promoter of alternative music who had joined the system and made a fortune.

The question was whether, in the harsher climate of the late 1970s and early 1980s, the fragments could be welded together to form a new force in British politics. The various Right-On movements, especially the women's movement, had grown enormously during the years of the Wilson–Callaghan government. The collapse of industrial militancy after the 'Winter of Discontent' in 1978 and the defeat of the Labour government in the election of May 1979 had tipped the balance of power in the Right-Ons' favour. They no longer lived in awe of their Big Brothers in the unions.

A conference, inspired by *Beyond the Fragments*, was held in Leeds in September 1980 – the first major Right-On gathering after the election which had ushered in the then relatively unknown doctrine of Thatcherism. As a Big Flamer Ben Lowe, like Henry Stewart from Big Flame in Newcastle, made attendance top priority. All this activity and talk of new Rainbow Alliances chimed perfectly with Lowe's newspaper plan, which he had always seen as partly being based on, and partly bringing about, greater co-operation on the far left. His discussion paper on the subject had now been drafted and re-drafted several times.

The trouble was that the paper never seemed to get off the ground, which was typical of the Big Flame and 'Beyond the Fragments' approach. The major flaw in attempting to get all the fractious fragments to work together, when nothing really united them except being Right-On, was the massive emphasis it placed on consensus. Endless meetings were needed, and there was deep dread of taking decisions in case anybody objected and walked out, causing the whole fragile alliance to fall apart.

Meanwhile the various splinter groups, whether they subscribed to Big Flame or 'Beyond the Fragments' ideas or not, viewed the post-election inquest in the Labour Party with their customary vulture-like intensity. As events unrolled they sensed that the noisy disarray presented them with new opportunities. Labour's traditional left wing, centring on the Tribune group, plunged into its normal Machiavellian schemings aimed at taking over the party. The outlook was good. Thatcherism was widely viewed at the time as a mad right-wing aberration which the people would not stand for long. It faced certain doom either at the polls or at the hands of the National Union of Mineworkers. Thatcher's rating in the opinion polls was crashing as the dole queues lengthened. All the left needed to do was to ensure that the next Labour government was a real alternative, and not led by another tedious old right-winger like Callaghan, who had gone back to his farm blaming the lefties.

The left's moment of revenge came at the Labour special conference at Wembley in 1980. The conference approved a series of structural reforms giving constituency parties and the unions more power over the appointment of the leader. The clear beneficiary was

Tony Benn, who immediately launched a six-month campaign to have himself elected as deputy leader instead of the hated Denis Healey, who was, in the opinion of many, the architect of the sell-out of socialist economic policy during the Wilson–Callaghan government. Benn's strategy was simple and well timed. Picking up the scent from 'Beyond the Fragments', he wanted to weld together the traditional Labour left and the newer Right-On movements. He encouraged Right-Ons to pile into the dilapidated inner-city party machines and replace the ageing right-wing old guard. The new single-issue groups, he believed, represented a potential new element in Labour's complex power brokerage which might tip the balance of power decisively in his direction.

For months Benn stomped the country addressing as many meetings attended by fringe pressure groups as he could, telling them they were good people wasting their time outside the Labour Party. But although thousands did heed him and join, it didn't quite work. The deputy leadership election was close-run, but in the end the party settled for the compromise of old-style left-winger Michael Foot, already in place as leader, with born-again 'democratic socialist' Denis Healey as deputy. The impression of division given by Benn's lengthy and vocal campaign, however, did immense damage to the party and the shambling, duffel-coated figure of Michael Foot walked straight into the delighted arms of the Tory press, which instantly fell on him and started taking him apart.

At first the arrival of considerable numbers of Benn-recruited Right-Ons in moribund inner-city Labour Party branches went unnoticed. But, putting to use the superior education unwittingly handed to them by the state or paid for by their parents, they soon displaced the handfuls of old faithfuls. Shocked old-guard MPs, who had imagined they were in cushy seats for life, suddenly found Right-Ons dominating their constituency parties with a potent mixture of brow-beating and attrition. Another, even less visible, result of the Bennite rivalism was the demise of Big Flame as a formal organization. Most of its best organizers and natural membership joined the Labour Party. And although Big Flame was never an 'entryist' party-within-a-party, like some of the Trotskyite groups, including Militant Tendency, everyone who had been part of it remained friends. A useful network of ex-Big Flamers emerged both inside and outside the party. Hayling and Lowe remained outside, though

Lowe worked closely with Benn and wrote a pamphlet about NATO with him.

Whether or not they were former members of Big Flame, the International Marxist Group, or any of the other sects which now dissolved themselves into the Labour Party, the Right-Ons' most effective weapon was an endless capacity to attend even the most obscure meetings. They used the skills acquired during the social science degree courses many of them had followed in the early 1970s to scrutinize rule books and exploit every line and loophole in their favour. Tactics which had been honed in the petty but ruthless world of student-union politics were now deployed in party meetings with devastating results. Throughout the press the cry went up of 'extremist take-overs' and 'packed meetings'. The Right-Ons fired back the unanswerable reply that meetings belonged to those who attended them.

Cheery tombola social nights at local Labour Clubs were replaced by showings of Peter Watkins's brilliant but heart-stopping anti-nuclear film, *The War Game*, which the BBC had commissioned in the 1960s but still wimpishly refused to screen. Similar grisly film delights, unsuitable for persons of a nervous, or even reasonably cheerful, disposition followed – some made by Hayling and his Newsreel collective.

The GLC

Nowhere was the Right-On bandwagon more apparent than in London, where it culminated in the elevation of Ken Livingstone to the leadership of the controlling Labour group on the Greater London Council the day after the local elections in March 1981. Livingstone had formed his political views during the 'new left' upheavals of the late 1960s. In 1968, the watershed year of the student riots in Paris, when most of the new generation of radicals were denouncing the Labour Party as hopelessly fuddy-duddy, he had joined up, believing it would one day become the focus for a new alliance of Right-On movements, Now, more than a decade on, his dream was starting to come true and the new radical politics were about to be released on an unsuspecting populace – with mixed results.

Local government, with its responsibility for sweeping the streets and emptying dustbins, had been essentially a humdrum business.

But this would never do for the gilded 1960s radicals. Many had started off working in the field as social workers, teachers, architects, planners or just plain clerks. Now, through their domination of the London Labour Party, they were running it, and they started putting into practice schemes hatched during their long hours in drab municipal offices. Local government was no longer boring – it was 'where it was at', and it became elevated to a collection of grandiose projects. Suddenly 'racism awareness' training, day nurseries, and sex-equality monitoring programmes were the order of the day. 'Chairs' were established, and town halls sprouted signs saying how many people were unemployed locally, although nothing effective was done about it. There was a mushroom growth of grant-aided housing associations, community advice centres, radical theatre groups and co-operative bicycle repair shops.

The headquarters of the GLC, the great pile of County Hall, changed from being a tedious and unloved administrative centre to become the Right-On rival to the House of Commons directly across the River Thames. The building was besieged by Right-Ons, many wearing dungarees and riding shiny hi-tech bicycles bought on credit in Covent Garden. In a parallel development, the old fruit and vegetable market was rapidly becoming the Right-On commercial centre where trendy shopkeepers cashed in with their hand-knitted sweaters, ethnic crafts and designer clothing.

There was nothing new in the preoccupations of the Right-Ons. Socialism has always attracted its fair share of cranks; as long ago as 1937, George Orwell wrote in *The Road to Wigan Pier* that the very word 'Socialism' seemed to act like a magnet attracting 'every fruit-juice drinker, nudist, sandal-wearer, sex maniac, Quaker, "Nature Cure" quack, pacifist and feminist in England'. He surmised that Socialism would remain unpopular as long as critics were able to say: 'I don't object to Socialism, but I do object to Socialists.'

But unlike their 1930s forebears, the 1980s Right-Ons had arrived in force. And they were no longer held in check by the culturally conservative trade-union movement, which was experiencing a sharp decline in its prestige and power. They swept the London Labour Party before them and established beach-heads in the other inner-cities.

Opinion about Ken Livingstone divided sharply. No politician had ever acted like this before, and people were genuinely shocked.

The tabloid papers, which make their money from guessing the prejudices of their readers and dressing them up as informed opinion, had a field day. But others thought: why not? Right-Ons were citizens and ratepayers too, and it was about time that local government began to represent them. A minority slice of the population loathed Livingstone with as much passion as the Right-Ons loved him. And in the middle was a larger group who had not yet formed an opinion. These people were prepared to accept Fleet Street's verdict that he was insane. But then again, most politicians were fairly mad. And there was great admiration for Livingstone's transparent honesty, self-effacing modesty and determination to stick to his guns. At least people knew where they stood with him, and the darkened corridors of local government, with their forbidding and ever-present whiff of graft and back-scratching, were now lit up in a blaze of publicity. That made a pleasant change.

The aspect which wasn't so popular was the business of giving grants to all and sundry, which was whipped up and wildly exaggerated by the Tory press. Until Livingstone, various Right-On pet publishing and campaigning projects had been largely confined to tedious discussion documents and papers wrangled over at interminable meetings. Now that there was a sympathetic hand at the helm, especially for the new sexual politics, they were shaped into formal applications for local govern funding. A stream of long, earnest and often hopelessly bureaucratic ideas flowed into the system, all with the same object of getting some cash. One of these was Ben Lowe's modest proposal to launch a new national newspaper. Compared to the GLC's plan to make London immune to all-out thermonuclear war by placing signs on lamp posts, it was small beer.

Those Right-Ons who had written off the Labour Party for ever now began to chew humble pie, and were drawn to Livingstone's GLC as though to a magnet. Jobs, as well as grants, were on offer, and people whom Lowe had met before started working there. His most important contact was Hayling, who had left Ford in 1983 and now had a job monitoring multinational companies in the GLC's Industry and Employment Branch. Hayling was also in charge of media initiatives, so Lowe naturally turned to him with the newspaper they had so often discussed as comrades in Big Flame.

The two men talked it over with Hayling's boss at the GLC,

Hilary Wainwright, who was head of the Popular Planning Unit. Wainwright was enormously enthusiastic, as she was about many things. A leading Right-On thinker, she had co-written the *Beyond The Fragments* book which had started as a mere pamphlet, but had attracted so much interest that it had been upgraded and sold an extremely respectable 20,000 copies in paperback, having a major effect on its earnest readership. Wainwright, an economist, possessed a first-class analytical brain powered by bundles of energy, and had lots of good political contacts within the Labour Party. Although she had little time to help organize the newspaper project, as she buzzed around discussing it with friends and jotting down ideas it began to get up steam.

On paper *News on Sunday* was a brilliant idea. Although to outsiders it was just a newspaper, to those in the know the concept went much further. *NoS* would provide a focus to weld together the splinter groups of the left into an unstoppable force which would sweep the Labour Party before it. The fragments would be reunited, and the hated paunchy old men of the traditional Labour movement would be overthrown. At the same time the tables would be turned, so that they could actually be used to help finance the project, along with the Right-On councils which had already thrown financial caution to the winds.

The boring old unions would be pushed out by a new Rainbow Alliance of media-wise radicals, alert and campaigning on the big issues of racial and sexual discrimination, nuclear power, and protecting the environment. The new obsessions, which were already making their mark in national politics abroad with parties such as the Greens in Germany, would take over.

The Big Flame would be rekindled.

A paper for the people

Even better for those who were thinking autonomously, the newspaper would cater for everybody who was Right-On. Each group would be able to campaign for its particular obsession in public. The wonderful vision arose of a publication which would be like the minutes of a gigantic nationwide meeting. Every cause – no matter how bizarre or obscure – could be represented simply by writing a story about it. Different causes and individuals could have their say on different pages, under an overall consensus umbrella which embraced correct Right-On thinking on all aspects of the paper's coverage – from news to TV to sport.

And the newspaper itself could provide a stunning example with its own employment practices of how to run an organization on correct Right-On lines. Blacks, gays, lesbians, the disabled and other disadvantaged people – all could join in demonstrating how the new thinking could be combined with commercial success. The paper would practise what it preached.

If Hayling had any doubts about swinging the GLC behind the paper, it was because of Ben Lowe's lack of experience and drive. But then he had a brainwave. Hayling had come across a man called Chris Walsh who was already getting funds from the GLC for his latest, faltering, business enterprise, a Third World Development unit based in Highbury, North London.

Hayling decided that the hyperactive Walsh, who was not afraid of any challenge, would be the perfect foil for the lugubrious and cautious Lowe. The two men would complement each other perfectly. Hayling met Walsh for lunch and explained the newspaper project. They hit it off at once. Since Walsh's Third World business was going nowhere, he was enthusiastic. He got to work at once, and an eight-page Walsh 'strategy document', the first of many, whizzed back to Hayling in the post. Hayling explained further that if the GLC was going to support the venture, Walsh would have to get some newspaper professionals – or at least semi-professionals – involved, including, of course, Ben Lowe. Shortly afterwards Walsh brought in Liz Cooper, the circulation manager of the ailing *New Statesman*, and Kit Sadgrove, a former advertising-agency executive now in market research. The GLC liked to work with committees, and one was formed with the addition of Mike Power, a *Daily Mail* compositor, trade-union activist and chairperson of the Campaign for Press and Broadcasting Freedom.

Together they wrote a short grant application, which Hayling pushed through the committees. The project was awarded £750 for a detailed pre-feasibility study, with Hayling, in his GLC capacity, responsible for making sure the report was properly written and the grant money not wasted.

The *Guardian*, the only national newspaper remotely acceptable to Right-Ons, was the logical starting-point. By now Ben Lowe had realized that a daily paper would be too difficult and costly, so the idea of starting a sort of Sunday *Guardian* seemed logical enough. The *Sunday Times*, under Rupert Murdoch, was moving to the right, and Right-Ons now only had the weedy *Observer*, which was rapidly disappearing into the abyss of consumer journalism for the comfortable middle classes. Since most Right-Ons would have been happy with a national version of a publication such as *City Limits* or *Spare Rib*, which specialized in redefining the world's priorities as their own, the comparison with the *Guardian* was daring.

Lowe was certain that if the paper was properly produced, with a GLC-funded journalistic team and regular national distribution, it could sell at least 250,000 and maybe 400,000. He didn't think there was chance of more than that. But his cautious frame of mind was already beginning to irritate some of the comrades. After frustrating years in which they had covered acres of print discussing the socio-logical theory and implications of newspaper readership, they wanted to compete in the more popular market. The defeat of the Labour Party for the second time in 1983 had been blamed largely on the media campaign which had glorified the Falklands, hammered Foot, and unleashed a campaign of unprecedented vitriol against Livingstone's GLC and the 'Loony Left'. It was time to hit back.

Livingstone himself had made a tentative start with the publication of the *Londoner*, a heavily subsidized but snappy tabloid free-sheet widely distributed throughout the GLC area. The expenditure was justified by the argument that the newspaper industry existed to vilify the GLC and the rest of the left, and that the public was being denied the chance to hear the other side. Fleet Street seemed to exist solely to praise the Tories and bolster the system. The posh end of the market was dominated by new-wave consumer journalism which was turning into a grotesque parody of the 'lifestyle' politics the Right-Ons had pioneered. At the bottom end, the masses were being fed on a diet of bingo, moronic competitions and 'news' reduced to a jumble of tits and bums, Tory propaganda and invented Royal Family rubbish.

The Sun was the most hated of the rabid tabloids, particularly for its 'Page 3 girls' and jingoistic coverage of the Falklands, which had caused widespread revulsion with headlines such as STICK IT UP YOUR JUNTA, and the infamous GOTCHA! on the sinking of the *Belgrano*. For the concerned middle classes, who could barely bring themselves to look at it, it was a horrible, violent, raucous vehicle out to destroy anything progressive or Right-On. Its huge success grated even more, especially as it had been a Labour paper until Murdoch had bought it and turned it into a cornerstone of his international media empire. But there was little they could do about it except wring their hands at each fresh horror in its columns, analyse its transparently partisan coverage, and point out how its competitors were dragging their standards downmarket to try to keep up with its soaraway sales. Most puzzling was that the worse it got, the more people bought it, and – horror of horrors – it was cheerfully read in large numbers by the very people who suffered from the hackneyed prejudices and stereotypes it dispensed – notably blacks, gays and women.

For the Right-Ons, many of whom had committed the cardinal mistake of taking other people's newspapers too seriously, it was inconceivable that this diet of trash should be allowed to succeed. It was now part of their ingrained thinking that the newspaper barons were imposing their standards on the population by rewriting the language of tabloid journalism. The proles were being forced to put up with this stuff because there was no alternative. Secretly (because the papers would never report it), behind the scenes a huge demand was building up for a 'decent' paper, one which – dare they say it – would Tell the Truth.

Another worry was now added to the complaints. Just as linotype operators at the *Sun* were breaking out the champagne to celebrate the arrival of £1,000 pay packets for a three-day week, the realization was beginning to dawn that sooner or later the power of the print unions would be broken by the introduction of new technology. In the north-west, Eddie Shah was starting to emerge as a hate figure as he replaced highly skilled union labour on his string of local papers with girls fresh from secretarial colleges. Shah was setting in motion a chain of events which would lead to the bitter Wapping strike, when Murdoch took on the print unions – previously assumed to be invincible – and won. The issue of jobs was now added to the left agenda, as the print workers finally lost their grip on the production jugular of the industry in the first fundamental update of print technology since the late Middle Ages.

So the idea of a mass-market paper for the Masses, rather than just the Concerned and Committed, began to surface. It didn't happen overnight. Most Right-Ons had to move from the Fleet Street 'heavies', the papers they actually read, to the unknown territory of the 'pops'. A mass-circulation paper was more risky, but it was much more exciting, and with the bigger sales that were on the cards, it could be very profitable. After the 'Sunday *Guardian*' came the next suggestion – a left-wing *Mail on Sunday*.

The snag in all this thinking was that most of the people involved knew little or nothing about producing mass-market newspapers. Lowe had worked as a researcher for the *Financial Times*, Hayling had done his stint with the BBC, and of course they had dabbled in the Big Flame paper and other fringe publications. Then Hayling brought in *News on Sunday*'s first top-drawer professional – John Pilger. Hayling simply rang him up, in the way that he was to cold-call others, asked for his help, and got it. Other good journalists, such as the *Observer* columnist Neal Ascherson and the ex-*New Socialist* editor and media studies lecturer James Curran, came and went, along with many lesser colleagues.

Pilger was immediately sympathetic. He was an immensely ex-perienced journalist, but had never found anything to match the heyday of the *Daily Mirror* under Hugh Cudlipp in the 1960s. In those days the paper had sold 5.25 million copies and had been respected for its powerful, picture-led campaigning journalism, its commitment to the Labour Party, and the chord it struck with its primarily working-class readership. Pilger was by now well into his forties and, like many other good campaigning journalists, more and more like a beached whale, increasingly irrelevant in the cynical new world of slick and sick journalism.

For journalists like him, and others who had made their names digging out scandals such as Poulson, Jeremy Thorpe, Thalidomide, and police corruption, or by trying to engage the sympathy of the nation and the government for the oppressed in society, life was becoming more and more difficult. Editors increasingly saw only the downside of tedious and expensive court actions and official or semi-official government pressure. They could do without it. And Pilger, an exasperatingly prickly individualist determined to expose the ills of the world, stubbornly refused to lower his standards and fit in with the new requirements.

When Hayling invited him in, Pilger listened to the Sunday *Guardian* versus left-wing *Mail on Sunday* argument. But he refused to compare the projected newspaper to anything on the present market, and insisted that only he could shape it. All he would say was that the paper would be completely new, but would hark back to the great days of the *Mirror*.

Lowe, a man of more modest vision, had a train-spotter's fascination for numbers which enabled him to take refuge in 'scientific' figures that endorsed his shyly offered judgements. He now proposed that the fundamental gut decision of whether the paper should be tabloid or broadsheet be tested by market research, until he was finally talked out of it by another newly recruited professional – Clive Thornton, lately of Mirror Group Newspapers. Thornton, a small, stocky, bespectacled figure with a Geordie twang from his Newcastle upbringing, was invited to join as an adviser by Lowe. He had come to the comrades' attention when he wrote an article in the journal of the Right-On wing of the Communist Party, *Marxism Today*, shortly before the £750 GLC pre-feasibility study was completed in November 1984.

Thornton had just left the Mirror Group after a brief but interesting spell in newspapers. He had been brought in by the conglomerate owners, Reed International, who were planning to float the Mirror Group off as a separate company and wanted someone to mastermind the move. Thornton was an unusual choice: his fame sprang from his period as chief executive of the Abbey National building society, where he had swept aside years of tradition, brought in a new management style (he was very proud of having abolished fifty-one committees), and had enormous success with initiatives such as Granny Bonds.

When Thornton started at the *Daily Mirror* he found the usual chronic Fleet Street over-staffing, and began to swing the axe to enable the paper to stand on its own two feet and ward off the inevitable predators, such as Rupert Murdoch and Robert Maxwell. But instead of just getting rid of jobs, as a 'committed expansionist', Thornton started work on plans to keep the unwanted staff, whom he described as 'almost to a man, dedicated, hardworking folk'.

Thornton's answer was a new left-of-centre Sunday tabloid, a 'seventh day *Mirror*', provisionally entitled the *Globe*. The paper was planned in enormous secrecy to run alongside the existing *Sunday Mirror*, which he thought had become 'a soft, ladies' paper'. The *Globe* was designed to sell in large numbers – anything under half a million was not worth considering. The second venture was a new London evening paper to challenge the *Standard*'s monopoly.

He was just warming to his task when Reed sold him out. Unbeknown to him, it had been negotiating with Robert Maxwell, and sold the *Daily Mirror* behind his back. When he walked into the office the next day he found the new proprietor's considerable bulk squeezed into his own chair, took the point and resigned. He eventually collected a £300,000 pay-off.

Maxwell, rooting about in his new office high up in the *Daily Mirror's* Holborn tower block, found Thornton's Sunday paper plan sitting in the in-tray and immediately rubbished it publicly as 'evidence' of Thornton's uselessness. But he took the evening paper suggestion more seriously, and it eventually emerged as the *London Daily News*, which was changed ambitiously at the last minute into Britain's first twenty-four-hour 'rolling newspaper', aimed at pulling both evening and morning sales. Despite some fine writers and good design, the paper was to fall heavily between two stools, and closed down ignominiously in July 1987 after its circulation had slumped to 90,000. The exercise cost Maxwell £30 million.

After leaving the *Mirror*, Thornton returned to his Lincolnshire home to potter about with his prize heifers. But he had been bitten by the newspaper bug, and various groups of disaffected newspaper people, including disgruntled employees and ex-employees of *The Times* and the *Sunday Times*, approached him with a number of implausible journalistic ventures. He even 'floated bread on the water', as he put it, with Harold Evans, the former editor of the *Sunday Times* who inspires guru-scale admiration among many hacks.

But although he listened politely to these ideas, Thornton became irritated that none of the people had done any business sums. As a man of action – as he never tired of telling people – he had stuck his multi-million-pound Granny Bond idea together on the back of an envelope in a couple of hours after the introduction of Budget changes which made it possible. He was just beginning to get heartily sick of the whole newspaper business, when Hayling phoned to follow up Ben Lowe's letter of invitation. Pleasantly surprised by how close *News on Sunday* was to his *Globe* plan, he agreed to meet. There was another pleasant surprise – Hayling and Lowe had actually done some work and had something on paper. Thornton, who prefers to follow a gut feeling, told them they had to move fast. There was a gap in the market which wouldn't last for ever. The Mirror Group would soon be back on its feet. Any delay would be fatal.

They nodded and invited him to a meeting.

Thornton is remembered by Hayling, Lowe and the others involved early in the project as being 'difficult'. His 'crimes', as they saw it, started when he insisted that if there had to be meetings they must be businesslike, properly chaired and follow the agenda. He had found the agendas clogged with 'all sorts of odds and ends, trivia and red herrings'. And when he tried transparent tricks to pull up vital business buried at the end of the list, he found himself making a number of enemies in the group. Worse, although Thornton knew that Hayling saw himself as a potential chief executive, he demanded that the business side of the paper be immediately put up under the direction of 'an upfront businessman with a solid track record'. Editorial direction should also be handed to an upfront, well-established journalist. He didn't think having been a member of Big Flame was a qualification for either post.

Thornton's demands caused consternation. Behind his back the group threw the Right-On book at him and, deeply paranoid as they were, came to the only possible conclusion. Thornton was trying to hijack their project – the baby they had nursed to its first hesitant steps. Co-operating with him might lead to a sell-out before they had even started. They were convinced he was plotting to make himself chief executive – a charge he recalls with a wry grin and shake of the head. Everything was wrong with him – he wouldn't always come to meetings and when he did he was 'difficult'. They decided that he was only in it for himself and was not the sort of person the comrades wanted to have with them, and definitely not part of the consensus.

Nevertheless, Thornton could not be ditched straight away. They had approached a GLC body, the Greater London Enterprise Board (GLEB), for money and been told that if it was to put money in, an established business person had to be involved. The only one interested at that time was Thornton, so he had to stay for the moment.

The original £750 grant from the GLC was one thing, but huge sums would be needed to get the real paper off the ground. Lowe had already calculated launch costs as at least £4 million. They wanted to raise as much of this money as possible from the City; Thornton assured them that he could fix it if they did what he said. This was good news, but they didn't want to rely entirely on him. Instead they decided to get money from the GLEB and the trade unions to do a proper feasibility study – one which would deliver an unanswerable case for investment. They would then be able to go to the City on their own, and not Thornton's, terms.

Thornton hammered at them that there was a 'window of opportunity' which had to be grasped. He laid out the argument: the *Mirror* had gone to Maxwell and dived downmarket, along with its Sunday counterpart; the *Mail on Sunday* was repositioning itself after its disastrous launch, but had still not recovered. There was a gap which nobody had yet stepped into. The Sunday market was still far larger than the daily market, though it had shrunk by 20 per cent in the 1970s. The heavyweight *Sunday Times*, *Sunday Telegraph* and *Observer* were more or less holding their own. But the populars had been harder hit. The market leader, the *News of the World* (sister paper of the *Sun*), was down to 4.2 million, a loss of 2 million in a decade, by the spring of 1984. Although it was recovering after a revamp, only it and the *Mail on Sunday*, boosted by massive spending on advertising, were actually gaining readers.

There were several reasons for this decline. Church-going was being abandoned in favour of the new religion of DIY and other time-consuming pursuits, and research showed that only 3 per cent of the population still indulged in the great British institution of the Sunday lie-in, paper included. In the 'pops' market, the distinction between the Sundays and the dailies was becoming fuzzy. It was no longer necessary to wait until Sunday for a dose of smut and scandal, when the *Sun* was offering it six days a week. But there was some evidence from the launch of the *Mail on Sunday* that the missing readers could be lured back by new papers. And there was a hunch that 'heavy' newspaper readers would be attracted by a tasteful paper with plenty of news, but which could be read quickly. A left-of-centre paper combining easy tabloid reading with heavyweight news coverage looked like a good bet.

Thornton spelled out how the new technology was rapidly opening up the newspaper scene, and offering enormous cost-cutting possibilities. The first paper to get it would be streets ahead of its rivals. A new left-wing paper sympathetic to, and backed by, the trade unions could be the first to sign new staffing-level agreements and steal a march on the competition.

The comrades listened. It was very interesting stuff. But they explained there was still a long way to go. A great many meetings needed to be held. There were thousands of people to consult, movements to co-operate with, reports to be written, consultation and 'accountability' structures to be built, agreements to be drawn up, codes and charters to be agreed. That could not all happen overnight. It was time for *News on Sunday* to set off on the trail of the people and organizations who had theorized about the prospects for a popular left-wing newspaper for so long. Now they were going to be given a chance to put their money where their mouths were.

And the person who was going to lead them to this golden opportunity was the new driving force who had come to the fore and already earned himself the nickname of 'the Eddie Shah of *News on Sunday*' – Chris Walsh. Walsh was a man who had surfaced in public life before. But the last time he had been in the headlines, people had known him by a different name – Chris Bott.

2 · Mysteries of the orgasm

Getting things moving

Orgasm, organism, organisation: the coming together of life forces to overwhelm the present constraints and repressions. Communality generalised. The libido building its own organisation. An organised resistance to oppression, but the building of new social relations, the realisation of desires now, taking place within the organisation as part of the struggle for state power and a new society in the future. An organisation embodying what its members want out of life now, the beginning of totality through total opposition, and what we do to change the world being enjoyable in itself, not a sacrifice.

The words of Chris Bott, anarchist or, more politely, 'libertarian left', as laid out in giant 36-point type and printed in lurid blue on a red background on the cover of *Ink*, one of the crop of underground papers that sprang up at the end of the 1960s. Bott was given huge amounts of space on the inside pages of *Ink* in December 1971 and January 1972 to set out the scrambled views on life which he was culling from a variety of standard left-wing and anarchist gurus. Prominent in his thinking at the time was Wilhelm Reich, the advocate of the practice of free love, which he believed would bring all power systems crashing to the ground. Hence Bott's concentration on orgasm.

Ink wasn't advocating Bott as a philosopher. The point about his thoughts, spelled out in a series of letters, was his current address – Brixton prison. There, as prisoner number 100485, he was being held on remand, charged with maliciously conspiring to cause explosions likely to endanger life. He was one of the Stoke Newington Eight – the Angry Brigade.

The Angry Brigade was the *cause célèbre* of the libertarian left during this period, for carrying direct action beyond the usual sit-ins, street theatre and noisy disruptions and demonstrations aimed at 'authority' and prominent politicians. It publicized itself with a series of military-style 'communiqués' to the papers, with dire threats against the 'pigs' and slogans such as: 'Blow it up, burn it down, kick it till it breaks.' Moving into action, it then carried out a series of bombings, the most serious of which almost destroyed the private house of the Home Secretary, Robert Carr.

The Angry Brigade never killed anyone. All the attacks were against property, and nobody was hurt. And the only thing Chris Bott had murdered was the English language. But, before the IRA and Middle Eastern terrorists made such things part of everyday life in Britain in the 1970s, the bombings caused huge outrage. The furore was increased by the ham-fisted police hunt for those responsible. Eventually more than ten people, including Bott, were arrested and spent over a year in jail before the end of the lengthy legal proceedings. The Old Bailey trial lasted 111 days, a new legal record. Four of the Stoke Newington Eight – John Barker, James Greenfield, Anna Mendelson and Hilary Creek – were convicted and given ten-year jail sentences. Four others – Angela Weir, Catherine McLean, Stuart Christie and Bott – were acquitted.

Chris had a normal middle-class background, with the exception of the fact that he had been adopted and brought up in Sutton Coldfield by step-parents called Bott. He went to Strathclyde University and then on to Essex in 1968. Described in press coverage of the Angry Brigade trial as a 'compulsive joiner of revolutionary movements throughout Europe', he dropped out of his Latin American studies course to go to Paris during the student riots of May 1968. The experience convinced him that Europe was on the brink of revolution, and he threw himself into revolutionary Anarchist 'Situationism', which rejected conventional left-wing political parties.

Drifting from Essex to Manchester and then London, Bott became a well-known figure on the briefly blossoming 'libertarian left' or 'underground scene'. In May 1970 he met Hilary Creek, another libertarian activist. Creek had an affair with Bott, and was also involved with John Barker, who, together with James Greenfield, emerged as the backbone of the group accused of the bombings.

Barker and Greenfield were working-class lads who both arrived at Cambridge University in 1968 and were repelled by their first ever contact with the upper classes. Greenfield told the court he had regarded the university as a 'playground for the wealthy' and decided, whatever he did with his life, it would not be to help the rich get richer and more powerful. The two men dropped out of their courses, moved to Stoke Newington in North London and stuck together as they became involved in the libertarian and squatter movements.

After the trial Bott continued to knock around his old haunts in Stoke Newington and the East End, gaining a professional qualification in urban planning which he used in community work with the homeless and unemployed. He worked for a time with Stopover House and the Newham Alternative Project, both designed to provide temporary help for the poor and homeless of the East End. But although he learnt such skills as writing feasibility studies, he soon tired of life in the grant-aided voluntary sector. He wanted to get out of the old activist scene and transform himself into a modern, successful businessman. All round his dingy housing-association flat in Stoke Newington, close to Amhurst Road, where he had been arrested at the begining of the 1970s, were the signs of the new affluence. A wine bar called Fox's had opened up a short walk away in Church Street, causing such amazement that the *Observer* printed an article about it. Bott wanted to be part of this new success story, along with the City people, young designers, clothes merchants, media persons and trendy local-authority and institutional workers – the Yuppies and Yeppies.

His first commercial venture was the Aardvark Transport and Trading Company, based in Wapping. It had sprung from his activities in the housing movement, but was run on straight commercial lines, providing an 'alternative' removals service and producing a nice sideline in salvaged Victorian fireplaces which were sold to the new rich. Aardvark taught him that the left was not just a movement but a market. He cut off his shoulder length hair, put on a suit, and started dealing with bankers. Associates were shocked by the transformation, and joked that he had become a plain-clothes policeman.

Now he believed that the people who supported left-wing causes, and shared in movements concerned with issues such as squatting, nuclear disarmament, ecology and environment, provided a cohesive group to be sold to. And although many of them might be poor in some ways, that didn't mean they had no money to spend. His thinking was based on the theory known in economic jargon as 'reverse income substitution effect'. This postulates that, although some groups may not have much money in relative terms, they will spend more in defined sectors. Students, because their money is not tied up in big items such as mortgages, spend a lot on goods such as jeans, beer and cheap travel, and are therefore a target group. On the back of this approach, which is sound enough, he was to evolve complicated and hopelessly over-ambitious merchandising plans.

By the time he got involved with the newspaper project, Bott had changed his name; he was now Chris Walsh. There was nothing sinister about this change – he had simply reverted to the name he was born under after a search to find the identity of his real parents. Although Walsh's main aim was to become a successful businessman, he kept most of his old political views, which were different from those of the other people starting up *News on Sunday*. He brought with him the 'direct action' theory and practice of the libertarian left. Politics for people like him was not what you said, but what you did. The contrast with Ben Lowe, the blushing withdrawn original founder whom he increasingly pushed to one side, could not have been more marked. Lowe represented what had always been the basis of the project until then – the concerned, upmarket readership of Right-Ons which was the perfect setting for a talking-shop.

But Walsh got stuck into the project with typical determination. He was quite clear about the paper he wanted. It was to be politically left, but above all popular, and designed to appeal to a big readership. He was contemptuous of soggy, concerned lefties and wanted the paper to be outrageous, noisy, controversial – an angry two-fingered salute to everyone in power – right, left or centre. Extrovert, cheerful and bursting with half-baked ideas and projects, he didn't see things the way the talkers did. What they saw as a problem, he saw as a challenge. He was thinking big, and thinking big meant a huge readership – a paper like the *Mirror*, to be read in equally large numbers by ordinary people who shared his contempt for organized politics. He wasn't interested in the heavy political stuff which bored the pants off most people. The required approach, rather like Walsh himself, was short, rude and snappy.

Thornton had been pushing for the same sort of readership, and the two men had another thing in common – they wanted action. Things must be got moving. But Walsh's position was not as polarized as Thornton's with regard to the others. He realized that there must be meetings, and he was prepared to go to them and fire off his battery of buzz words which signified he was 'one of us'. He had been around the scene for long enough to know how to manipulate meetings without getting everyone's back up. His loathing for committee-bound inactivity was not new. In his outpourings to the readers of *Ink* he had compared bureaucrats to the police, the army and prison officers. Instead of traditional forms of organization, which for the Labour movement meant committees and conferences, Walsh confusingly advocated 'the overthrow of the present set-up, the development of self-organisation, of consciousness, of strategy, power, for this to take place, the creation of community resources, shared pleasure, the spreading of present alienation'.

But at the same time he had another libertarian trait – he was shambolically organized. Nothing was worth doing unless it gave pleasure, he had argued in *Ink*. And being organized did not give him pleasure. For a start he was a night-bird, and would often only surface in the middle of the day. He didn't like the tedious business of routine, and rapidly became notorious in the group for missing meetings and failing to make appointments. The complications of the laborious paperwork and endless reports of minutes which obsessed other members of the project held no interest for him. He often only glanced at the reports. Like Thornton, his philosophy was to back his hunches and do it now. The rest he saw as just bureaucracy. Walsh thought that if it was left to the others they would go on talking for ever. Unlike them, he had 'a strategy'.

Outside his own environment, however, in the more sober and conservative world of conventional business, Walsh worried people. Thornton knew of various incidents which confirmed his opinion that Walsh made a distinctly negative impression in the hunt for backers. A typical occasion was when Thornton used his contacts to set up a meeting between the paper and the trade-union-sponsored Unity Bank to borrow £10,000 to keep things going for now, and to test the water for the millions of pounds that would be needed in the future.

The meeting was not a success. Unity Bank's Terry Thomas, who represented another backer which it was hoped would look favourably on the project, the Labour Party-linked Co-operative Bank, turned them down flat. Much of his decision was based on his assessment of Walsh and Hayling, who was also present, and of their business plan. Walsh, bedecked with new suit and executive glasses, had pitched in with his usual aggressive style. Head tilted back, and firing out ideas like a machine-gun in his nasal North London voice, he had presented himself as a man with his finger on the modern business pulse. His conversation was spattered with recently mugged-up marketing and business phrases. It all led to only two possibilities: he was either a whirling business genius or a complete headbanger. And since he was in his late thirties and apparently without a cent to show for it, the conclusion was obvious. Hayling, who was much smoother in his appearance and approach, just seemed to Thomas to be very ignorant of business and how it worked.

After the two had left, Thomas confided to Thornton that he found it quite extraordinary that these two people, who were so naïve and inexperienced, could be at the top of what was supposed to be a concrete business proposal. What they had told him about the paper was 'positively negative' – an endless list of what the paper was not going to do, rather than what it was going to do. He could see no future in their hopelessly optimistic sales forecasts.

With this thumbs-down from a part of the financial world whose support was expected, Thornton was losing his 'window of opportunity' argument. It didn't worry the comrades too much. The Right-On alternative to the City was sitting under their noses in the form of the Greater London Enterprise Board. The negotiations which followed were mainly handled by Alan Hayling. Hayling was still not a formal member of the group starting the paper, but he was getting more and more interested, and in his official GLC capacity acted as a go-between between the paper and GLEB, smoothing over the difficulties and piloting the paper round bureaucratic pitfalls.

GLEB had been set up by the GLC in 1983 to provide venture capital to start up enterprises and provide jobs in the London area. An endless stream of proposals had poured in for the £20 million a year it had to dispense. Many of the earlier ones came to grief, especially workers' co-ops, where money was handed out for projects such as a vegetarian quiche restaurant in Deptford. Some were simply misguided, others were closer to the edge of the law, but predictably many crashed. However, GLEB made progress with more sane ideas, and was credited with creating or saving 2,000 jobs in 116 different enterprises. Whether this added up in terms of cost per job was another matter.

When *News on Sunday* made an approach, GLEB was concentrating on how to replace the rapidly disappearing jobs in the print industry, and any proposal in this area was high-priority. Critics of the organization say it gave away money indiscriminately, whilst its supporters maintain fiercely that all projects were minutely criticized for viability. Certainly, as *News on Sunday* found out, it involved a vast amount of bureaucracy and meetings before any money was handed over. By now, in 1985, the GLC bandwagon was slowing down and the Department of the Environment had imposed swingeing cuts on GLEB's expenditure.

News on Sunday asked for money to produce a dummy newspaper, which would then be market-researched, and the results would be wrapped into a feasibility study. The research would determine likely sales levels, and also settle the division between a left-wing *Mail on Sunday*, with projected circulation of 400,000, and a 'Sunday *Guardian*' selling 250,000. If the green light came on for either project, the paper would go straight to capitalization as a commercial company. Investment would be sought from the City, councils, trade unions and rich individuals. GLEB would be paid back with shares in the company when it was floated, and be given a say in the structure of the company.

The paper pitched for £56,000. GLEB offered £39,000 with strict conditions. The funding money had to be matched pound for pound by other backers; the people who believed in the paper had to put up £5,000 of their own money between them; and the paper had to have a controlling group to protect it from an outside takeover which might change the political line. This group also had to be made up on strict equal-opportunities lines, with the requisite number of minorities and women. Two GLEB representatives, including information director John Palmer, previously a *Guardian* journalist, joined the *NoS* executive committee.

Walsh, with Hayling fronting the show to add that important touch of Cambridge class, threw himself into raising the matching funding required by GLEB. He was given able assistance by Mike Power, a long-standing member of the Communist Party with high-level contacts in the left-wing unions. Thornton had good contacts as well, and proved very useful in arranging meetings. He was friendly with Ron Todd, the head of the giant Transport and General Workers' Union, with more than one million members. The T and G was the paper's greatest union supporter from the beginning, and was to end up as the biggest single investor. Thornton had also earned the respect of SOGAT, the print union, and Manchester City Council for his previous efforts to re-employ the redundant workers at the *Daily Mirror* plant in the city.

Although the amount *NoS* had to raise at this point was small compared with what was to come later, those involved say that in many ways it was harder work. The unions posed the same problem as the City. The proposal did not yet have concrete facts to back it up. And the unions had also been through this scene recently. At the beginning of the 1980s, the TUC had asked Lord McCarthy, a Fellow of Nuffield College, Oxford, to examine the feasibility of a daily newspaper sympathetic to the Labour movement. There had been great difficulty raising the £40,000 contribution from the unions. McCarthy's report had proposed a £6.7 million plan for a national daily along the lines of the *Sun* or the *Mail*, based in or near London, with a staff of 230. The paper would need a minimum circulation of 300,000 to make money, and with an annual expenditure of £13.3 million would make an annual profit of £6.4 million, if it reached a circulation of 500,000. But the idea never got off the ground. The diminishing role of the unions, disillusionment among workers, and falling membership due to unemployment had put many of them in considerable financial difficulties. Although the idea was superficially attractive, money was too tight.

Ben Lowe had studied the McCarthy report carefully and had answers for a lot of the scepticism, even though the unions' enthusiasm had been blunted. And Walsh, zooming about, was tirelessly energetic and ruthless in his determination. Mike Power and Clive Thornton pointed him in the right direction and sent him in like a terrier down a rabbit hole. He and Hayling emerged with £11,000 from Manchester City Council, £7,000 from the TGWU, £6,000 from SOGAT and a total of £10,650 from six others – National Union of Public Employees (NUPE), £3,500; National Communications Union (NCU), £2,000; National Union of Journalists (NUJ), £2,000; National Association of Local Government Officers (NALGO), £2,000; Association of Cinematograph, Television and

Allied Technicians (ACTT), £650; and the tiny TGWU-dominated Bakers' Union, £500.

The people who wrote the original GLC-funded pre-feasibility study – Chris Walsh, Ben Lowe, Mike Power, Liz Cooper and Kit Sadgrove – met in a flat near Kings Cross and formed themselves, with the addition of five others, all friends, into the Founders' Trust. The Founders put up the required £5,000, making a total of £39,650 – enough to match GLEB and trigger the promised grant.

But while Walsh and Hayling were raising the money, relations with Thornton were becoming increasingly strained. He began thumping the table and insisting the paper instal experienced management. The comrades were horrified. One of the key elements of the paper had always been that it should be run on consensus lines, with broad agreement among the group, often expressed by a vote before any decision was taken. The trouble with 'meetings management' is that the viewpoint adopted is that of the people who turn up. If you miss a meeting, or a crucial decision within one, it is very difficult to have anything reversed afterwards, as it has then been approved by the consensus and therefore stands. Decision-making and prioritizing therefore fall more and more to the kind of people whose forte is attending meetings and getting the support of those present. It is management by attrition. But the decision to use it was deliberate. *NoS* people were not just inexperienced in business, but were opposed to its methods, and consciously trying to do things in a different way to prove the rottenness of the capitalist system. Thornton, on the other hand, understood a lot about the caring side of capitalism, but was firmly wedded to the way it operated. He grew more and more dismayed at this well-meaning amateurism, which he could not see working in practice.

The two sides might have parted company there and then had it not been for the GLEB's condition that someone with newspaper business experience should be on the executive. Thornton agreed to stay, but insisted that his name be kept secret. As he was only a member of the executive, with the same status as everybody else, they agreed, but then promptly let him down. James Curran, the left-wing media intellectual who had been advising on market research, leaked his involvement to *Tribune*, the established semi-official paper of the traditional Labour left. Thornton exploded, and successfully demanded that Curran be booted out.

RSGB

The leaked news that a figure as credible as Thornton was involved put *NoS* on the public stage. Thornton then insisted that although his name was known it was not to be used for fund-raising. He would remain on the sidelines, and do some more work if and when they were ready to launch the paper. He also advised them again to get a high-profile chairman and a well-known editor. Pilger had already been sugggested, but Thornton was unimpressed after coming across him in his *Daily Mirror* days. He was more interested in offering the post to John Lloyd, one of the most respected journalists on the *Financial Times*.

With Thornton dropping into the background and the money coming in, the comrades progressed to the next stage, the dummy edition. It was a marathon process. The paper was first scheduled to be printed in June, but in the end didn't go on the presses until four months later in mid-October. It was preceded by the involvement of hundreds of people in discussion groups devoted to different sections – home news, features, music, the arts, international and foreign news and sport. At great length, and with considerable idealistic heart-searching, they worked through the various problems and anomalies of the paper in comparison with its rival newspapers.

The discussion groups were relatively open, and many people came along as friends of friends. Some were journalists, others political activists, and many were interested in working on the paper for wages once it got going. One of the attractions of *NoS* was that, in breaking away from the Fleet Street mould, it was also looking for a different sort of employee. A major part of the paper's thinking was that it could employ people who would have been good journalists if they had pursued journalism as a conventional career. They were therefore unrecognized, as they knew only too well, and were attracted by the idea of the possibility of a job. Some were qualified, others wanted to learn.

Most of the group members were quite young, Right-On, middle-class, intellectual, and had their own particular obsession which they wanted to see in the paper. There was a high attendance by women, who formed a major part of the thinking. A count at one meeting revealed that all twenty-seven people present were *Guardian* readers, and it was obvious that many of them knew little about popular papers. This persuaded one faction, representing experienced news-paper people such as John Palmer, to try to push the paper back upmarket. Palmer, seconded by GLEB to work with *NoS*, felt many people were naïvely attracted to the pops because they thought they were easier to do. Fleet Street, which has been spending millions for years trying get the formula right, holds the opposite point of view. Working on a quality paper, where journalists have more room for the finer points and a more informed audience, is considered to be much less demanding.

Although these new contributors were welcomed, the central organization of *News on Sunday* remained secretive and close-knit. Instead of being directly involved, radical supporters were diverted into the groups where their thoughts could be sifted and selected at will. Walsh, ever eager to stick his finger in someone else's pie, gravitated towards the foreign affairs discussion group. The agonized hand-wringing about internationalism and the finer points of world politics were thrust aside. Instead Walsh put in simplistic suggestions with blockheadedly dramatic headlines like: 'South Africa – Is it going to blow?' It was exactly what Palmer feared.

Ultimately, though, which way the paper was going to go was decided by market research, a new obsession and an antiseptic surrogate for contact with real tabloid readers. 'Concept research', followed by an omnibus quantitative survey, produced a brief for the dummy which came out in favour of the more 'downmarket' left-wing *Mail on Sunday*, rather than the 'Sunday *Guardian*'. Walsh was pleased. For him this was a move in the right direction, though not far enough.

The brief suggested a paper with sixty-four pages, 'strong on photographs, highly readable and written to be taken seriously'. But the brief also instructed that it was to be 'a lively, humorous paper that covered all aspects of life and not just current affairs. The paper was to be open and frank on political as well as personal issues; it was to be investigative and campaigning, internationalist, but also accessible, and radical but clearly independent of any political current or party.' Not surprisingly, people in market-research panels up and down the country had said they would be delighted to buy a paper like that. Now all the comrades had to do was produce it.

The job of pouring vintage Right-On journalism into mid-market 'quality-tabloid' bottles fell to Hayling. He was now the member of the newly formed executive committee with special responsibility for both structuring the company and liaising with discussion groups and with adviser John Pilger. After a series of delays, more discussion groups and a conference in Manchester, work started on the actual dummy. It was put together at the Camden New Technology Centre, which was loaned by the council, and administered from *News on Sunday*'s recently occupied headquarters in Caxton House near Waterloo station, the London offices of the print union, SOGAT. The dummy took three weeks' work by a team of volunteers, mostly part-time and helping when they could. The operation was overseen by Pilger, who put in an occasional appearance in person with suggestions for improvement.

Nobody knows exactly how many people were responsible for input, but by the time the dummy was finished more than two hundred had played a part one way or another. Some of the work went smoothly, but a lot was chaotic, with much confusion and many meetings to dole out coverage in accordance with the relative worthiness of various campaigns. Brian Whitaker, a former editor of the *Sunday Times* 'Insight' team who was responsible for much of the last-minute layout, found himself interrupted by the constant political hubbub. At one point a furious gay activists delegation turned up. It had heard that the paper was planning to include an item on AIDS and demanded to be consulted. A cardinal error had obviously been made, as the paper had made huge efforts beforehand to consult pressure groups about tackling their subject in an approved fashion. Naturally the activists got their meeting at once. Whitaker thought this was all wonderful stuff and great fun, but at one stage when his patience was wearing thin he was heard to exclaim: 'This is worse than working for Murdoch!'

News on Sunday, when it eventually emerged, was pronounced a fair effort by the rest of the industry. It had its sixty-four pages, some in smudgy *Today*-style colour, some in glossy heat-set colour, and most in good old black and white. The front-page story was about a waste pipe dribbling low-grade radioactive waste into the Thames, which, by Fleet Street standards, was not a great story. Clive Thornton contributed a personal finance column. The paper was an extraordinary jumble. So many people had to be pleased or mollified, and it was trying to do so many things at once, that the pages were hopelessly crammed with bitty stories. But it was particularly strong on international news, and contained a good consistent political line which pleased most of the people involved. The design, however, was almost universally condemned within the project. At a glance, the paper resembled a specialist publication like *Motorcycle News*, with elements of *Socialist Worker*, *New Musical Express* and the *Mail on Sunday* stirred in. The new obsession with trendy design was indulged in by scattering diamond-shaped symbols around the pages.

The paper was immediately put out for market research by RSGB – Research Surveys of Great Britain Ltd, one of Britain's largest and most respected market-research companies. The company, which is a wholly owned subsidiary of AGB Research, had been chosen by Ben Lowe partly because it had done market research for other papers, including an abortive workers' co-operative, the *Scottish Daily News*. (It was later to do work for the *Independent*.) It was also felt that it was a company which nobody could attack on the grounds of political bias in favour of the project – if anything, thought Walsh, the other way round, after he had seen a portrait of Margaret Thatcher prominently displayed in its Ealing headquarters.

After two weeks RSGB's thick brown-covered report thumped on to Lowe's desk. It contained nearly a hundred pages, densely covered with rows of figures – the results of interviews with 1,072 people from Land's End to John O'Groats. Lowe liked crunching numbers anyway, but as his figures skittered across the rubbery keys of the calculator, he began to gasp with amazement. After a desultory fifteen minutes looking through *News on Sunday*, 5.6 per cent of interviewees had said they were 'certain to buy' a paper like Hayling's dummy. In a national Sunday paper market of around 20 million, this amounted to 1.1 million 'certain' sales every week. Add in 9.8 per cent who said they were 'very likely to buy', and you had three million customers.

When the shock had worn off, Ben Lowe and Henry Stewart – recently drafted on to the executive committee from the Newcastle regional group – started examining the figures in detail. Their findings were summed up in the feasibility study published in February 1986, which predicted a minimum weekly sale of 800,000 and a maximum of 1.5 million. There were a number of warnings from RSGB which were included, and which were later to be added into the company prospectus. 'Newspaper sale prediction is open to wide margins of error, as are any sale predictions . . . primarily because the quality of the product will change from week to week depending on the available content, the number of editorial pages and so on.' There were other factors to be taken into account – the effect of the pre-launch television advertising campaign, the launch of new opposition titles, and the 'variability of the product from the impression given by the dummy'. Lowe and Stewart concluded that all these factors were 'likely to increase sales'. They thought the pre-launch promotional campaign would easily counter any moves by the opposition. The other new launches planned were Sunday *Today* and *Sunday Sport* – neither aimed at the same sort of readers. Most important, the real paper, as opposed to the dummy, would be 'produced with professional staff, an extensive newsgathering network and extensive resources, and it therefore seems certain that it will be more impressive than the dummy issue', they grandly announced.

The most extraordinary factor was RSGB's advice that they should go ahead and publish – the opposite to what the company had told the *Scottish Daily News*. And the advice was on the back of the most comprehensive research ever carried out for a new paper.

Though Lowe tried to hang on to the original concept, RSGB's figures finally killed off the 'Sunday *Guardian*' approach. The paper had now taken a major turning. The market gap which Lowe had guessed was there was bigger than he had expected. Walsh was ecstatic: now the paper was looking far beyond the Right-On supporters' group and being told what he had always wanted to believe – there was a large group of solid working-class people fed up with the frivolity in the existing tabloids. Added to the Right-On readers, they effectively expanded the core group and provided a viable number of buyers.

The readership identified by RSGB broke down equally between men and women. Most – 65 per cent – were working-class in socioeconomic groups C2, D and E. The rest were white-collar, middle-class and upper-class from groups A, B and C1. The readers were younger than average, with 45 per cent under thirty-five, compared with 37 per cent in the population as a whole, and the paper was confirmed as northern, with 67 per cent of its potential readers beyond the Watford Gap. It seemed that *NoS* was going to be the first to tap the huge reservoir of people who had given up on the papers altogether. An impressive 17 per cent of the potential readers were not buying a Sunday paper at the moment. Of the ones who were, half would come across from the *News of the World*,

Sunday Mirror and *People*. More than a third of sales would be to Labour voters, another third to Alliance or Tory (12 per cent), and the rest to people who could not say which party they supported. As an aside the research revealed that just under half of the women questioned did not support the women's liberation movement.

To this day RSGB stand behind their research. The fact that it was proved to be an overestimate is blamed on various horrors which took place on the paper's route to market. But at the same time, the fact has supported those who have a low opinion of market research in estimating 'self-image' matters such as which paper people will buy. Now, after various newspaper disasters, it is being recognized that allegiance to a particular paper, whatever others may think of it, is not something people change lightly. Even when the study appeared, there was a great deal of scepticism within *NoS*, but the attitude was that they had consulted the experts and got the evidence. If this was the reply, they were prepared to go with it.

The next step was to turn the feasibility study into a detailed business plan which would be presented in a share prospectus aimed at attracting the target £6.5 million now estimated to be needed to launch a paper selling between 800,000 and 1.1 million copies. The key to this was finding a Chairman. And although Thornton seemed the obvious choice to the outside world, relationships with him had reached a new low in October 1985. Immediately after the dummy was produced, Thornton found that money had been raised in his home city of Newcastle by using his name without permission. He was furious. He had already noted, with some concern, that money raised was immediately 'dissipated' into a range of fringe activities. But this was too much; he picked up the phone and left his resignation on the answering machine at Caxton House. The next morning Tom Picton, a former lecturer at the Royal College of Art who had worked as picture editor on the dummy edition, played back the tinny message. 'This is Clive Thornton. I resign here and now.' Thornton was eventually smoothed down and persuaded to stay on condition that the paper find a Chairman at once – a reputable businessman whose name could be used instead of his.

Finding someone was a question of asking round in likely circles. Matthew Evans, head of publishers Faber and Faber, was the first to get the call. Hayling reported to the unenthusiastic executive committee that he was 'favourably disposed', but nothing came of it.

Sir Denis Foreman, of Granada Television, excited a little more interest. He told Hayling that he was keen to help, but could do nothing until he retired in April, more than six months away. The IBA rules prevent chairmen of television companies having substantial national newspaper interests. But he would be happy to be 'Godfather' to the project.

Christmas came and went, and it was three months since Thornton's answering-machine ultimatum. Since nobody else had been found, Hayling offered Thornton the Chairmanship, but the executive attached two humiliating conditions. First he was to endorse publicly the *NoS* Equal Opportunities approach, and second he was to agree to allow negotiations with the unions to 'run their course' quietly.

As Hayling, Walsh, Lowe and the others must have known, Thornton could not accept either condition. He was on record as saying that he regarded the agonizing over Equal Opportunities on a paper which did not even exist as – at best – a red herring. And he felt even more strongly about the union issue. He had told them a year ago that one of the main reasons he was interested in the paper was his conviction that the 'new realism' of print unions made it financially possible to seize the 'window of opportunity'.

Thornton wasn't interested. *NoS* had mucked him about for more than a year. He had attended endless meetings which they accused him of dominating. If he didn't turn up they moaned at him later for not being there, and they had used his name for fund-raising without permission. All he had intended to do was bridge the gap until they got a Chairman, or 'Chair' as he was supposed to call it.

With Thornton's final refusal the comrades could not fudge the Chair issue any longer. They tried Walter Runciman of the Child Poverty Action Group and Peter Hughes of Logica, the computer company. Runciman was not interested and Hughes told them he was busy turning round his company, which had temporarily bombed – an ideal qualification in retrospect.

As they culled *Who's Who* there was a debate on the executive about the 'Old Lord approach' – finding someone who had been a financial force in the past, and would prove the paper was commercially sober. But at the same time, through being virtually geriatric as they saw it, the Lord could be expected to stay in his castle and not spoil the fun. Lord Lovell-Davis, Lord Kearton (Labour financier and former head of the National Enterprise Board), Lord Wedder-burn (Professor at the London School of Economics) and Joel Barnett (merchant banker and former Labour Treasury Minister) were put in the frame and sounded out. But, employing the commercial sobriety for which they were being approached, they all refused.

Then Hayling struck gold. A call to Nicholas Horsley, the Chair-man of the Hull-based food-supply giant, Northern Foods, led to a meeting at Glendor House, Clarges Street, the company's plush Mayfair duplex flat off Curzon Street. Hayling lavished the famous charm in unprecedented quantities, making an immediate and long-lasting impression on the fifty-two-year-old Horsley.

It didn't take long to get things sorted out. At Northern Foods Horsley's brother-in-law, Chris Haskins, was taking a bigger and bigger part in the running of the company, leaving Horsley with more time, and he was delighted to have a chance to help in a project which instantly appealed to his idealistic nature. He accepted at once and was almost ready to start tomorrow. He promised, as his first task, to sort out Thornton. All that remained was to get his appoint-ment approved by the comrades.

The *NoS* executive reacted to the Horsley option with character-istic lack of grace. Ben Lowe was dispatched to comb the radical food supplier's background for things to complain about. The verdict was that Horsley had about as clean a bill of health as it was possible for a real, live capitalist to have. Northern Foods was even tussling with one of its customers – the 100 per cent un-Right-On McDonalds hamburger chain – over its activities in South Africa. This was just the sort of attitude the paper wanted – in another context it would have been a good news story. And Horsley had given money to miners' families during the 1984–5 strike.

Horsley passed the test and went off to see Thornton, who was still simmering and had nothing but dire warnings for him. 'They're driving me mad,' he fumed. He had been let down several times, they had done all sorts of things without asking him, and sometimes he only found out what they'd been up to when the papers rang for comment.

'They've no idea. And it'll be you who'll be in the public gaze as the figurehead. You'll get the reporters, the TV, the media all in-truding into your private life asking you to explain what's going on. It's not worth it,' he stressed.

But to Thornton's surprise, Horsley assured him that *NoS*'s naïvety was its greatest asset. The stories of his own radical youth flowed out. 'You know, they remind me of myself thirty years ago when I was a student activist at Oxford,' enthused Horsley.

Hayling's invitation had brought it all back. When Horsley had left university in the mid-1950s, with a third-class degree in philosophy, politics and economics, he had planned to conquer the world as a footloose roving reporter in the mould of his great hero, the foreign correspondent James Cameron. He set off with rucksack and typewriter on a round-the-world trip, but only got as far as New Orleans, where, ever the hopeless romantic, he fell in love with a girl he met on a park bench. Before the first blockbuster clattered from his typewriter he was back in Hull, settled down with his new wife, and started in middle management in the family business, then called Northern Dairies.

Thornton was unimpressed. While Horsley had been cavorting about at Oxford, he had been on the first rung of an entirely different social ladder, as a solicitor's clerk. Horsley didn't think much of Thornton either, and later complained (as did others) that he talked mostly about himself. But to seal the deal he offered Thornton a place on the board of the nascent company, Jeboda, which was to be *News on Sunday* until flotation. Thornton accepted, agreeing to stay around and possibly play a larger role again if things looked up.

But he gave a final warning to Horsley. He was going to find he had an enormously difficult job on his hands. The people in *NoS* had to be made to realize that if they were going to go after big money, professional management had to come in. And that meant them moving over. Thornton saw no sign that they were prepared to do so.

Horsley just smiled, his large relaxed frame and confident bonhomie contrasting sharply with the abrupt style of the little self-made Geordie. He looked down at Thornton and informed him of the new management attitude. His hero, James Cameron, would have approved.

'They've got a dream, Clive. A dream. And we've got to help them make it come true.'

3 · Serious money

Moving up north

With Clive Thornton out of the way, the media spotlight began to warm up on Nick Horsley. And he began to sweat. At this stage the media hounds were sniffing *News on Sunday* for signs of Loony or Hard Left activity. It was partly for a story, and partly to size the paper up as competition or business. Files on the paper were being opened in cuttings libraries and (behind the scenes) on executive computers. Newcomers – especially such crucial ones as the Chairman – were being inspected carefully as the jigsaw of the company began to fall into place. But Horsley's reasons for joining the paper were entirely respectable. He was a pacifist professing the admirable, old-fashioned virtues of his Quaker upbringing.

Horsley's CND activities went back to his days at Oxford, when the time he spent on demonstrations was one of the reasons for his third-class degree. He remained an active supporter of CND, boasted that his daughter had been conceived on an Aldermaston march, and had once horrified Margaret Thatcher by wearing his CND badge when he met her at a gathering of northern business people. He even had a CND sticker in the back window of his car, a Jaguar XJ4.2 – and he claimed that no other Jaguar in the country displayed one. *Campaign*, the advertising industry trade paper, noted that he had happily accepted the deletion of the suffix 'man' from his title of Chairman of News on Sunday Publishing plc. The article made a weak joke about his CND beret.

There was no questioning the fact that Horsley was an extremely successful businessman, even if his clothes sometimes looked more like *Country Life*. His big frame, slightly unkempt, thinning blond hair and florid appearance smacked of outdoor activity and a 'hearty' attitude. He had been a keen sportsman in his youth, and now followed cricket avidly. And he was well known in the City, where there was still respect for a solid Yorkshire businessman. Northern Foods was one of the largest and most successful companies in the country, with a steady record of expansion which was beginning to attract foreign investment. At the same time, the company's interests had spread all over the world, far beyond the milk-round set up by his father.

The company had been well placed to take advantage of the 1960s consumer boom, and was already prospering by the time Horsley joined the Board in 1963, at the age of twenty-nine. He became Chairman seven years later; under his chairmanship profits rose from £1 million to £60 million, making him by far the most successful businessman in the East Riding. A particular coup for the firm was the contract to supply the rapidly expanding Marks and Spencer chain.

But Horsley hadn't sacrificed his humanitarian principles whilst presiding over such speedy business growth. Northern Foods had always had a good name locally, and had earned respect for its relations with its workers. Horsley personally insisted the company practise Equal Opportunities, and have fully unionized factories where managers and employees addressed each other on Christian-name terms.

In some ways, though, Nick – as he insisted people call him – lived in the shadow of his father Alec, a renowned pacifist who had set up a Chair of Peace Studies at Bradford University on the sensible grounds that everywhere else seemed to study war. It was through this initiative that Nick finally got to meet his great hero, James Cameron, and after the collapse of his first marriage, he married Cameron's step-daughter, Sabeita. When she left him in 1983 he was devastated. But after that he met up again with Olwen, a childhood friend. The two of them had often met socially in the old days, with their respective partners, at evenings in the Green Dragon, the local pub in the village of Welton, ten miles from Hull, where Horsley lived in a magnificent stone house which, he always stressed, did not have a drive.

Olwen had had her troubles as well. Her marriage had broken up, and she had gone to live with a man who was starting an art gallery in the Lake District. The relationship didn't work out, and early one Sunday morning she rang Horsley pleading for help. He told her to drive to him immediately, and when she arrived treated her to a breakfast of kippers and Chablis. They had stayed together ever since, and Nick referred to her as his 'partner'.

Olwen was not at all sure about the *NoS* offer. She thought it would be a big mistake for Nick to devote two or three days a week to the newspaper at the expense of the family business. And she was worried about his health. Horsley was being slowly crippled by a rare type of paralysis spreading from his ankle, which meant that he now had to walk with a stick, and which it was feared would eventually put him in a wheelchair. Frequent travel made his leg swell up, and caused him a considerable amount of discomfort. Olwen didn't know at that time that the commitment was soon to become twenty-four hours a day, seven days a week. At one point she told Nick that if Hayling – whom she referred to as 'that nice-looking young man with the curly hair' – came round again she would refuse to let him in. But she did, and was another won over by the famous charm.

Horsley cheerfully admitted when he took up the post of Chair that he knew nothing about newspapers. He would rely instead on his successful general business experience to pull him through. His language was full of nautical metaphors. The Board was the bridge; he was going to keep his hand on the wheel. This was a perfect frame of mind for chairing Northern Foods, a great supertanker of a business forging steadily ahead through the profitable waters of supermarket supply. But *NoS* was more like a racing power-boat, and Horsley soon found himself in the position of a water-skier rather than a captain. Instead of being at the controls, he was desperately clinging on while the engines, at full throttle, thrust the boat violently from side to side as a host of faction fighters wrestled to grab the wheel – or in most cases to avoid touching it. Shrewd observers, such as Paul Johnson of the *Spectator*, pointed out that there was a world of difference between running a food-supply business – however large and successful – and a newspaper. The former was a relatively stable affair. Newspapers, even ones unencumbered by the exceptional problems *NoS* was creating for itself, need quick decisions and highly interventionist managers who know the business inside out.

But Horsley was popular with the Founders on a personal level. His politics didn't cause any problems. He was a self-confessed old-fashioned Liberal, who believed in people being nicer to each other, and he had a warm and generous manner to which they responded. Hayling got huge enjoyment from introducing the two sides, and he and others were beside themselves at the incongruity of the meeting. Their attitude was part of an exaggerated respect for the English class system, and they did not seem to realize that an open-minded person like Horsley could easily have had the same sort of meeting at, for example, a CND conference.

Horsley, as a Yorkshireman, was naturally a fan of the north, and hoped that *News on Sunday*, as part of its political stance, would help halt the growing north–south divide. The paper had originally intended to base itself in London, where large-scale funding from the GLEB and the GLC seemed certain under the banner of creating jobs. But now that the GLC was about to be abolished and GLEB in trouble, the paper, with Horsley's enthusiastic support, decided to move to Manchester.

Horsley and Hayling were in disagreement about the Manchester move. But the two men had quickly developed a peculiarly close and mutually protective relationship, and could agree to differ without falling out. It was said that Horsley treated Hayling as the brilliant but wayward son he always wanted, but never had. He could criticize 'Alan', but nobody else was allowed to. Others said that Horsley saw in Hayling the image of what he had always wanted to be – idealistic, full of derring-do, glamorous, and free from the tedious baggage of conventional business life.

The *NoS* pro-Manchester lobby had a strong moral argument which appealed to both Horsley and the Founders. The paper would be whisked out of the cynical ghetto of Fleet Street, and away from distorted, degenerate London priorities – back to basics and closer to 'the people'. Supporters of this argument seemed to believe that the paper could defy the laws of journalistic and financial gravity. All the nationals except the *Daily Star*, which had been specifically based there by its owners to soak up the spare capacity left by their other declining title, the *Daily Express*, had either closed down, moved to London or drastically reduced their Manchester operations. The *Guardian* left at the beginning of the 1970s, and even the *Star* was shortly to move to the Smoke.

The anti-London lobby, however, was well organized and had financial arguments to back its case. There was the possibility of large-scale investment from Manchester and other northern councils hoping to stem the tide and keep a vestige of the newspaper industry in the city. EEC training grants would also be available. To bolster the argument, Kerry Marcus, a radio journalist from Manchester, was hired on a £6,000 grant from Manchester City Council to produce a convincing financial case. Marcus calculated that by taking into account property costs – estimated at a third of those in London – and salaries on average £2,000 lower, the paper should save £658,000 a year by being based in Manchester.

It could also get £140,000 in grants and investment from the council and the local equivalent of GLEB if it moved north. By this time many of the London borough councils, such as Islington, Brent and Southwark, were confidently expected to invest, regardless of where the paper was based. There was hope that locating the paper in the north would swing other, non-London councils behind it. As much as £750,000 extra in investment from Manchester and other northern councils was estimated to be available if the paper moved. And, to top the argument, market research indicated greater reader-loyalty amongst *NoS*'s target audience for a northern-based paper – indicating an extra £1 million a year in sales and advertising revenue. Added together, the anti-London lobby said, there was around £2.5 million to be gained by moving to Manchester.

But in the end, like most decisions on *NoS*, the Manchester move was 'positively negative'. It was not so much pro-Manchester as anti-London. As the paper was to be printed on contract presses with pages faxed across electronically, its editorial offices could in theory be based anywhere. But the plan had another side to it – it was a vital factor in the faction fighting which was beginning to engulf the paper. For the comrades it was a back-handed way of ensuring that the increasingly suspect and disliked Pilger would be ruled out as editor. And it would cut his ally Hayling down to size. Both men had fought a long and isolated battle against the move from London.

Globe-trotting Pilger regarded even London as provincial; Manchester was beyond the pale. He described the city as 'an interesting train ride away from all the talent and all the good stories.' He might visit from time to time should a story miserable enough to write about crop up, but there was no way he was going to edit the paper from there. After all, Pilger was a citizen of the world. He virtually commuted between London and Sydney, his Australian birthplace, where he would stay for months at a time with his parents, making award-winning films, before returning to London in his safari suit, sun-bleached and fit. He saw himself, with some justice, as towering above the rest of the *NoS* people. He admired some of them as determined but ordinary folk. Others, like Hayling, obviously had talent, but none of them had even a fraction of the experience or ability which had twice earned him the Journalist of the Year award for his coverage of Vietnam and Cambodia. Though Pilger was a committed left-winger, he was lacking the finer points of the new feminist-influenced Right-On etiquette. The maverick and often exasperating individualism which had served him well in battles against conservative-minded executives at the *Mirror* became a major liability at *NoS*, where the premium was on conformity to group objectives. Like all outsiders, he was automatically a focus for suspicion, and his casual dismissal of the Manchester plan had gained him enemies.

Hayling, who was now working closely with Pilger, sensed the Manchester decision had been made in advance by the Founders, and assembled a team of journalists to explain what was wrong with it. He wanted to use Pilger as his main gun, but the globetrotter had disappeared abroad again. As a substitute Brian Whitaker, the second most experienced journalist continuously involved with *NoS*, was drafted to write a journalist's case for the paper remaining in London. Whitaker's report explained how newspapers worked. Just because the paper was in Manchester would not even mean that it would be easier to report on the north. All the lines of communication were routed through London. London had the City, the Government and all its departments, the headquarters of all the major companies and pressure groups, all the people in the know – in short, as Pilger had said, all the stories. And the crucial support elements, such as press-cuttings and picture libraries, were in the capital. Even the Founders recognized that a London presence could not be abandoned altogether, so by choosing a northern HQ the paper would turn itself into a two-site operation. This would throw up a host of attendant problems.

But the Founders and their political allies weren't interested in these facts, which, with their ignorance of newspapers, did not mean much to them. They decided that Pilger, Hayling and the journalists simply couldn't be bothered to make the move. Hayling had let them know that the move would complicate his personal life. He was a pro-feminist 'new man', and therefore saw himself as required to do his fair share of the housework and of looking after his young daughter at home in Shepherd's Bush. But the Founders' vote for Manchester was also supported by Walsh, who was excited by the possibilities of fund-raising from the northern councils. The decision was not unanimous, but it was clear-cut. Hayling recognized at the time how the project had been damaged. It was only later that he described the mistake as 'terminal', but he knew originally that it was serious.

By the time the paper was launched a year later, it was clear that he was right. The economic advantages evaporated, and large-scale investment by Greater Manchester Council's pension fund never materialized, although other northern councils did invest. The move was a major handicap in recruiting journalists – who, after all the fuss, were mostly hired from the south, and not from the local redundant talent which was said to have been available. The costs and confusions inflicted by the twin-site operation were huge. *News on Sunday* ended up with the worst of both worlds – a paper with metropolitan Right-On concerns, produced in a city that had fallen off the edge of the Right-On world.

Hayling's authority as chief executive was severely dented by the decision, and his defeat contributed to the creating of an un-manageable company where authority was beginning to dissolve into competing committees and rival cabals. He considered resigning, for the first and not the last time, but failed to do so. And the argument over Manchester polarized the two ends of the company. The Founders and the closely allied management team, recently formed from the old executive committee and resolved to work by consensus, began to close ranks against Hayling and the intruding alien business world which he came to represent.

The main voice for the growing suspicions was Liz Cooper, a member both of the management team and the Founders' Trust. As a staunch feminist, she grew alarmed as all the positions of power were taken by men. It seemed that the men were welshing on the Equal Opportunities policy so as to make the paper more attractive to investors. And the feeling grew that the women had been out-personoeuvred. Instead of being at the top, they were being concen-trated in middle management, where all the hard detailed work had to be done.

Walsh, lecturing the others on how they must junk 'traditional left-wing fund-raising methods', had the most important job of the moment as fund-raising co-ordinator. He was now presenting himself as a cynical hard-nosed East End wheeler-dealer. He had recruited John Hoyland, the recently redundant editor of the GLC freesheet *Jobs for a Change*, as his assistant and general factotum. Hoyland saw his job as trying to impose some order on his boss's whirlwind operating methods, which had caused such irritation amongst the others that there had been demands for his dismissal.

Hayling, now describing himself in Trotskyite jargon as a 'commercial rightist', and wearing a three-piece suit to prove it, seemed determined to become a City gent. He was disappearing regularly into the bowels of the City to meet various moneypersons, all of whom were assumed to be faintly threatening male chauvinists. And he had formed an exclusive and close personal relationship, which went beyond mere business, with another powerful man, Nick Horsley. Horsley, in turn, was followed around and virtually nursed, as the women saw it, by the embarrassingly doting and un-feminist Olwen, whose old-fashioned attitude towards her man sickened them. Hayling and Horsley were obviously lining up yet another man, Pilger, to control what the paper would say with its editorial content. Without consultation, Hayling had invited Pilger to move up from being a mere adviser to the new post of editorial director.

The Horsley–Hayling–Pilger axis, with Walsh spinning round it in a erratic orbit, symbolized the male domination of the project. The feminists thought the whole structure was rotten, but they had taken a particular dislike to Pilger. He embodied everything that was wrong about men. He was arrogant, powerful, patronizing, self-assured, and would sweep into rooms and dominate space and conversation. For Liz Cooper it was somehow summed up by his big feet, a typical male defect, which she would complain about whenever possible.

On top of this, there were plenty of people in *NoS* who were opposed to the idea of having an editor at all. Supporters had been split into regional groups throughout the country, and John and Joan Bohanna's Merseyside Regional Group directly confronted Pilger, telling him that 'ultimate *NoS* editorial control rests not with the editor, or the Board of Directors, but the Founders', and the editor would have to do their bidding at all times. There were only four things that the editor could do without consulting the Founders. He could work out the house-style; take legal responsibility for libel; make sure nothing went in the paper which was against the editorial Charter when the Founders were not looking; and he could put 'scoops' in the paper should the reporters come across some. The traditional notion of an editor, hired to get on with it, was out. This arrangement represented 'the same top-down white patriarchal model of leadership that surrounds us in our daily life in capitalist society and most left-wing organizations in this country. The success of *News on Sunday* in financial terms *does not depend on this outmoded politically sterile model of operation.*'

Not that the success of *News on Sunday* in financial terms was very high on the list of priorities. 'In the first place we can never forget the main objective in establishing *News on Sunday* was not to make money,' the Liverpool comrades continued, adding the muddled rider: 'It would be lovely to ignore money, but we can't.'

There was little enthusiasm, then, as the paper moved towards the alien financial world of the City to set itself up as a public limited company. Suspicion intensified that a sell-out of its principles was on the cards.

Raising the money

The manner of the capitalization was that the shares would not be publicly quoted and dealt in like ones on the Stock Exchange, but would be offered to investors who would have faith that the company would grow and their shares would increase with it. A great inducement of 'start-ups' or 'green-field projects', where the original investors are in on the ground floor, is that they will make a killing if the company one day goes on to the Stock Exchange, or is gobbled up by a predator in a takeover bid.

But to attract the funds needed to capitalize, *NoS* would have to persuade a merchant bank to sponsor it, which would inevitably lead to confrontation over the Right-On organizational principles on which the project was based. The first merchant bankers approached were Samuel Montagu. They were interested, but their fees were considered to be too high. Instead they recommended Guinness Mahon, part of the giant Guinness Peat group. Hayling went along to meet Anthony Everett, the director who would be handling the issue. Everett, an extremely experienced chartered accountant, was captivated by Hayling and became personally very interested in the paper and the job opportunities it would create. Hayling in turn was delighted to meet a man whose friends described him as a 'non-conformist' compared with most City types, and one who had strong views about the way City investment was dominated by political advantage. Everett had difficulty convincing some of his colleagues, but the involvement of Horsley 'put it all together', and he was authorized to take the share issue on.

The share offer was to be made through the normal prospectus, summarizing the business plan for the paper and projected profits, endorsed by relevant professional advisers. Guinness Mahon, in conjunction with solicitors Jacques and Lewis, had the responsibility of drawing up the document, a complicated matter strewn with legal pitfalls. Such a process is always lengthy and complicated, as each line has to be verified to ensure no false promises or claims are made. It produced some odd scenes: when *NoS* wanted to state that the paper was going to be 'progressive' and 'accessible', articles from the dummy had to be scrutinized to make sure they proved this was true. There was constant pressure from Everett to make the company more attractive to investors by dumping various Right-On commitments. Hayling relayed the pressure back to the ever more suspicious comrades. There were two specific worries – the lack of management experience and the extraordinary Golden Share proposal, giving the Founders power over the financial control of the company. But, like Horsley, Everett was immediately infected by the challenge of the project and the admirable enthusiasm which it represented, and he put himself out on a limb to help.

It was decided that the company should be capitalized at £6.5 million, to be sold in shares of £1 each. Hayling, Walsh and the others gravely signed undertakings to appear in the prospectus that they would look after the shareholders' money and manage the company in a 'responsible and profitable manner'.

There was much discussion as to who should and should not appear in the prospectus as the management team. The original plan had been to leave all the top posts open, with a promise to find people as soon as the investors had parted with their cash. Everett pointed out this was ridiculous, and reminded the comrades that management was everything, especially in a risk-capital venture such as this. Many new companies are floated on the reputation of the team alone, and although *NoS* did not have one which would bring investors flocking, it had at least to state that one existed. Eventually Hayling agreed to appear in the prospectus confirmed as chief executive until the launch. Up until then he had been acting temporarily in the post, awaiting the arrival of a more experienced businessman. Walsh did not appear, but Cooper and Pilger went in as non-executive members of the Board. Hayling was pressuring Gerry Taylor to appear in the prospectus. Taylor, former managing director of the *Guardian*, was cagey. He had talked to the paper and was agreeing to join, but had not yet committed himself. Anyhow, he had other contractual commitments, so he refused to allow his name to be used.

The lack of experienced management was commented upon when the prospectus was issued, but there was an even more serious problem – the powers given to the Founders' Trust. The Founders had to agree everything to do with the paper, including the appointment of the sponsoring merchant bank. Everett was duly interviewed for suitability in a hall in Shepherd's Bush on a Sunday afternoon. It was a bizarre scene, with the City merchant banker being interrogated about his views on a number of subjects. When asked about his attitude to Equal Opportunities, Everett promptly offered a half-hour lecture on why women should be ordained as priests. The Founders moved on to the next question.

The Founders' powers had emerged in the long wrangle with GLEB. Essentially a self-appointed and unaccountable élite, lacking any national-newspaper or big-business experience, they were put in a position of control of both the company and the editorial side of the paper. The objectives were laudable and in some ways romantic. The Founders were to be the guardians of the purity of the paper, protecting it and keeping it in touch with the grass roots which they represented. Membership of the Founders' Trust had changed frequently in the quest to find more women, working-class people and blacks, but at the time the prospectus was issued the original five Founders – Lowe, Walsh, Cooper, Sadgrove and Power – had been joined by a mixture of others. Walsh's ex-partner Jo Robinson, ex-Big Flamer Henry Stewart from Newcastle and New Zealand journalist Kerry Brown had become Founders, along with Maxine Johnson, an industrial-relations lecturer who lived in Manchester.

The group had been completed by Steve Riley, a T and G shop steward at Fords in Dagenham and two people from Liverpool – Yussef 'Joe' Farrag and Joan Bohanna, shop steward at Glaxo. Bohanna's husband, John, was the secretary to the Trust and its public spokesperson. They were all friends, or friends of friends, of the original group and highly politicized. Hayling had been excluded from becoming a Founder first because of his job policing the project for the GLC grant, and then because he was working for the company. Founders were not allowed to take *NoS* jobs without giving up their place on the Trust, which determined from the beginning to act as a collective. Hayling nominated Riley and Bohanna, who were cronies from his days as a 'workerist' Big Flame activist at Fords.

The Founders appeared in the prospectus as holders of a Golden Share which gave them six powers. The most important was the right to prevent any single investor from owning more than 15 per cent of the shares, which effectively gave them the right to veto a takeover bid. The object was to prevent takeover by a rival paper, or even by a consortium of people opposed to *NoS* and its politics which might try to build up a majority shareholding. Because of the Golden Share, Murdoch and any others would be forced to stand on the sidelines gnashing their teeth as *News on Sunday* forged ahead, slicing huge swathes off the readership of their titles. The next target was already in sight. Founder Henry Stewart had produced costings for a daily paper financed out of the profits of *News on Sunday*, which would be protected by a similar fiendish arrangement.

The second most important power which came with the ownership of the Golden Share was the right of veto over the hiring and firing of the editor. This was to ensure that he or she would not be pressurized to publish things against their judgement or be got rid of in favour of an outsider who would change the paper's political line. With the final umbrella of the Charter, which theoretically laid down the principles of the paper and what it stood for, the last bricks were put in the edifice.

Everett argued that the Founders would have to give up some of their powers if *NoS* was going to attract any regular City investment. Nobody, he said, would put money into a company controlled by an outside body like theirs, with no financial liability or incentive to make the company profitable. In the first feasibility study for GLEB in November 1984, *NoS* had planned to raise £1.5 million from the

City, either in the form of venture capital or debenture stock – a hefty 29 per cent of the launch costs, then estimated at £4.45 million. There was no chance, Everett told them, of raising that sort of money with the Founders' powers. But they didn't care, tending to the view that the City was a viper's nest of scheming capitalists, whose sole reason for investing would be to take the paper over. And they had decided that they could keep more control by financing the paper with capital raised from 'the movement'.

Shares in News on Sunday Publishing plc, registered company No. 1989364, went on sale at 10am on 9 July 1986. The offer was of 6,500,000 shares at a cost of £1 each. The prospectus offered investors a return of either 18 per cent, 34 per cent or 45 per cent over a three-year period, depending on the accuracy of the sales projections, based on the RSGB figures, with all the appropriate caveats cautiously attached. Because the issue was not underwritten, if any shares remained unsold when the statutory forty-day issue period ended at 5pm on 12 August, the company would fail to capitalize. The whole thing would be over, and all the money raised would have to be sent back.

Everett tried a quick tour of 'neutral' investors – the big pension funds, particularly those belonging to the nationalized industries, and the major insurance companies. But he did not waste much time. He knew the projected return for such a risk venture was 'at the lower end', and felt the companies were very wary of anything with a political content. As he expected, he drew a blank, and found the main objection was the Founders' powers. Everett was convinced that part of the lack of enthusiasm was due to the fact the paper would actively support Labour. He knew it was in the interests of the City that the Tories win the next election. But there was nothing he could do. (There was, however, another side to this coin. The City was beginning to wake up to the fact that the Labour movement all told, had a great deal of money at its disposal – especially in the pension funds of Labour-controlled local authorities. Pension-fund investments across the country amounted to billions of pounds, and by helping *News on Sunday* investors could score many brownie points, and find a possible way in to this exciting and under-exploited source of money. But even that argument failed to raise any investment.)

In any case, most City people put politics to one side and looked at the nascent company as a simple business proposition. Merchant bankers N. M. Rothschild were completely dismissive. Mentioning 'optimistic' circulation forecasts and the key problem of inexperienced management, they stated: 'There is a very real possibility that the business will run out of cash and that investment returns will be negligible.' They forcefully advised clients not to invest. Phillips and Drew emphasized that there was no finance director to look after investors' money, and added that the return being offered was much too low for such a high-risk project. 'The Founders' rights make it difficult for *NoS* to be taken over,' they warned. 'This is a disadvantage in raising the capital because the possibility of profitable acquisition appeals to investors.' It was as Everett had feared – the Golden Share was being seen as a kind of sterilization pill which would prevent a takeover, and a profitable union.

But the comrades were prepared for everything the class enemy could throw at them. Walsh, as fund-raising co-ordinator, and Hayling, as 'poacher turned gamekeeper' (as Everett described him), had been sounding out potential 'movement' investors for months. Reluctantly realizing that major investment from the City was increasingly unlikely, they had been concentrating on the unions and council pension funds. Now they joined in with Everett's strategy of going where the big fish were. The Founders had always thought that they might get some pension-fund money. But it was Hayling and John Hoyland, Chris Walsh's new assistant, who knew exactly how it could be done. Hoyland, like Hayling, had taken an interest in the campaign being run by their GLC employers to 'disinvest' – withdraw investment – from companies involved in South Africa. In an effort to avoid any financial contact with South Africa, the GLC had devoted considerable attention to its pension fund and the way it was managed. It had been pleasantly surprised to find that, after years when nobody had bothered to find out, political control over the investment decisions was more direct than anyone had realized.

The GLC introduced a new vogue for councils to take a far more active role in their investment decisions. Now, just as the GLC had been abolished, *NoS* was going to step into its shoes and teach other councils how to use their pension funds to back risk ventures, within the limits which were laid down. In many cases *NoS* was to be their first experiment. The paper homed in on its discovery that councils could use 5 per cent of their pension funds on risk ventures. In one example – Haringey, which covers an inner-city area of North London including Tottenham – the 5 per cent limit worked out at £7 million. Larger Labour-controlled county councils had even more money available. Cleveland, in the north-east, had £13 million to invest. Most important of all, much of this risk capital – adding up to hundreds of millions right across the country – was at the disposal of the *NoS* core group's close political allies. All they had to do was hit a tiny fraction of the total available and they were in business. A target of £3.5 million was set for the councils. Hayling and Walsh had already probed the possibility of getting their hands on some of this money, but it was only when Horsley arrived in March 1986 that things really began to move.

For the next three months Walsh, Hayling, Horsley, Everett and the ever-present Olwen raced around the country in the black Jaguar. Under Walsh's overall co-ordination Horsley and Hayling, assisted by John Hoyland and Henry Stewart, handled the councils. Walsh, Hayling and a new assistant, Marisa Casares-Roach, looked after the unions. Hayling had introduced Casares-Roach to Walsh after meeting her at a Ford workers' conference in Benidorm where she had been the translator. She was a small, fiery Spanish woman who was experienced in marketing and had once worked for Athletico Madrid football club. Casares-Roach had moved to England in 1968, and had a multitude of contacts through her trade-union activities, especially in the T and G, where she was a member of one of the national committees.

The *NoS* roadshow was idiosyncratic but effective. Olwen drove, and evolved a schedule of visiting her numerous girlfriends or looking for bargains in the shops whilst the others pitched the local council or union. The bureaucracy of both institutions caused numerous problems, particularly with the councils, where there were endless fixed meetings to attend, return trips, official hands to be shaken and backs to be slapped.

As the programme of meetings rolled on, sometimes with many presentations on the same day, Horsley was exhilarated, amazed and excited. Everett, similarly enthusiastic, described it as 'being on the stump'. The close-knit team found it exhausting, but tremendous fun – a bit like a rock tour, with half-hour presentations of the business plan instead of 'gigs'. After years of dealing with the likes of dullard and truculent supermarket purchasing managers, Horsley was suddenly meeting all manner of fascinating and powerful people. And he was having the time of his life. There was a Westminster hotel meeting with Neil Kinnock, a fellow CND supporter. Finding that broking in political power was more fun than selling milk, Horsley self-importantly told Kinnock he'd better stick to his socialist principles after being elected Prime Minister, or there'd be trouble from *NoS*. Kinnock's more realistic reply was: 'That's fine, Nick, so long as you help me get to Downing Street first.' Of course the paper would, Horsley assured him.

One day in April, Horsley, Walsh and Everett spent the morning in Manchester meeting the Co-op insurance company and asking them for a £750,000 investment, before rushing straight round to the Council Economic Development Committee to pitch for another £500,000. In the afternoon they sprinted over the hills to the offices of Derbyshire County Council in Matlock. Horsley asked for £500,000. And Walsh piled on the pressure to get promises of advertising business. On a typical evening, and sometimes in the small hours, it was back to the Caxton House HQ in London for strategy meetings.

Whether *NoS* could be classified as 'Loony Left' or not, the majority of its council backers were to be the big names on the *Sun* hit list. The paper started by zeroing in on the inner London boroughs. Top-priority councils for fund-raising efforts were Lewisham, Haringey and Newham. Islington, Southwark, Camden and Hounslow were thought to be in the bag. The operation was run on a 'me too' basis, so Greenwich, for example, was only to be approached after Haringey and Newham had committed themselves. Their investment advisers might try to stop them, or limit the investment if it was being made on social grounds, but the Labour Groups could be relied upon to over-rule the objections. In Islington the financial advisers set a maximum of £50,000, but the council decided to invest five times that. Hounslow came up with £100,000 after being given a limit of £10,000.

On 12 July Southwark council received a report from its finance director concluding that *NoS* was high-risk, low-return. He strongly recommended against investment 'unless the aim is to support the editorial charter'. The inadequacy of the *NoS* management, described as 'enthusiastic but inexperienced', was mentioned once again. Nevertheless, Southwark invested £300,000.

There was another problem with some of the firm political allies such as Lambeth, Brent, Haringey and Hackney, who still tended to leave investment decisions to their advisers: *NoS* had to teach them what to do. At one south London council, which had left the fund in the hands of stockbrokers and been happy to rubber-stamp their annual report, nobody could remember who was in charge. He turned out to be an elderly ex-colonel, who was tracked down to his retirement home in Surrey. At Haringey it needed the direct inter-vention of council leader Bernie Grant, later to become the first black MP for Tottenham, to change the policy of leaving all invest-ment decisions to the advisers. The outcome was an investment of £250,000. In Brent, council leader Merle Amory had to organize an emergency meeting of the pension-fund investment panel. Brent came across with another £250,000.

The campaign did well in London, but in the rest of the country the pickings were thin. Derbyshire was a rare, and expected, northern exception, investing £300,000 after the Matlock meeting. (When Southwark promised £300,000, matching Derbyshire's investment, the council insisted on putting in another £5,000 to stay the largest single shareholder.) The West Midlands and Cleveland County came up with £300,000 and £250,000 respectively, and that was all for the north of England – a paltry sum compared with the £2,325,000 raised from twelve London boroughs. A Walsh whirlwind tour of Scotland yielded a meagre £300,000. Walsh found many of the councils quite backward. Strathclyde, a huge left-Labour-controlled council, had not even set up the required risk-capital fund. Walsh and Everett began to advise them how to do it, but it was too late. Wales only added another £150,000, but the operation was still an overall success. The target had been £3.5 million, and the total raised from the council pension funds was £3,630,000.

'We have a newspaper!'

Next came the unions. An initial target of £4.7 million, later reduced to £2 million, was set for investments, which could be drawn on the unions' general funds. The target was ambitious, but by no means impossible had the fund-raising campaign been properly organized. It was not. When it came to it, the unions were badly handled and the strategy badly thought out. Seasoned pressure-group activists advised Walsh to combine the presentations to top officials with pressure from the grass-roots. The standard tactics were explained – alerting the membership in each union, by letter or leaflet, dispatching activists to local branches to pass resolutions supporting the paper and to make sure they got on the agenda of the union's conferences. General Secretaries would then be obliged to satisfy the membership and could be put in a classic squeeze when they were approached at top level, even if supporting *NoS* was against their better judgement.

Walsh sneered at such suggestions as 'traditional left', old-hat and boring. He didn't think much of the unions and their so-called democracy, preferring to rely on direct contact with the leaders. In many cases he had left the unions to the last minute and missed the relevant conferences anyway. Instead he was backing what he called the 'peer group domino approach'. The first promise of money would be hardest to get, but once it was in the bag the others, not wanting to be left out, would fall in line.

Ignorance of the union world was underlined early on by a detailed target list itemizing the amount sought from each union. It included a target of £150,000 from the National Union of Mineworkers, even though it had emerged penniless from the strike in 1985, with its assets in the hands of the sequestrators. Another £100,000 was put down for the National Union of Journalists, despite its clear and well-known policy of not investing in newspapers because of the inevitable conflict of interest in its role as champion of higher wages for journalists. Another £100,000 was targeted from the National Union of Students, which as a federation of local student unions and associations is barred by law from spending or investing any of its constituent members' money.

The Transport and General Workers' Union was the first domino to fall in Walsh's strategy. The T and G is a weathervane union closely connected to the Labour Party leadership. Other unions would wait to see the attitude of its General Secretary, Ron Todd, before making up their minds. Todd, supported by his executive committee, promised £550,000 – which was £50,000 above target. This was not entirely unexpected, as he had been a firm supporter of the project, and the union had put £7,000 into the earlier feasibility study, but it was still a useful bonus, and provided the sort of result *NoS* needed to wave around.

The real hunt, though, was to find a union less clearly aligned with the labour left. The breakthrough came with the middle-of-the-road National Union of Railwaymen, which promised to come up with their target £150,000 'subject to a positive reponse from a number of other unions'. The NUR did deliver, and the victory was heavily emphasized in a letter to John Edmonds, leader of the General and Municipal Workers, the largest union led by Labour right-wingers. They nevertheless declined to invest, and the whole 'domino' strategy was soon in tatters.

Even though the overall union target had been cut back from £4.7 million to £2 million, only four unions came in on target: NALGO came up with £250,000; the National Union of Seafarers and Fire Brigades Union with £50,000 each; the fourth was the Amalgamated Union of Engineering Workers, led by the vociferously right-wing Gavin Laird. It was something of a shock that the AEU had invested at all, let alone met its target. But the decision was made only hours before the share sale closed, and too late to cause a domino effect among other right-leaning unions. The only union to exceed its target was Ron Todd's T and G.

Other unions which had either supported the earlier feasibility study, or might otherwise have been expected to be sympathetic, came up with only feeble amounts. The print union, SOGAT, targeted for £150,000, invested only £10,000. NUPE (target £250,000) invested only £5,000, and the nurses' union COHSE (target £250,000) was little better with £15,000. Fourteen large unions each targeted for more than £100,000 failed to invest anything. They included the National Communications Union, contributors to the earlier feasibility study, and left-wing unions such as TASS, UCATT and Clive Jenkins's ASTMS.

In the first week of the forty-day share sale period, the unions only invested £871,000, and two weeks before the closing date the total had only crept up to £927,500. Despite frantic last-minute appeals, only £1,634,000 had been raised by the time the offer stopped – still well short of the new lower target of £2 million. Between them the two major planks of the strategy had yielded £5,264,500.

The third target group was of individual supporters and commercial investors. This turned out to be an even bigger disappointment, and showed how few people were really heavily committed to the project. The target was £1 million, which Walsh wanted to collect through the 'thousand times a thousand' approach which had been mentioned in the original feasibility study. The idea was to persuade 1,000 'rich radicals' with incomes of over £12,000 per year (the Walsh criterion for being rich) to put up £1,000 each. Everett vetoed the suggestion as unorthodox and cranky, totally scotching a Walsh proposal that an advertisement be placed in the *Guardian*. He explained that if the money wasn't raised it would destroy confidence, and anyhow such an unusual move would be very close to breaking the rules about soliciting investment.

As a substitute, Walsh frantically instructed everyone to turn out their address books. Long lost 'friends' suddenly received phone calls which edged quickly round to the appalling standard of the existing Sunday papers. If the conversation didn't quickly progress to the bottom line, it was swiftly terminated. Various individuals came up with useful sums. Horsley's father, Alec, put in £7,000. Nick Horsley, for once, bettered him with £10,000. Hilary Wainwright, the co-author of *Beyond the Fragments* who had joined the Board of the new company, bought £1,000 of shares. Her brother Martin, a *Guardian* reporter and steam-train enthusiast, did likewise. Hayling did not invest as he had no money. Some left-wing celebrities were persuaded. Julie Christie and guitarist John Williams each bought £1,000 worth. Best-selling thriller writer Ken Follett, a former newspaper reporter himself, put in £10,000.

But it was touch and go all the way. As they entered the last fortnight of the share sale there was still a shade under half the £6.5 million to be raised. Most of the London councils had paid up by then, though some of the large sums promised by the unions were still churning their way through committees. Then, a body blow. Just two days before the share sale was due to close, the Greater Manchester Council superannuation fund failed to come up with the expected £250,000. Like the GLC, it had been abolished, and its responsibilities passed to a joint organization of ten Manchester boroughs. All had to agree to the investment, and at the last minute Stockport, the only council where Labour had lost overall control to a mixture of Tories and Liberals, vetoed the decision.

Caxton House and Guinness Mahon's City offices saw frantic activity as existing investors were begged over the phone to increase their contributions in a desperate bid to bridge the gap. The NUR was the only one to oblige. Others, including the London councils, were sympathetic but explained that it would take months, not hours, to get the decision through all the relevant committees. The last nerve-wracking day was 12 August, the 'Glorious Twelfth' which marks the opening of the grouse-shooting season. The red line on the thermometer on the wall of Caxton House crept up with agonizing slowness. If the £6.5 million target was not met in full by 5pm, it would be too late.

And the target was not reached. At the end of the day the company was still short by £719,000. Everybody had known it would be a close thing, and the invitations sent out to the party that evening had hedged bets by inviting people to a 'congratulations/commiserations' party. But the day was saved by Everett, who agreed – after pressurizing his boss, Alastair Morton – that Guinness Mahon would take up the remaining shares.

The closing rules about share issues are very strict; ironically, this is to protect investors in successful issues. The argument goes that if an issue has been over-subscribed, people who come in late already know that it has been a success and are therefore cutting down their risk. But in this case, Everett argued, Guinness Mahon could take up the slack as the company fully expected other investors who had been too slow to meet the deadline to come in. One of the disadvantages of the issue's timing had been people going on holiday, exacerbating the delays caused by the bureaucratic structures involved.

But the Guinness Mahon decision, although it had saved the company, had introduced a sobering note. Everybody knew that if Everett had not stepped in to buy all those unsold shares, the company would have been a dead duck. But Horsley put these thoughts to the back of his mind as he headed for the party at Caxton House, determined to enter into the spirit of things. 'We have a newspaper!' he yelled as he crashed in, mopping the sweat from his brow. At the *NoS* offices the champagne corks had been popping. The celebrations were for having pulled it off, but it was also time for many people who had been involved in the project to leave. For them this was the high point. With the Charter and the political precepts of the paper firmly in place, all that was needed was to drag a few journalists out of the pubs and set them to work. The rest would follow automatically. Henry Stewart returned from a last-minute fund-raising pitch and changed out of his three-piece suit into his familiar jeans in the corridor. It was the first suit he had ever owned and three sizes too big. As he gulped the warm champagne he swore he would never wear it again.

Three days later Everett and Horsley went north to collect on the promises that had been made. Though the Greater Manchester pension fund investment had been blocked by Stockport council, the Greater Manchester Passenger Transport Executive was still game, and Everett picked up a cheque for £175,000 from a suspicious representative who demanded proof that he was really the man from Guinness Mahon. Everett told him not to be so ridiculous, grabbed the cheque and ran. Back in the Jaguar with Olwen, they motored north up the M6, turning off close to Lancaster to make their way up a private road to a grey stone castle at the top of the hill, overlooking the beautiful valley of the River Lune.

The forbidding-looking castle, Claughton Hall, belonged to Owen Oyston, a flamboyant fifty-one-year-old self-made multi-millionaire known for his good local Labour Party connections. Oyston had been brought up the son of a Durham miner and had moved to Blackpool with his parents when they went to open a boarding house. He had made his millions by first cornering the estate-agency business in the gaudy resort, and then expanding throughout the north-west. He showed Horsley and Everett politely round the castle, explaining how parts dated back to the fifteenth century, and telling the preposterous, but true, story of how the building, formerly the family home of the Fenwicks, had been shifted stone by stone from the foot of the hill in the 1930s to give it the spectacular view it now enjoyed.

Everett and Horsley were both intrigued. They had heard of Oyston, who had originally been contacted as a cold call, but they had never met him. He was an interesting character, with the raffish air of a nineteenth-century showman and a goatee beard and longish hair to match. He even kept six shaggy bison in the grounds of his castle, and had a Wild West hat which he donned to complete the pioneer image.

Oyston's estate-agency fortune had been based on the sort of direct contact with the people to which *NoS* was aspiring. He had moved in and taken the stuffiness out of the business, slaughtering its 'professional' pretensions, and bringing it on to the High Street long before the present new wave of trendy estate agents. His slogan was

'NO SALE – NO FEE!' If he did not sell a property there was no charge, and at a time when other agents charged for everything down to advertisements in the papers, this was a popular and profitable revolution, which added to the image of 'man of the people'. This had been further enhanced recently by his appearance in television ads for the estate agency chain, which suggested his decision to give up an earlier acting career had been a smart move. That career had peaked with a part as a junior barrister in Granada TV's *Crown Court*. Now, in the television ads, he cheerfully delivered some hammy lines before falling backwards into a swimming pool.

Other Lancashire businessmen watching his progress had come to respect him as a red-hot entrepreneur and ruthless opponent in business dealings, for whom profit was the consideration that overrode every other. They noted with some awe the way he had risen to become one of the richest men in the county.

Oyston was now moving across into the media, using the same formula of low overheads, tight management and aggressive advertising. He had bought up the loss-making Radio Aire in Leeds and Red Rose in Preston, and turned them round. Both, along with Red Dragon in Cardiff, which he also picked up, were now showing a healthy profit. Next had come the much bigger step in to cable television, which he believes will one day be a major community resource and the source of enormous profits through home-order shopping on two-way TV lines. By the time Horsley met him he had won the franchise for Lancashire Cable, had a controlling interest in Merseyside Cable, and was looking for other cable companies.

Politically Everett and Horsley also found him intriguing. Oyston kept close connections with local Labour parties, and helped with schemes to provide jobs and start small businesses. He had been one of the founders of Lancashire Enterprise, started in the early 1980s by the controlling Labour Group on the county council, and financed by a 2p rate. The organization, based in nearby Preston, put money into promising new businesses in return for a share in any future profits. Although it had originally been derided by the other parties, it was now a local success story, backing businesses which employed a total of 2,500 people, and had gained all-party support.

The project was typical of Oyston, who is a 'corporatist', advocating co-operation between government locally and nationally, the

banks and private entrepreneurs such as himself. He believes this
'tripartite alliance' is the reason for Japan's rise to domination in
world markets, and the only way that Britain's true industrial base
can be saved. It makes him a hard man to place on the political
spectrum, as he is in some respects an avowed admirer of Thatcher.
But at the same time he totally disagrees with the way she has given
the banks a free hand to put resources behind new 'non-industries'
such as the service industries, and concentrate economic wealth in the
south. Oyston sees the north being reduced to Third World status,
and is alarmed that the country is being taken over by foreign investment.

The tour of the castle over, Oyston seated his *NoS* guests in the
draughty baronial hall and explained his views as they sipped some
of his own-label champagne. Olwen found this incredibly vulgar –
she had not been impressed by the mixture of genuine antiques and
large hideous brass objects which gave away Oyston's boarding-
house background. Nobody had been quite sure either what to make
of the stuffed animal heads on the wall, and the large crocodile
sprawled across one of the floors. She suppressed an embarrassed
chortle as the men began to chat about the paper.

Oyston knew *NoS* was desperate for money, but Everett thought
his decision to invest was quite impulsive. After consultation with his
lawyer and right-hand man, Michael Connolly, Oyston wrote out a
cheque for £100,000 and made to hand it over. But as he was passing
it across he paused halfway, holding the precious piece of paper up
by three fingers. There was one condition he hadn't mentioned – he
wanted a seat on the Board as a non-executive director, in line with
his standard policy when putting a significant amount into a company. Everett and Horsley consulted each other quickly, then agreed.
They waved goodbye at the door and got into the Jaguar well
pleased at the chunk which had been taken out of the Guinness
Mahon share mountain. Back at the castle, Oyston had already
written off the £100,000.

Down in London there was only one thing spoiling the continuing
party atmosphere. Now was the time the comrades had dreaded,
when they would have to move over and allow the company to be
managed by the 'persons of experience and ability' as they had
promised in the prospectus. But Horsley did not seem to see things
like that, and he had cheered them up mightily with a little speech

congratulating them all and insisting 'the team' must stay together. It had already been decided that Hayling was to remain as chief executive, and everyone who had been doing a specific job for the company was invited to carry on. Walsh became Marketing Director on a salary of £20,000, and with a £1.5 million budget. But the two of them had had a falling-out on the night of the capitalization party. Walsh had accused Hayling of keeping financial information from him and the others, and Hayling had countered saying Walsh had no need or right to know. It had been a bitter row.

Ben Lowe was the only person doing a specific job for *News on Sunday* who demanded a competitive interview. He wanted the job of national regional manager – in charge of the complex network of local committees which he had himself established – and was distraught when Walsh and Hayling offered him only the assistant's job. Brought in over him was Tony Cook, a good-natured and permanently jolly *NoS* regional activist and successful businessman who had invested £6,000 of his own money in the paper.

Other management jobs only went to outsiders if there were no internal candidates. There were three such positions. Gerry Taylor, the ex-managing director of the *Guardian*, came in to organize advertising sales as principal consultant to the Board. The two other new jobs went to people who could hardly be described as outsiders, even though they had not been either Founders or members of the Executive Committee. Vince Luck was brought in as finance director from Northern Foods. Christine Jackson, a Manchester-based national officer of the Equal Opportunities Commission and personal friend of Horsley for thirty years, became Director of Personnel in charge of Equal Opportunities. After some agonizing over whether they were confident enough to do their respective jobs, ex-Big Flame member Tony Hodgson became Production Manager and Liz Cooper gave up her job as Circulation Manager of the *New Statesman* to take up the same position on the new paper.

At the capitalization party a number of well-wishers had wandered in from the various Labour movement campaigns and organizations which shared the Caxton House office block with *NoS*. One of them had been Keith Sutton, taking a break from editing the anti-Murdoch strike paper, the *Wapping Post*, in the office below. Hayling had seemed unusually pleased to see him and offered him some champagne. Sutton, who had gone teetotal, refused. 'You've done the easy bit, Alan,' he joked, sipping orange juice. 'Now all you've got to do is produce the paper.'

It was an obvious remark to make, but Sutton was surprised by the response.

'Well,' Hayling whispered with a twinkle in his eye, 'that's largely going to be up to you, mate!'

4 · Officegate

Choosing an editor

Raising the £6.5 million, 'the largest sum ever attracted by a radical project in Britain' according to the publicity blurb, had been either a heroic achievement by selfless, dedicated humanitarians or the blag of the century. John Pilger had no doubts.

'I had little to do with raising the money, but I watched in considerable awe those who did: Alan Hayling, Horsley, Chris Walsh and others. As one door would close, they would move on to another, never surrendering faith in the need for a popular paper that, in Hayling's words, "at the very least reflects the decent humanity in this country",' he wrote in the journalists' trade paper, *UK Press Gazette*.

Under the title 'How we will revive the lost arts of the tabloids', Pilger laid down the criteria: 'dramatic, uncropped pictures which the old *Express* displayed with such flair; original well-written investigations which the *Sunday Times*' Insight Team pioneered (I count the old *Sunday Times* as a great popular paper); and the use of writer-photographer teams which *Picture Post* and the *Mirror* used with such power.' The paper's job was to warn its readers when they were being conned by 'governments, opposition parties, vested interests, food manufacturers, sporting authorities, the media, powerful individuals and so on'. The paper would challenge authority, never 'preach' to its readers, and would not just publish political tracts of the left.

To the outside world it seemed that the man who was providing such a detailed vision of the paper would be editor. Pilger was the only nationally known journalist mentioned in the prospectus; one muddled council had even noted: 'The editor will be John Pilger of the *Financial Times*.'

But Pilger was not prepared to move to Manchester. He wanted to 'shape' the paper from London, and took the job of editor in chief, with an editor to work under him. The editor's primary responsibility would be the tedious business of bringing the paper out every week. But it would be more than just a production job. The editor would also have the authority to make decisions when Pilger was away on one of his frequent trips abroad, within guidelines which Pilger would lay down. This was an unusual arrangement which might have worked in a perfect world. But in reality it was a compromise designed to bring the long factional struggle about Pilger's role to an end. Pilger would be allowed to be editor in chief, but to take the job he would have to resign from the Board of Directors. Pilger and Hayling wrote a job description outlining the editor in chief's total power over the editor, which was to be shown to applicants for the editor's job so they would know the position. Pilger, as editor in chief, would have 'overall editorial control', and his vision, ideas and contacts would essentially create the paper. The editor would edit on a 'day to day basis' in Manchester.

There were about twenty applications for the editor's job, which were marked up under headings of 'politics' (most got zero) and 'experience'. Politics, of course, was not just a matter of party or creed, but how many Right-On points were scored for being black or female. Unfortunately no blacks applied, and only one woman. To help sort things out, little comments such as 'sincere/wet', 'over-zealous', and 'pompous' were attached to the more promising applications. Most were not considered worth interviewing, but a shortlist was drawn up for interview at the Northern Foods flat in Clarges Street.

The interviewing panel of Horsley, Pilger and Hayling, with Kerry Brown and Maxine Johnson representing the Founders, was supplemented by Christine Jackson, sitting in and limbering up for Equal Opportunities. The candidates had been asked to supply a dummy paper with a lead story and some idea of content. The best was supplied by an immensely experienced journalist with a suitably northern background. His dummy, leading on the story of a northern factory which was allegedly poisoning its workers, had been marked down as brilliant and just the sort of hard-hitting stuff the paper wanted. But his interview was a different matter. He arrived forty-five minutes late and entered the room in an oddly measured fashion.

He took off his jacket with exaggerated deliberation, folded it with studied care, and placed it on the floor, parroting a curious sales pitch of clichéd adspeak. 'I can produce you a great paper,' he drawled. 'A really great paper . . .'

He was white, male, middle-aged and middle-class and therefore scored zero Right-On points. But as they started to grill him on such matters as his attitude to South Africa and Northern Ireland, it was his actions, not his befuddled replies, which riveted the panel's attention. He appeared to be searching for some key document. He emptied out the contents of his briefcase one object at a time before moving on to his pockets. Each item he retrieved was examined with great care, and he took the opportunity to do some elementary housekeeping by discarding unwanted minutiae of his life. Scraps of paper looking like old bus tickets were placed neatly on the carpet. The panel sat mesmerized until it slowly began to dawn that the applicant appeared to be suffering from the old Fleet Street problem of being tired and emotional. After twenty minutes Christine Jackson passed a tart note to Horsley, who looked up sharply and abruptly concluded the interview. Until he got Jackson's note he had been convinced that the man was suffering from some sort of regular illness. The other interviews went smoothly enough. The female candidate, Barbara Dalzell, a New Zealand journalist from the *Financial Times*, made a good impression and was reluctantly rejected as lacking experience.

But what the rest of the candidates did not know was that Pilger had already earmarked someone for the job – the man who had gatecrashed the capitalization-day party – Keith Sutton of the *Wapping Post*.

Pilger had met Sutton whilst making a film for Australian television about the Wapping dispute. They had a common cause against Murdoch, publisher of the filthy *Sun*, and Pilger was impressed that Sutton was bringing the Wapping strike paper out on a shoestring. The two men found they agreed on many points about today's press. Sutton, a former sub-editor on the *Sunday Times* colour magazine, explained how he had started the *Post* with only his faithful assistant Carmel Bedford, a former *Sunday Times* copytaker. He had laid out the pages, subbed copy, written articles and thought of stunts and headlines.

As more people arrived to help, the *Wapping Post* became a focus for the 'refusenik' journalists, who got their nickname from their refusal to go to Wapping. Many, particularly from *The Times* and *Sunday Times*, had been on the papers in Gray's Inn Road and Printing House Square all their working lives, and for most of them the strike was about more than trade-union principles. The *Sunday Times* had always been a special paper, particularly in the Harold Evans days, when, with stories like Thalidomide and the Insight coverage of Northern Ireland, it could lay claim to being the greatest in the world. For the journalists, resentment at the move to Wapping and the slaughtering of 5,500 print workers' jobs was combined with bitterness at Murdoch's destruction of the papers' *esprit de corps* and journalistic standards. Murdoch's motivation was simply profit, and his cynical attitude had already led to a mass exodus of high-minded journalists. *The Times* had been reduced from being the 'top people's paper' to running a form of bingo based on stock-market prices.

Wapping had split the staff on both papers. Many of those who moved were deeply ashamed and riddled with guilt as they were bussed into the plant, hiding under the seats from their former colleagues on the picket at the gate. Many of the others – broke and sickened by the attitude of their non-refusenik colleagues, who included most of the staff of the *Sun* and the *News of the World* – experienced personal traumas as they struggled with the difficulties of what was obviously becoming a futile protest. The *Post* was a way to fight back using their undoubted journalistic skills. Lew Chester, one of the paper's greatest reporters, turned up and started knocking out his usual classy feature articles. Brian Whitaker, who had been editor of the Insight team, and had remained alone in the old Grays Inn Road *Sunday Times* building finishing a book on the sinking of Greenpeace's *Rainbow Warrior*, brought along his production skills.

Sutton's energy and commitment had bound the people on the *Wapping Post* together with fierce loyalty to each other and their publication. His most notorious story was a psychoanalysis of Rupert Murdoch based on material from sources including the office cleaners. It was incredibly rude. A cartoon of a naked Murdoch, complete with tits and with his privates covered by a copy of the *Sun*, appeared under the headline MURDOCH ON THE COUCH and the subhead IT'S RUPERT THE BARE WEEK IN YOUR PEACEFULLY PICKETING POST. Inside Sutton dredged up personal details, such as Murdoch insisting the fringes of his Indian carpets be combed into regimented lines every morning and that there must be no marks left behind by the wheels of the Hoover. Details of the state of his toilet had been supplied by the cleaners and 'a Harley Street analyst' concluded that the Australian media mogul had never overcome struggles with his mother over toilet training. Sutton gleefully added a further strapline: THE DIRTY TRICKS IN LITTLE RUPERT'S POTTY WORLD.

The story was a riposte to a similar stunt pulled on Tony Benn by the *Sun*. Delighted, Benn told a refusenik rally that if the striking miners had had a paper like the *Wapping Post* they would have won. Sutton had been deeply moved by this compliment. He had begun working on plans to turn the *Wapping Post* into a national strike paper when Pilger tipped him off that he was first in line for the editor's job at *News on Sunday*. As a leader of a protest against a key Thatcherite hate figure, he was the obvious choice. And his general background, a useful blend of the traditional and the unconventional, fitted well with *NoS*.

Born in 1945, Sutton was brought up in a Nissen hut, the son of a mechanic and a hairdresser. He made it to grammar school in Woking, leaving at sixteen with enough O-levels to get a traineeship on the local *Surrey Advertiser*. By the age of twenty-one he was on Fleet Street, married with a mortgage, and was living in suffocating respectability in Rayleigh, Essex.

His progress up the ladder of the Street was rapid, from the *Daily Mail* to Associate Features Editor at the *Express* and then Features Editor on the London *Evening News*. His main rival at the *Express* was another young rising star, Kelvin Mackenzie, who handled news. But whilst Mackenzie carried on and ended up editing the *Sun*, Sutton began to question what he was doing. He took nine months off between jobs and dabbled in commune life, with a period at Laurieston Hall, the alternative centre on the Scottish Borders. Then in 1975 he 'dropped out' altogether, moving into the alternative society full-time as a squatting activist in south London.

Sutton was one of the organizers of the famous occupation of Harry Hyams's Centre Point office block in the winter of 1975. With another group of activists he later co-ordinated another well-publicized protest after the GLC's 'Fare's Fair' cheap public transport proposals had been overruled by the Master of the Rolls, Lord Denning. As a stunt Sutton and thirty others queued at a bus stop, got on the bus, and changed into home-made 'Lord Denning' gowns, complete with wigs made out of carpet tiles. The bus was made to stop on Westminster Bridge, where the 'Lord Dennings' filed off for the benefit of the world's press, to the accompaniment of a reading by Heathcote Williams, the alternative poet.

Throughout this period Sutton continued to work Saturday-night shifts at the *Sunday Mirror* as a sub-editor, and decided to catch up on his education by taking a BA in history at Goldsmiths College, part of the University of London. After graduating he moved to the Royal Holloway College to research a Ph.D. on nineteenth-century radical newspapers. He became enormously interested in these papers and the effect they had at a time when many people thought Britain was on the brink of popular revolution. And he was delighted to find that these forerunners of pop journalism had used the same skills as those on which he prided himself to stamp events into the nation's consciousness.

Most impressive of all was the reporting of the 1819 'Peterloo' massacre, when the Manchester Yeomen of the Guard slaughtered destitute hand-loom weavers protesting about their version of new technology – the mass-production steam mills. The massacre really took place on Saint Peter's Field, but a sharp writer on the radical *Manchester Observer* linked the outrage to the battle of Waterloo, coming up with the headline 'Peterloo'. The phrase caught on, and although Peterloo was only one of several similar incidents around that time, it became the one people remembered. That, for Sutton, was what journalism was all about. But his research ended when his grant ran out, and he took a mundane job as a sub-editor on the *Sunday Times* colour magazine just before the Wapping dispute began.

Sutton's political credentials helped win the approval of the Founders. And whether he knew it or not, he could be marked down as one of Wainwright and Hayling's 'Fragments' – a talented 1960s person who had now matured and wanted to bring his skills back into the mainstream. Pilger, on the other hand, was more interested in Sutton's production skills and in satisfying himself that he could be entrusted with that side of the paper – not easy with a new start-up and the complexities of the new technology.

Sutton had taken great care over his written application for the editorship; even his later detractors say it was brilliant. His dummy was excellent, but there were doubts in the question-and-answer section of the interview, when Pilger thought he detected a certain woodenness in his replies after the initial pitch. Sutton was called round the day after the formal interview to double-check, and was much more relaxed in sweater and jeans. But although Maxine Johnson of the Founders still had doubts, he clinched the deal with his easy and cheerful manner. There was a slight hiccup when he demanded a salary of £40,000. Pilger supported the payment, on the grounds that the editor should not feel a poor relation in Fleet Street. Hayling, however, was scandalized. In an interview with the *Guardian* when his dummy had been published almost a year previously, he had specifically said the paper 'would not pay £40,000 wages'. But someone had to be got into the job quickly and there were no other obvious candidates. It was only after his appointment had been confirmed that Sutton demanded a nine-month notice period, which was in such stark contravention of the paper's equality principles that Christine Jackson took his contract to the Board. It was approved.

Two days after the interview, Sutton's appointment was ratified by the Founders, who had the right, as holders of the Golden Share, to veto his appointment if they chose. They asked him how he proposed to work with Pilger and, to his surprise, told him that he had far more power than Pilger had led him to believe. Walsh pointed out to Sutton that it was he, and not Pilger, who had the final say about what went in the paper. Joan Bohanna was worried that Pilger might use the paper to say what he, rather than they, wanted. Sutton promised to make sure this did not happen.

Maxine Johnson, who had been uneasy at his interview, was worried about whether Sutton would 'be able to stand up to Pilger'. But for the moment that remained to be seen, for the jet-setter was about to leave for Australia again to make a three-part film assessing his country on its bicentennial. The film was to be broadcast in January 1988.

The formalities over, editor in chief Pilger laid out his plans to his new editor. Colleagues he had worked with all over the world were to form a network of stringers. An investigations unit would be set up in London, staffed by reputable heavyweight journalists he had already selected. The three women who made up the much-admired *Daily Mirror* Reader Service, introduced in 1944 but cut by Maxwell (on New Year's Eve 1985, the same day as Pilger himself had been 'purged', as he put it), would come *en masse*, providing an unmatchable advice forum for the paper's buyers. A first-class woman columnist would come from the *Liverpool Post*, along with the man to fill the key job of chief sub-editor.

Leaving Sutton to chase up and entice these people, Pilger got on the plane and disappeared Down Under.

'We want journalists'

With Pilger out of the way, Sutton began to find his way around the organization on his own. He was getting on fine with the Founders. He had even discovered that John Bohanna, their honorary secretary, shared his admiration for Robert Tressell's classic novel, *Ragged Trousered Philanthropists*. In contrast to Pilger, Sutton was approachable and friendly. He was enthusiastic about the paper being located in Manchester, whereas Pilger had clashed with them over the move. They called him 'Keith', whereas Pilger was pointedly called by his surname. And now he was to have his first big test as editor at a gathering at an old Big Flame haunt, the Beechwood conference centre near Leeds, a worker's co-operative, complete with wholefood canteen. The conference was being arranged for the Founders and regional activists to meet the newly arriving senior staff. The agenda gave Sutton a golden opportunity to stamp his authority on the paper. They asked him to make a speech entitled: 'What kind of paper and how we're going to sell 1.5 million.'

Sutton pitched straight in. He told them there was no point in producing a more expensive, national version of *City Limits*, the Right-On London listings magazine started by former employees of *Time Out* and helped into the world by the GLC. The only game in town was mass circulation, and that was to be achieved by *NoS* becoming an aggressively popular tabloid. He whipped the 10 October edition of the *Sun* out of his pocket and brandished the front page. The splash read: THE LIARS – WHOPPERS ASIANS TOLD AT HEATHROW. Below was a racist article about immigration control.

It was Sutton's chance for revenge on his old foe Kelvin Mackenzie. He changed from his normal calm self into a frenzy. The veins standing out on his neck, he shouted at the top of his voice: 'We're going to crucify this stuff. It's filth!' He began punching the paper, sending flurries of cheap newsprint showering to the ground. 'We're going to go round to Mackenzie's house and we're going to ask his daughter what she thinks of this and we're going to take pictures of him and we're going to run our own front page with a picture of him and a bloody great headline which says RACIST!'

The meeting was thrilled. This was no simple production assistant. This was a man with spirit! The Founders and regional activists loved it. But Hayling felt sick. It was so vulgar. This was not what he and Pilger wanted at all – he had better let him know what was happening. News of Sutton's sudden elevation from humble production editor to rabble-rousing orator reached Pilger in Australia from Ben Lowe as well as Hayling. He was slightly alarmed. Lowe wrote claiming that Sutton was trying to undermine him and forge an alliance with the Founders.

Now, pushed to produce a dummy for potential advertisers, Sutton had started interviewing and recruiting journalists. The editor in chief, from Australia, tried to keep in touch. His anxiety mounted as telexes were left unanswered and calls blocked by Martin Huckerby, another Wapping refusenik whom Sutton had recruited as the paper's managing editor. Huckerby, a worried-looking, balding man, had a responsible position which basically involved overseeing editorial expenditure and running the paper day to day, but was best known for fussing round the office collecting old coffee cups and switching off the lights last thing at night. He infuriated Pilger, who referred to him as Sutton's 'butler'. Pilger was worried by the descriptions of Sutton's Beechwood performance, but was more concerned that progress should be made on his list of key editorial appointments.

Left behind in England, Sutton had found many of the people on Pilger's list unenthusiastic about leaving secure and well-paid jobs for the uncharted seas of a Pilgerite Quality Tabloid edited by Sutton. John Merritt, a young reporter then on the *Mirror*, by whom Pilger set much store, was particularly difficult to pin down. And there were further problems presented by *News on Sunday*'s GLC-type Equal Opportunities commitments. The Founders were particularly keen on these, and urged more efforts to recruit blacks and women – unqualified if need be, and to be trained on the job. They criticized Christine Jackson for not doing enough. They minuted 'grave reservations' about her, and resolved to 'bring to the attention of the board the limitation of Christine Jackson's skills'.

Jackson ploughed on regardless. An extraordinary advertisement simply headed 'Journalists' – giving scant information on what jobs were on offer and what qualifications were required for them – was placed in the *Guardian* and black papers such as the *Voice*. An equally extraordinary number of replies found their way back in a deluge to Manchester. Nobody knows exactly how many there were, but estimates range up to 5,000. Each received a bizarre open-ended application form, a baffling collection of leaflets, including the Charter and material about Equal Opportunities, and a list of a large number of jobs open to anyone who fancied trying one of them. 'Ever worked on a street barrow?' one leaflet asked. Why not apply to be editor of the paper's glossy colour section? – the equivalent of a colour supplement and usually put together by large teams of highly skilled and experienced specialists. A nineteen-year-old insurance agent was one who did just that. He didn't get the job.

Pilger, in drawing up his list for Sutton, had cheerfully ignored Right-On methods of recruitment, bypassing and snubbing the Founders again. Bending the Equal Opportunities rules, he had used the normal method of tipping off chosen journalists and assuring them their applications would go through smoothly. But those on the list who actually applied, as opposed to expressing vague interest, had no way of knowing whether their completed application forms had been weeded out or simply thrown on to the paper mountain along with everyone else. The whole process quickly got out of control.

Applications varied wildly in calibre and content. Some were superbly typed or run off the ubiquitous Amstrad printer. Others were handwritten and virtually illiterate. Long political screeds were attached about what the paper should be like, pleading justifications of position and talent. Hopefuls who wanted to be journalists promised bounds of enthusiasm, and optimistically said they would learn the rest. Burnt-out old hacks explained a sudden new lease of life, promising their days in the public-relations ghetto were over. There were lots of hopefuls who would have been journalists if they had pursued a career, or who now wanted to learn. All, of course, were hugely talented.

Once the usual carpetbaggers, liars and opportunists had been discounted, there was a heart-lifting common thread, a real desire to work for a paper promising to lift them out of the cynicism and virtual despair of the current newspaper scene. Older reporters fed up with the declining standards of Fleet Street; younger ones condemned to the grind of sycophantic local newspapers owned by disinterested big groups; good freelances – all were ready to start work. Contained in the application forms was the core of a first-class and committed newspaper staff. Here were the people who were now convinced the paper existed and wanted to join the venture. Motives were mixed. A few were prepared to take big salary cuts and throw away the security of their present employment – others were just grateful for a job or the chance to work on a national. Some were doubtful whether it would actually work, but all shared a hope of something new, and all were to be given an equal chance.

As teams of temps struggled to cope with the mounting chaos, Jackson tried to keep the Equal Opportunities flame burning. She reported sternly to a meeting of the management team that word-of-mouth recruitment might be taking place. Anyone doing this, she said, 'is likely to be acting unlawfully'. The team, as usual lacking expertise in the particular field, agreed, and laid down criteria for positive discrimination to fight back. Each department was set a minimum target of 52 per cent women and 10 per cent ethnic minorities. As an aside Jackson promised to investigate providing the blind with the paper on weekly cassette.

But she had already lost her balance as she impossibly tried to juggle Equal Opportunities, shortage of staff and time, and the torrent of 'open access' job applications. And by now there was pressure to hire staff, with the launch date less than six months away. If any reporters were to be poached from other papers, they would mostly need to give three months' notice.

The Founders and other people within *NoS* kept up the pressure to go even further down the Equal Opportunities road. The equal opportunities committee, set up by London office administrator Zoe Picton-Howell, had gone into mothballs after getting the executive committee to co-opt Sylvia Collier as 'editorial co-ordinator'. Now it sprang back into life. Picton-Howell's main mission in life was to record faithfully the minutes of the many meetings she attended. But she had spent many years perfecting the art of the memo. She was a shy, quiet woman in her mid-twenties with a tinkling nervous laugh. Her father, Tom Picton, was the *NoS* photographer. Picton-Howell had worked hard for the project since the early days, and had kept her old job as London office administrator on Equal Opportunities grounds that the post should not be put out to competitive interview after capitalization. The logic of this 'Equal Opportunities' argument escaped most people.

Picton-Howell, who later became an editorial researcher, now bombarded Jackson with demands about maternity leave, paternity leave, day-nursery facilities and more mundane and familiar matters such as car mileage allowance and overtime payments. With determination in her large, watery blue eyes and a doleful expression permanently on her face, Jackson moved to quash the revolt. A crèche was written off in favour of a child-minding allowance and the demand for equal paternity and maternity leave refused. Taking the traditional and un-Right-On view of child-bearing, Jackson told the staff that women needed time to recover physically.

Equality did apply to some things. The staff were informed that the company could not afford to pay overtime to anyone – regardless of sex, race, age or disability. The car allowance, a key item in reporters' lives and in getting them out of the office – was fixed at Option B – 15p a mile. One of the sub-editors, a former vicar with a most un-Christian vocabulary, later pointed out that this was less than the Church of England paid the clergy.

Whilst Jackson struggled not to offend black outreach workers, the system for processing the application forms buckled under the weight of numbers and its inbuilt defects. Under the 'open access' policy, people applied for different jobs in as many as three separate departments. Each form had to be copied and sent to a different department editor. Some went to London, others were returned to Manchester. And then there were other copies for the Founders, who were to attend interviews and vet applicants. Soon the demands grew so heavy the photocopier could not cope, and originals began to fly about the system.

Hayling added to the confusion by taking away applications from blacks, which were put aside for positive consideration. There were disappointingly few. Hayling had realized that although women's interests were being looked after on the paper, there was already suspicion of *NoS* in the black community. Blacks were right to be suspicious. They had met Right-Ons before.

Soon the system was in total chaos. There is no record to say how many applications, and for what jobs, were finally considered. Cuttings and examples of previous newspaper or magazine work were separated from the application forms, depriving the editors of the main thing they needed to judge them by. Some were lost by hapless temps. For months afterwards copies of forms turned up all over the Manchester office. They were found at the bottom of drawers, in filing cabinets, and stuffed in amongst other papers. One large pile of forms with attached items of a non-standard size was uncovered, apparently untouched, weeks after they had arrived. All over the country hurt and disillusioned journalists and would-be journalists wondering why they had never received a reply could only presume that they had been rejected.

Pilger managed one brief telephone conversation with Sutton while he was in Australia. He was very worried about the lack of progress with recruiting the people on his list. Pilger told him they had better get together for a serious talk the minute he got off the plane. *News on Sunday*'s temporary London offices in GLEB were available for the summit, but Pilger instead hired a room in the Kennedy Hotel, a modern businessman's establishment next to Euston station. Sutton was told to get on the first train from Manchester.

The two men have different versions of the meeting which followed, and there were no witnesses except for a waiter who interrupted them in the middle of the shouting match and asked if they wanted any sandwiches. They did not. They agree, however, on four points: the pleasantries lasted about thirty seconds; there was a terrible row; one of them stormed out; and the word 'cock' was used.

According to Sutton, Pilger made him cancel interviews which had taken a long time to set up. He had not got very far with Pilger's list. He did not know the people on it and they did not seem as keen to join as he had expected. And more and more the fast-approaching deadline of the next dummy edition was pressing on his mind. He met Pilger in the foyer and they went up to the room. Pilger had laid on a lot of beer. Sutton got the impression Pilger was 'going to really put me through it'. He found him agitated and anxious and thumping the table, demanding to discuss the two men's roles in relation to each other.

Sutton says Pilger 'went bananas' and kept repeating: 'Listen, cock! Listen, cock!' He strode round the room shouting: 'I am number one, cock. You are number two. What's more, cock, I expect you to treat your number two in exactly the same way.' Sutton says he was astonished. He had been in scenes like this with his teenage daughters, and he kept thinking: 'I must stay cool.'

Pilger then got even more upset and accused him of wanting to produce the *Daily Star*. Then Sutton got narked and asked Pilger why he hadn't applied for the editor's job himself. Pilger said he couldn't because of Manchester and added: 'I suppose there isn't even an office there for me?' Sutton replied that there wasn't. He'd decided that if Pilger was only going to be there one day a week he could share an office with Hayling. Then he started winding Pilger up, saying over and over again: 'Why aren't you editor, then?' Pilger, furious, was eventually provoked enough to shout: 'You've had it, cock! I'm going to see Hayling and Horsley.' He stormed out, paid the bill at reception and disappeared. Sutton peeped round the door and, when he realized Pilger had gone, followed him. The beer was abandoned. He went round to the *Observer* where his girlfriend Stephanie Thompson worked and told her what had happened.

Pilger remembers it differently.

According to him, Sutton was uptight from the moment he walked in. He set the tone by drawing out a plan of the Manchester office. First he pointed out his own editorial cubicle, then the adjacent one which he explained was for his personal assistant, Carmel Bedford. Pilger was certain that Sutton's accent dropped several social degrees and ended up strong south London.

Sutton looked Pilger straight in the eye, jabbed at his chest and announced: 'There's nowhere there for you, cock.'

Pilger says he was flabbergasted. When he got his breath back he told Sutton it was imperative they sat down that night, the next night, the night after – however long it would take to thrash out a plan for the paper. He ploughed on, trying to outline his plans for the paper, and engage Sutton's attention. But Sutton suddenly seemed weary. He slumped in a chair with his head in his hands and told Pilger he was already exhausted by the workload and the pressures. Suddenly Sutton snapped, got up and announced sharply: 'I'm not having any of this editor-in-chief bullshit.' The meeting ended abruptly and both men walked out. Pilger couldn't believe it. He rang both Hayling and Horsley. 'We've got a real problem,' he told them.

Obviously only one of these recollections can be correct, but whichever it is made little practical difference. From this point the foundation of the editorial side of the paper, the working arrangement between the two men, collapsed.

For Pilger the drama reached almost Shakespearian proportions. It was not quite the end of the world as we know it, but it was close. In a letter to Horsley nine days later he wrote: 'I believe that if the decision is made to go the way of the *Sun*, the tragedy will be of historic proportions. Keith Sutton . . . brings us the worst of Fleet Street, the *Sun*, disguised as "radical" . . . you cannot be radical and look like the *Sun*; it is a contradiction in terms. The way the *Sun* looks is an integral part of its violent approach to almost everything: its anti-humanism. It is laughable to suggest it represents "a tradition". I want no part of that "tradition". Nor should *News on Sunday* be part of it. "Noble failure" was mentioned yesterday. Worse than that would be success by means that in no way reflect the need for a radical, popular paper.'

He concluded that he shared responsibility for hiring Sutton. 'I think, via him, the *Sun* "tradition" will hijack *News on Sunday* . . . The prospect of a betrayal of everything *News on Sunday* has meant to so many people is there . . . I believe Keith should go.' And although Sutton had offered to continue working with Pilger, the answer was quite clear: 'Of course I won't be able to work with him.'

The Pilger–Sutton split had an immediate effect on staff recruitment. Both men had to approve senior editorial appointments; now they were deadlocked. Each appointment became a battle in the war between them. To get things moving, Sutton skirted both the Equal Opportunities and the Pilger problem by hiring people on temporary consultancy contracts. Brian Whitaker, who had worked on the *Wapping Post* and the Hayling dummy, had applied for the job of editor and, although he had not been interviewed, was taken on by Sutton as his deputy.

Another key job, Features Editor – or Assistant Editor (Features) in *NoS*-speak – had been filled by Polly Pattullo, who had served more years than she cares to remember on the *Observer* colour supplement before wilting under its increasing consumer bias. Weary of the general air of malaise in the *Observer* office, she had written round. Although she was a feminist, her primary motivation for joining *NoS* was the challenge of working on a tabloid. And she saw another plus point. Living in Manchester would allow her to escape from Yuppified Clapham.

Pattullo and Whitaker were in turn lining up staff. Sports editor Bob Edwell, who had come from the *Daily Express* in London, was looking for sports writers, and above all the paper needed its back bench staffed by the all-important sub-editors, who prepare the reporters' words (the copy) for the paper, and write the headlines. On *NoS* they were being treated to the miracle of new technology, bypassing the National Graphical Association compositors who, before the age of 'direct entry' computers, retyped the articles on Linotype hot metal machines after the subs had marked them up in pencil. Most important of all, a chief sub was needed. The chief sub, more than anyone else, would be responsible for the look of the paper. Sutton, to the alarm of Pilger and Hayling, had lined up John Hetherington of the *Daily Star*, a scarcely less provocative choice than the *Sun*. The appointment was immediately blocked (two months later, when the ban was lifted, Hetherington was no longer interested). The fight over appointments became more and more bitter and added to the all-engulfing problems of Christine Jackson's recruiting operation, with its Equal Opportunities commitments.

As Sutton pushed each new recruit through on the grounds of urgency, he would gain a new ally. He and Pilger were now at each other's throats, with the showdown already on the horizon – the dummy edition of Sunday 7 December. The dummy was needed, Hayling said, to show to potential advertisers and help start up the advertising sales process. It was also to be used to feed the market-research obsession.

Sutton's first dummy

This was to be the first chance to see what Sutton could produce. He had made it clear at Beechwood that he believed the paper had to be pop, pop, pop if it was going to sell a million. And to do that it had to follow the successful formula of the present day, of which the leading exponent was the *Sun*. Sutton's focus on the *Sun*, and on headlines like 'GOTCHA!', was not just rivalry with its editor, Kelvin Mackenzie. Sutton was looking at what the public bought today. Not for him the good old days of the 1960s, when the *Mirror* – social conscience and all – reigned supreme and Pilger was churning out his hard-hitting reports. People used to drive around in Austin A40s then. Papers had changed as much as cars. Nowadays this heavy investigative stuff was a liberal wank – 'concerned' middle-class people trying to raise up the working classes. The way to make *NoS* popular was to put lots of people in it. They could be used to bring home the sort of things which should be exposed and campaigned about in the paper – like housing conditions, or unemployment.

And there was no reason why *NoS* could not be like the *Sun* and still talk to the left. It just had to be upfront and radical. The 'Up Yours' mentality which people liked was nothing to do with politics or being right-wing. The sort of rude things you got in *Private Eye* weren't right-wing. And his Ph.D. studies of radical tracts had covered a period without any of today's party politics. It was getting through to the readers on a human level that counted.

Sutton had recruited Bill Packford, who had worked with him on the *Evening News* in the old days, to lay out pages for the 7 December dummy edition. Packford summed up a lot of the negative reaction to left-wing journalism. He saw Sutton's interview dummy and was not impressed. BLACKS UNDER THE LIQUID COSH and STRIP IN THE NAME OF THE LAW was not what he thought people wanted to read about on Sunday morning. They didn't want to be hit over the head like that, he concluded with his characteristic weary shrug.

Packford was an active member of his local Labour Party, sympathetic to the idea of the paper, and liked Keith. He was, however, a hack, a dyed-in-the-wool Fleet Street man. He knew what worked in popular national Sunday newspapers and what didn't. BLACKS UNDER THE LIQUID COSH didn't. Like Sutton, Packford had dropped out of papers as a career. He had moved to Penzance in Cornwall, commuting to London for work. The two had met up again when Packford helped on the *Wapping Post*. But apart from that, he offered his skills to the highest bidder and would produce any type of paper to order. He went round his customers, the publishers of trade magazines and in-house company newspapers, like an interior decorator with a book of samples. He would show them examples of different sorts of pages and wait until they found one they liked. 'Make it look like that,' they would say, pointing to one of his sample pages, and that is what it would look like. He had won an award for his Glaxo house magazine.

News on Sunday was more difficult than Packford's normal

customers. He had been amazed when Sutton rang to say he had become editor, especially as the British Telecom line had been so bad that he had misheard and thought Sutton had taken over at *Today*.

Though Packford was happy to experiment with all kinds of design, his work on the launch and re-launch of the *Mail on Sunday* had only confirmed the view that he and Sutton shared. The *Mail on Sunday* had been launched with all sort of fancy design ideas. It had immediately bombed and Sir David English, editor of the *Daily Mail*, had had to be brought in to rescue it by throwing out the new design ideas and making it look as old-fashioned as its daily counterpart. Sales had picked up and the paper was now established. It proved exactly what Sutton thought: whatever the intellectuals might think, the punters did not want designers mucking about with their newspapers.

Sutton and Packford both cut their teeth on the old hot-metal newspaper production process. In those days newspapers were filthy, grubby things, often virtually illegible, with smudgy pictures and layers of black ink which got all over your hands. New technology might have improved the print and production quality, but as far as Sutton was concerned nothing else had changed. Designers were effete trendies from art college. They might be all right for magazines or even upmarket newspapers, but they were useless on pops. They charged you a fortune and left you with nothing but a hopelessly constricting grid. The only bit they could cope with was designing a trendy logo. But whereas Packford had adjusted to the age of new technology and the design possibilities it offered, Sutton remained wedded, at heart, to the old hot-metal approach.

Hot-metal men knew how pop papers were really composed. Instead of being 'designed', the mishmash of typefaces, type sizes, screaming headlines, jumbled-up articles and unrelated snippets came from an organic process. To the unpractised eye it might appear a hotch-potch thrown together at random. But really it was a skilled, even magical, craft, evolved over two hundred years. Papers looked like this because the ones that did not went bust.

Pages were put together by gathering the material up and roughing it into a layout based round the principal hooks – the headlines and pictures which were the only things that really mattered. It was a fast, intuitive process. The object was to pack together the secrets of the trade – WOBs, NIBs, blobs, bullets, underscores and over-scores, starbursts, barkers, screamers, gobbit-boxes, straps, rag-outs, bastard measures and cross-heads. Anything that would grab the eye was jammed together to make the page frantically busy. The words of stories were secondary. Power over those was delegated to the sub-editors. The reporters tipped in roughish copy which the subs could slash to fit the allocated spaces.

This was to be the formula for *News on Sunday*. After all, it wasn't a coffee-table production for the middle classes. It was a pop paper, not the Bayeux Tapestry. Ten years ago you would have wrapped your chips in it. As for the committed audience, they would have to live with it. They were in the bag anyhow. Sutton thought getting them was 'a piece of piss'. Still high on the *Wapping Post*, he told Packford it was worth giving *News on Sunday* a chance. Sutton was later going to have to cope with marrying up this formula to the new direct-entry computer system, which was being sorted out by systems editor Eugenie Verney, a sub-editor made redundant from the *Daily Express* in Manchester, who had previously worked on the *Guardian*. She had already fallen out with Sutton, who regarded computers with unconcealed loathing. His lack of new-technology experience had been ignored by Pilger and the others when they chose him for his production skills.

For the moment, anyway, he was using the old methods on the 7 December dummy. It didn't work out very well. He and Packford had to work under appallingly difficult circumstances, with a skeleton staff and a jobbing printer who had never done anything like it before, and the actual paper was printed on cheap newsprint. But it was still unmistakably mediocre.

Under the strapline of 'The People's Paper' there were thirty-two pages. The front page, headed uninspiringly WAS THE PRIME MINIS-TER A SPY? was a good story, an early revelation from Peter Wright's book *Spycatcher*. There was more heavyweight material with a double-page investigation into the mystery plane crash which killed President Samora Machel of Mozambique. A black-and-white 'Life on Sunday' section in the middle carried an illustrated feature advising women how to feel themselves for signs of breast cancer. A section called 'Relax' covered entertainment and television with features on Lenny Henry, Batman and Boy George. There were eight sports pages and the football results. The glossy colour section was entitled

'More on Sunday' and immediately truncated to 'Moron Sunday' by Sutton's critics.

But it was the news pages that had really gone off the rails. They were hopelessly bitty, and the real mistake was on page 3, with a hopeless attempt at humour in a picture story headlined THE POPE'S HOROSCOPE. There was a large picture of the Pope in tarmac-kissing mode and the story of how the paper had entered his birthdate on the British Telecom horoscope service. For good measure the piece whined about the cost of the call.

Behind the scenes Pilger, still fuming from the Kennedy Hotel showdown, was working separately. He did not think people wanted harmless fun on Sunday. They were desperately keen for information. Under his leadership, the heavyweight investigative team was to produce reports which were a cross between the old *Sunday Times* Insight team and the occasional 'Shock Issues' which are all that remains of the old *Mirror*. These would hit the popular audience – the old-style *Mirror* readers who wrote in bemoaning the trivial-ization of their paper. Pilger had kept a lot of these letters, which had moved him deeply. His experiences in covering the miners' strike had reinforced his conviction that people were begging for his sort of paper.

Pilger was not at all convinced that the *NoS* sales target was viable, but it was not his job to worry about that. He believed that if the paper made a big enough impact and was raved about by the industry, there would be a rush to save it even if it didn't sell enough to make a profit. Some sort of re-financing package could be organ-ized. And even if it went down, at least it would be a heroic failure – a genuine attempt to break the mould and bring back standards of quality and decency. And it would not just be decent in its coverage – it would look decent. It would be a quality product and not ashamed of it. It was the least the people whose letters he kept and treasured deserved.

So while Sutton had been frantically interviewing and trying to cope with real stories, Pilger had been to the Regent Street studio of Carrol, Dempsey and Thirkell, designers of the two-month-old *Independent*, described by the middle classes hoping for better papers as 'a good deed in a naughty world'. Working with Thirkell, Pilger had drawn up sample pages of a new design, using gobbledegook text except for the headlines. The front-page splash was an old Pilger chestnut – the latest of a series of articles which he periodically wrote based on the diaries of a seven-year-old Asian girl in the East End in which she faithfully recorded racist attacks on the family.

The result was quite unlike any current national paper in Britain. The front page was a picture of the Asian girl below a long headline in lower-case type. The typeface was clean and simple. The inside pages used classic 1970s magazine design. Pictures and illustrations were used big, and the wide column layout packed a lot of words on to the page. The layout was powerful and grabbed your attention. Each page concentrated on one article. There were no hooks like those of the Sutton formula to send your eye skittering round the page. You went straight in. Overall it was crisp, tight, and committed. You either loved it or hated it. It was a designer newspaper – its nearest equivalents the trendy but established continental papers such as *Libération* in France.

There was one unfortunate mistake. 'Siege', in the front-page headline, had been misspelt as 'seige', which caused Pilger opponents to fire back the 'Moron Sunday' jibe with racist jokes about stupid Ozzies who couldn't even spell.

Now the two rival versions had been completed, it was time for the multiple power centres of *News on Sunday* to deliver their verdicts. The chosen day was 16 December, when there were meetings at the GLEB offices to discuss Sutton's dummy. Sutton knew his dummy was not that good, but he wasn't prepared for what came next.

The day started with a meeting of the London staff. They had no particular reason to like Sutton. The ones who had worked on the previous Hayling dummy, including photographer Tom Picton and his daughter Zoe, had good reason to fear that Sutton, given a free hand, would get rid of them. The journalists who had been hired by him were based in Manchester. The administrators and Walsh's marketing department minions, who had been invited in to criticize as well, were suspicious of 'outsiders' like Sutton anyway. But there was an emotional element as well. They had been shocked by the dummy, which they thought was far worse than the Hayling one. But because many of them knew little about journalism, they didn't appreciate the difference. Hayling's dummy had been a marathon performance over months, whilst Sutton had had only a short time and few people.

When the London staff, gathered round specially for the occasion, began to deliver their verdict and the litany began to roll, Sutton was staggered by their ferocity. Some were veterans of *News on Sunday*'s many faction fights but now, for once, they stopped ganging up on each other and ganged up on Sutton. The paper had no stories in it, they said. It bore no relation to the Charter, it wasn't irreverent and anti-establishment, the pictures weren't strong enough, it did not have enough on ethnicity or women, it wasn't exciting, different, political or inspirational. And another thing – it had no humanity. Someone said it was the worst paper they had ever seen. Sutton was goaded about his statements that he would bring 'real people' into the paper. Instead they'd got the Pope and an article about a highly paid journalist, Simon Winchester, eating a dog for dinner. They didn't even like the editorial, which had been written by Packford on half a bottle of Scotch. On and on it went. Each new speaker had a separate catalogue of complaints.

Sutton was devastated. There he was, just off the picket line, where he knew people had loved the *Wapping Post*. They had queued up for it, even if the committee people had worried about it. A copy had been auctioned on the spot for £35. Now he was trying to get something done in this nightmare, and this was all the thanks he got. Becoming editor had been the greatest day of his life, and now these people were telling him that his paper was apolitical and had a lack of analysis and editorialization. Though his critics maintain they were trying to be constructive and wanted him to stay, Sutton was convinced that the criticism had been organized in advance as a warning that if he did not go, as Pilger was demanding, they would make life hell for him. It was like a kangaroo court, he thought. No, he decided, it was worse – a lynching party.

Then came the *coup de grâce*. Pilger raised a copy of Sutton's paper disparagingly above his head, and solemnly pronounced: 'This is a travesty of journalism.' He produced from his briefcase his own alternative, Thirkell-designed sample pages, beautifully printed on glistening white bromide paper.

Next it was the turn of the Founders. Their meeting was a grade up from the mob justice represented by the staff. The Founders at least had the semblance of a court. But they were no more complimentary, and complained bitterly that the paper was devoid of politics. Sutton was allowed to say his piece. He blamed chaotic production arrangements, lack of time, people and resources. He didn't think much of his dummy himself. And Hayling had told him to tone down the politics to smooth away advertisers' fears that it was going to be a Commie rag. They had seen his passion and anger at Beechwood. It would come out later, along with the politics. Sutton pleaded with them to have confidence in him. Pilger had been giving him a hard time. 'I've been living in fear, undermined over the past few weeks,' he complained.

Pilger was called in, and he summarized his position. He blithely asserted that Sutton's dummy 'said it all'. It was a paper devoid of politics and didn't represent any of the spirit they had thought of and encapsulated in the Charter. The last one, done by Hayling with his advice, had been far better. They all knew what he thought should be done; the Founders were on a 'disaster course' if they fudged it. The earlier staff meeting had shown that journalists would not work under Sutton. He sympathized with one of the Founders who had said that there must be 'no blood on the floor', but blood was now clearly necessary.

NoS had not been hijacked – that was too strong a word. But they had all made a serious error, himself included. And now Sutton had formed a coterie of cronies round him and was appointing the wrong staff, which had to be stopped at once. All applications for jobs had to be routed through Pilger.

'I can't do any more,' he concluded. He wanted Sutton sacked that very day. Hayling would take over as managing editor until somebody else could be found – he'd done well enough on last year's dummy. Pilger himself would remain editor in chief as agreed.

There was a skirmish at this point. The Founders had been suspicious of Pilger for wanting too much power long before Sutton was appointed. They had offered him the position of editor in chief with, apparently, more direct control over the content of the paper, but only if he came off the Board. Pilger had agreed but had apparently not realized how this weakened his position. The Founders now told Pilger that the role they had given him was something less than total editorial control. Pilger was furious. He hated the intricacies of the *NoS* management system. He replied that without total control he didn't have a job. They'd better make their minds up quickly whether he was in charge or not. He'd got other things to do if they didn't want him on his terms.

Pilger left the room and the Founders mulled it over. It was quite a dilemma. Sutton's dummy was awful. They didn't trust either of them, but if either left there would be trouble. If they sacked Sutton now it would be seen as a victory for Pilger and agreement to his total control over the paper. They would be rendered powerless – there was no way they could do anything with him. But if they backed Sutton at least they stood a chance of controlling him – even if he had turned out to be, as some thought, a bit of a duffer.

After this Sutton was spared what he had thought was going to be his third inquisition of the day, the Board meeting. The result was a foregone conclusion. As Pilger waited outside he was passed a note telling him Sutton was to stay. He still went in and showed his pages. Steve Riley, one of the Founders' representatives on the Board, asked him to stay. If he had to go, he should go quietly and give continued moral support to the paper. Though he got some support from Board members Hilary Wainwright and Vella Pillay of the Bank of China (who changed his mind and agreed that Sutton had to go as soon as he saw Pilger's pages), there was no real point.

Pilger was disgusted by what he saw as a load of hand-wringing, indecisive amateurs. Their main worries seemed to be not the paper, but bad publicity and the left being seen fighting amongst itself. Bitterly disappointed, he later complained he felt like a Spanish general without a horse. He was the principal architect of the paper's style and the only journalist involved with the original Founders. Three months previously he had been invested with 'overall editorial control'. Yet now he had no editorial powers at all. The committees, which he saw as 'aspiring to mediocrity', had betrayed him.

He walked out and never came back.

Two days later the Founders, Board and management team met together to discuss the crisis. They took the *NoS* way out by setting up another committee – the product development committee – to keep Sutton in line. This was to be headed by Hayling, who became the 'new Pilger' in the position of editorial director, to which he was appointed in the New Year. Hayling's place as chief executive was taken by Gerry Taylor, who had been hired as the paper's advertising consultant.

Two days before Christmas Hayling circulated a memo to the staff. 'The trauma is now over', he wrote. Many of them were now much clearer about the paper, and he explained the latest changes in management structure. He wished them all a peaceful Christmas break. 'We certainly deserve it', he concluded. A last memo from the London office manager, Anne Diamond, promised that the Christmas party, which had degenerated into a drink in the wine bar opposite GLEB, would now be held in January.

5 · No tits but a lot of knockers

The Grumbly Brigade

The sprightly figure of Gerry Taylor is a familiar sight in the London restaurants where the financial wheels of the media industry are lubricated. Everybody knows Gerry – loquacious, clubbable, with a touch of radical chic. But while *News on Sunday* was being put together he was a bit off the normal circuit, and toying instead with the delights of retirement in leafy Beaconsfield.

Taylor had just finished nearly two decades working for the *Guardian*, first as advertising director, and then managing director. For his last ten years he had also been deputy chairman of the parent company, owners of the *Manchester Evening News*. He had moved with the *Guardian* from Manchester to London at the beginning of the 1970s and, although there were high losses to start with, the move had finally paid off. When Taylor retired in 1984 at the age of sixty, circulation had topped 500,000 and the paper had moved into profit for the first time ever. It had been a fitting time to leave.

But Taylor had soon chafed at life in Beaconsfield, and he had taken a job as Director of the Radio Marketing Bureau in London. He was in his office in Old Marylebone Road in February 1985 when he got a call out of the blue. 'My name is Alan Hayling and I am trying to launch a newspaper,' said the voice on the other end of the line. Taylor had never heard of him, but, ever alert to an opportunity, agreed to lunch. Before they started, Taylor stressed that he was fully employed. He was not a newspaperman in the strict sense of the word. His interest was in the commercial side of the industry, not editorial, and he worked in fields like PR and advertising which journalists generally ignored. But he liked the newspaper game, and he was looking for a bit of excitement. He had even set up a company called Media Village with an old friend 'to do something', but nothing had come of it and the company was still dormant. And although Taylor was not politically minded, he was sympathetic to the idea of *News on Sunday*. He immediately saw potential challenges similar to those on the *Guardian*, but this was a smaller operation which would be easier to handle, and could be fun. As Hayling explained *NoS*, Taylor found him persuasive and interesting, and was impressed that he was just as chic as himself, in a beautifully cut grey suit.

He was equally impressed by the amount of work which had already been done. He asked to see the market research, and studied it with a practised eye. It was good research by a good company, and he found it encouraging. He scrutinized the RSGB analysis especially carefully, knowing the real skill lay in the interpretation of their interpretation of the raw data. The results were not quite as good as they first appeared. The fact that 17 per cent of potential readers did not take a Sunday paper did not necessarily mean to him that they would buy *NoS*. They might not like newspapers, or they could be too busy with other things. They might even be illiterate or disabled. (At one stage arm-ache induced by holding up broadsheet papers was suggested as a reason why people might switch to tabloid-sized *NoS*.) No brand manager, Taylor decided, would have taken the results as literally as the paper had. But he still found sales of 800,000 a week acceptable – providing the paper was done properly. There could be more – 1.2 million, or even 1.3.

Taylor trusted his own interpretation of the RSGB research, so he visited Clive Thornton. He had no particular regard for Thornton, with his short newspaper experience, but he was interested in what he had to say about these *News on Sunday* people. At that stage Thornton was still smarting from having his name used in the Newcastle fund-raising exercise, and he told Taylor the full saga. Then he gave his standard moan about *NoS*, which he was telling everybody – the endless meetings, the 'Chair' business, and the lack of experience of the people involved. He told Taylor he was thinking of baling out. 'They're obsessed with trivia,' he emphasized. 'It's driving me mad.'

Taylor listened carefully, and then considered the other person he had met from *NoS* – Chris Walsh. Hayling had towed Walsh along to lunch, and Taylor had found him a 'ratty-looking fella'. His dislike for him had intensified when Walsh started tearing the

Guardian to pieces. Taylor had winced. In his urbane world, 'fellas' did not do that sort of thing – or at least not over lunch. He came to his conclusion and rang Hayling. *News on Sunday* needed a figurehead – somebody people could focus on. Hayling immediately offered him the job. Taylor refused – he did not want to get in that deep. But he had decided to keep an iron in the fire. 'Why not go out and find someone?' he suggested. 'Then come back to me.'

The result had been Horsley.

Now he was in the Chair, Taylor was invited round to the Clarges Street flat and pressed to become commercial director with a salary of £30,000 and a car. Mention of the car brought back the horrible company status game. Taylor remembered it all. How big would the stereo be, would Fred be jealous, would the machine have extras like wire wheels? (Taylor had a slightly outdated concept of car design.) He had been through these endless wrangles at the *Guardian* and suddenly realized he was enjoying his comparative freedom and did not want to be part of a company again – even if it was a small one. There was another consideration. There would be tax problems if he had to go on PAYE.

'Tell you what, fellas,' he proposed. 'Employ me as an outside consultant, forget all the fringe benefits, and double the salary.'

They settled on £55,000.

Taylor went round to see the friend with whom he had set up Media Village. 'I've come to buy you out,' he said, slapping down a coin to purchase his partner's £1 share. 'I've got my first client.'

Taylor's appointment was announced at a Board meeting in September, a month after capitalization. Horsley introduced him as 'Gerry Taylor, who has come to teach us how to run a newspaper'. Horsley put Taylor straight in charge of promotion. He did not like advertising, did not understand it, and wanted nothing to do with it. 'This is your baby, Gerry,' he said, handing him a £1.3 million budget for a national poster and television campaign.

The job brought Taylor into immediate contact with Walsh, who, as Marketing Director, was rapidly expanding his influence throughout the paper. Taylor regarded Walsh as one of those people he had come across before who put signs on their doors and their chests saying important things like 'Marketing'. He was not impressed by what he thought of as Walsh's minuscule grasp of the advertising scene which he himself knew so well. No respectable agency would talk to Walsh, he thought. The man kept badgering him about how they made their profits and threatening to interrogate them to find out. Taylor shuddered. That was a subject you certainly did not discuss in their presence.

But Hayling implored Taylor to give them a chance to get the feel of the ad world, so the three went to a small agency to offer it a poke at the account. But within forty-eight hours the agency had been bought out by Saatchi and Saatchi, architects of the Tory propaganda machine. That was the end of that. Anyway, Taylor was not interested in the normal wining, dining and pretty girls which accompany rival bids for an account. He had seen it all before, thought it 'boring crap', and had already chosen the agency he wanted.

Just before leaving the *Guardian*, Taylor had fired J. Walter Thompson and selected the replacement agency from two contenders – Boase, Massimi, Pollitt and Bartle, Bogle, Hegarty. BMP had got the *Guardian*. Now BBH was to be given second prize – *News on Sunday*. It had no other newspaper accounts, was *Campaign* magazine's Agency of the Year and had a reputation for young, daring, imaginative advertising. BBH was only five years old – formed in 1982 by the three-man team of John Bartle (planning), Nigel Bogle (account management) and John Hegarty (creative). All three had become jaundiced with the clients they dealt with in their jobs at bigger agencies. Thinking life was too short for all that, they had determined from the beginning that at BBH they would only work with people they liked. Many of their clients had since become good friends. The agency's best-known campaign was 'Vorsprung durch Technik' for Audi cars. They had also run a small-budget campaign for Levi 501 jeans, with roughly the same spend as *News on Sunday*, which had been so successful that ads had to be pulled when the shops ran out of stock.

But the agency had had a run-in with the Right-Ons over its campaign for Robertson's Golden Shred marmalade, which used the familiar golliwog symbol. Islington council had complained to the Advertising Standards Authority that 'Big Golly' was 'an offensive caricature of a black man', and the GLC had joined in by banning Robertson's products from its canteen. Consolation had come in adland when the campaign won two coveted DADA Awards. But the memory of the brush with the councils still rankled, even if it had been dismissed as 'Loony Left' activity. Hayling saw the golliwog ads in the BBH 'bullshit pack', as Taylor called it, and told Taylor he was worried about them. At a pre-meeting with John Bartle and Nigel Bogle to fill in some background, Taylor offhandedly mentioned Hayling's remarks. The ad men reacted sharply. Bartle said they had a young black woman at the agency who wore a golliwog apron out of choice. Everybody thought it was great fun and there were no problems. And Bogle said he did not want to get involved with 'golliwog people' – you never knew where it might lead. But when creative director John Hegarty was consulted he was more relaxed and said he did not foresee any difficulties. The agency decided to go for the account.

The next stage was to liaise with the client to find out more about the product and the market it was aiming at. The individuals had their own newspaper preferences to go on. Bartle read the *Sunday Times*; so did Bogle, along with the *News of the World* and another he just chose on the day. Hegarty was another *Sunday Times* man, but described himself as 'increasingly disillusioned'. All the papers were unfortunately owned by the *NoS* hate-figure, Murdoch.

The relationship started well on the surface. BBH knew Taylor of old, and liked him. And he was bringing two more people to the paper who were familiar to them – Karen Needham, who was to run the advertising department, and Jill Armstrong, who, although ostensibly in Walsh's marketing department, was to work under Taylor on day-to-day liaison with the agency. Armstrong had previously worked for Saatchi and Saatchi, and only landed at *NoS* by accident through an old friendship with Henry Stewart. They met up and he told her about the paper – which she had never heard of before. Because she was a Labour supporter and between jobs, she had written in. Taylor had snapped her up.

BBH set to work on getting to know their clients. Advertising agencies, from the account management to the creative teams which think up the actual slogans and commercials, have to get inside their clients' thinking and the market first. Not until then can they start coming up with ideas. Often they drift off course, and it is the client's responsibility to apply corrective touches to the tiller. Misunderstandings on both sides are taken as a matter of course during the process. But, as with others who bumped into News on Sunday Publishing plc as it steered its erratic course through the choppy waters of commercial life, what followed was no normal misunderstanding. It was, as Taylor said afterwards, 'in a league of its own'. The agency put it more simply – 'a catastrophe'. John Bartle, the planning director, who comes from a working-class background in Leeds, was even more blunt: 'It was the worst experience any of us have ever had with a client in our whole careers. We never want to go through anything like it again.' And afterwards BBH stuck by the old adage – clients get the advertising they deserve.

To start with, though, the agency was very bouncy, and everyone was interested and excited by the theory of the paper. BBH were proud of their own principles – the reasons for setting up the agency; their small size compared to juggernauts like Saatchi and Saatchi; the way it was run informally on Christian-name terms; and the clients who were also friends. They saw *NoS* as fitting in with all this. The account seemed a worthwhile challenge to their skills and a wonderful addition to their stable of like-minded people. Although the £1.3 million spend was a shoestring budget for a newspaper launch, in general advertising terms it was a 'medium spend', and especially for a project as laudable and well-researched as this, it was enough.

The overall brief as they understood it was quite simple. *NoS* was to be a popular newspaper. Therefore the advertising had to get as many people as possible to sample the product. In Taylor, Needham and Armstrong they were dealing with capable people in whom they had confidence. It was just like old Gerry to come up with something interesting like this. And Karen Needham was very good news indeed. They had liaised with her a lot when she was working for Haymarket Publications. Now they started meeting other key people at the paper to get the full picture.

Walsh rasped out his 'strategy' for them. He was not afraid of a sensationalist paper. It would be 'youthful . . . irreverent . . . controversial . . . punchy . . . a modern breath of fresh air . . . campaigning and anti-establishment . . . taking the side of ordinary people'. It would concentrate on 'the human angle' and 'go beyond stereotypes'. What's more it would be 'radical'. (The word 'radical' was to crop up a great deal in *NoS*-speak as a substitute for 'left-wing'.) Walsh racked his brain for a simile. *NoS* would be to other papers as *That's Life* was to television, *The Boys from the Blackstuff* to soap opera, and *EastEnders* to *Coronation Street*. And just for good measure it would have more – more sport, more television, more fun, more news, more of everything.

The Hayling and Pilger approach was more measured and sober. Looked at from their angle, *NoS* would 'entertain as well as inform', but would be primarily a 'powerful, campaigning newspaper'. Hayling explained with smooth but typically agonized sincerity: 'It will confront the real issues of the day: the bad housing, the dilapidated schools, the embattled Health Service and the decimated public transport with which ordinary people have to struggle every day.' It would be 'investigative' and tell people 'what is really going on' in the Government and the City, and always take the side of the individual against the establishment. Editorially it would be on the left. Humanity would be put back into 'human interest' stories. People would be treated with dignity, and the paper would reflect the 'lives, joys and struggles of people' in a way which would touch the hearts of readers. It would contain 'fine writing' and would be 'entertaining and fun'. *News on Sunday* wanted its readers to relax and laugh along with it – as well as being informed.

The agency decided to call in the editor to get his viewpoint. Sutton duly arrived and gave a repeat of his Beechwood rant, complete with the fist-smashing exercise into the filthy *Sun*. BBH were quite staggered. Though they had never seen a performance like this before from a client, they were delighted. What depth of feeling and passion! There was no doubt that this was going to be a bold newspaper – to put it mildly – with a man like that running it!

Brian Astley, the account director, was happy to address his new clients with a mixture of naïvety and optimism which he thought matched their own. But Astley was no fool. Under his mandatory Right-On ad-agency clothing and black 1960s shoulder-length locks was a sharp brain which had already got him a law degree at Cambridge. He had been called to the Bar nine years earlier, but had left to go into advertising, joining Saatchi's and then BBH. He had been there just six months.

And now he and the others at BBH started to pick up another side of the coin. Because of what it stood for, *NoS* seemed to be planning to leave out the very things that sold normal Sunday papers. It was anti-Royal Family, against stories about soap-opera stars, did not want scandalous gossip about famous people, and – above all – it was very definite there were going to be no cheesecake pictures of women, with or without their clothes. Although very praiseworthy, of course all this could lead to problems in terms of sales. It would be up to the agency to see how these aspects could be portrayed positively.

At this early stage, before they had really begun, BBH and *NoS* were already beginning to sail off in different directions. By now John Bartle had formed the idea of trying to capture the old *Daily Mirror* in the advertising. As he explained later, it was not just Astley but he and Gerry Taylor who were very naïve to start with. Although they understood that one of the great attractions of the paper would be that it helped redress the right-wing bias in the press, they saw *NoS* first and foremost as a popular Sunday newspaper. Sunday was not the day to lay heavy politics on people, and although there would obviously be an undercurrent of politics in the paper, they thought the primary attraction would be that *NoS* was fresher and brighter than the others. 'Vibrant' was John Bartle's word. The thought that it was going to be a political journal never occurred to them.

BBH were not the only people who came across *NoS* to have this problem. In its publicity, and when it talked to outsiders, the paper deliberately glossed over the political background of the people behind it. Few people ever grasped the full intricacies of the politics underlying the project. The Charter was often displayed, though it aroused widespread questioning about how it could possibly work, and there would often be objections to one or two of its clauses. But these were invariably waved aside as minor details, and many people on the paper said quite breezily that they only supported parts of the Charter. The real significance of the background of Big Flame and *Beyond the Fragments* was never explained, and was so obscure to most people that even those who take an interest in politics would often have been hard put to it to understand it. But although it was difficult to grasp, it was crucial because it changed the paper from what it was masquerading as – a broad-left paper supporting Labour – to a paper which was the sum total of a large number of obsessions, a completely different matter. Such economy with the truth about the real political intentions was particularly cruel on the unions and their members.

The reluctance to go into background was extended on a personal level to professionals who were brought into the paper. It was only long after they had joined that many people began to get an inkling of what was behind *NoS*, and some never understood a word of it.

There was some sense behind this approach, as the people who had started the project originally were now being 'respectable'. But it was a major reason for their failure to build bridges with the professionals. If they had been more open about the paper and themselves a lot of misunderstandings would have been avoided. But by now all the pioneers of the project had bedecked themselves in suits – in many cases the first they had ever owned – and at a casual glance appeared quite normal in the business world they were so new to. BBH, like so many others, were only told what they 'needed' to know.

The presentation of the client brief showed what the agency was making of all this. BBH's imagination had been caught by the key words 'youthful, witty and irreverent'. The brief explained: 'We observe that we are increasingly in the era of the "individual". There are fewer "mass trends" than in the Sixties and the Seventies. Herd instincts are on the wane. There appears to be a desire for less government, less bureaucracy. If *News on Sunday* can adopt the role of Popular Crusader, expressed with the irreverence that has characterised so much British humour with regard to our institutions, then to us there is the basis of a very competitive new entrant . . .' (The agency had just chosen the logo of the *Daily Express*, which carries a Crusader on its masthead.) BBH concluded: 'If the newspaper is to be challenging, campaigning, anti-establishment and irreverent, then so should the advertising.' There was a cautious rider about the Independent Broadcasting Authority code, which has strict rules about television adverts which can be construed as 'political'.

BBH considered it would be important to 'manage' the paper's political stance, a process which they did not describe. *NoS* was warned: 'Almost without doubt your competition will attempt to represent it [the paper] in a way which suggests extremism, voice of the Labour party and other misrepresentations . . .' There was hurried coughing at this point, and great hilarity afterwards.

A profile of *NoS* readers was emerging. Astley had looked through the RSGB market research and decided to dump it and start from scratch. According to the new definition, *NoS* readers had a youthful outlook on life and 'street cred'. They were not highly educated, but bright and concerned enough to be interested in real news. They lived in council houses, high-rise flats, Victorian terraces and pre-war semis. They aspired to XR3is (sporty Ford Escorts), coloured bathroom suites, Wimpey homes and, curiously, G-Plan furniture. This was indeed a different world to that of the Right-On.

And so BBH intended it to be. As John Bartle said afterwards, if the paper had been intending to reach the smaller committed 'Sunday *Guardian*' readership Ben Lowe had started with, the agency probably would not have taken the account. There would have been no point in the sort of advertising they were doing, which was to sell to the much wider audience of what Bartle called the 'GBP' – the Great British Public.

The brief also revealed, though, that there was a crossover between the GBP and the Right-Ons. *NoS* readers fought valiantly against the tide of consumerism. They were 'independent thinkers – shepherds rather then sheep'. Although they were not natural non-conformists, they did feel a healthy scepticism towards the establishment, and believed they had to be alert to the many 'cons' in life. But they were not uncaring – they would be the first to complain that elderly people were being given a raw deal, or that the local bus service had been discontinued. 'They are happy with their existing Sunday paper (*Sunday Mirror, Sunday People, News of the World*). They enjoy the fact that these papers are titillating and sensational. They appreciate the short, sharp, shocking stories. They probably even quite like the tits and bums they come across in them . . . More than anything they are out to enjoy themselves as they sit and relax and browse through their Sunday paper.'

The way in for *News on Sunday* was to provide a paper which was enjoyable, but which also 'provided a satisfying level of information content about issues that have relevance and importance to them'. Although the paper would be 'launching broadsides left, right and centre it must keep a sense of both humour and perspective to avoid being "just an Angry young newspaper".'

There was the message from BBH. The readers would be good people with normal consumer ambitions who liked enjoying themselves, but who still cared for others. But there was a caveat. BBH added: 'If we are honest, they are probably grumblers rather than doers.'

This was the nearest the two sides ever got. BBH were touching on the core *NoS* Right-On readership, with its multitudinous obsessions for which the various fragments campaigned and protested. But the crossover was almost entirely by accident. By now

the agency, which was thinking it had got the full picture, instead
had only seen the full façade. And for one person at least times had
changed. It was no longer the Angry Brigade who were the committed and the concerned fighting for a better society. The readers
NoS was after were its new 1980s successors – the massed ranks of the
Grumbly Brigade.

The slogan is approved

Bartle, Bogle, Hegarty proposed an overall approach of 'no-holds
barred' advertising. They were after something which would cause a
sensation, and which might come close to being banned. The ad men
were going in over the top. Walsh, keeping closely in touch, had
accepted the brief, though he found it a bit too 'yuppy'. The first
results were shown to *NoS* at the beginning of the year under the
strapline of WE DON'T KISS ANYBODY'S . . . BBH laid on a 'concept
presentation' for the paper at their trendy headquarters in Great
Pulteney Street, Soho. At this stage in the development of a campaign,
ads are produced which may not finally be used, but give clients a
clear pointer to the direction of the creative team.

The *NoS* delegation, ushered into the adland designer interior of
black woodwork and silver walls, sat down in the air-conditioned
room where the 'concept posters' were displayed on the wall. There
was one of an old man coming out of soup-kitchen, wearing his
medals and walking with a stick. The copy read: 'He's 78 and fought
in two world wars and he's still fighting. Only the dictators have
changed.' Another showed a coffin on a chair with a sign on the wall
reading 'Waiting Room'. The copy told you the NHS waiting list
would be the death of you. A third showed the Pope reclining on a
chaise-longue. 'What does a man who has never had sex and wears a
dress know about abortion?' it enquired.

The agency waited breathlessly for the reaction. This was the 'no-
holds barred' approach that had been promised. To their dismay it
was Gerry Taylor who thought it was over the top. Too gloomy,
was his immediate reaction. He did not like the Pope poster at all –
'gratuitously offensive', he said. There wasn't sufficient justification
for this tone. It would lose the paper goodwill. (The Charter committed *NoS* to supporting British withdrawal from Northern Ireland,
a stance which might attract Catholic readers.) Astley watched as the

others echoed Taylor faintly. He noticed they were rather reserving judgement. Walsh, who had been pushing the line that the advertising ought to be political, liked the posters in a way, but immediately side-lined himself. He picked up on the idea that the ads were based on the theme 'on our side – the side of the ordinary people'. He was to pursue this idea fruitlessly through the rest of the drama. From Astley's point of view, Taylor won. Although, obviously, not everybody agreed with him, none of them was bullish enough about the concept to fight for it. And Taylor was formally in charge.

Taylor turned the posters down. He did so reluctantly, aware that it was a tricky time. The creative team of Barbara Nokes, BBH's head of copy, and art director Warren Brown was well advanced. Nevertheless he asked them to rethink.

By now John Hegarty, the creative director, was becoming more confused, and Taylor and Walsh were beginning to part company. Taylor thought much of the 'no-holds barred' approach had been due to Walsh's input. Sutton hadn't helped. And Walsh was not too impressed with Taylor, who was beginning to commit the *NoS*-speak crime of being 'difficult'. To Walsh he seemed to have no sympathy with the radical project. He said disparaging things about the print unions and seemed to be trying to impress on everyone that just because he was from the *Guardian* it did not mean he was woolly-minded. Walsh got a stiff memo in which Taylor, noting the expansion of his department, pointed out that he seemed to be masterminding 'a massive amount of activity'. They both knew things were not going well with the agency. 'I sense that relationships with BBH are a bit "iffy"', Taylor wrote. 'They ought to be busier on our behalf and closer.' Taylor pointed out that Walsh's merchandising plan, which projected a monster series of special offers, had landed him in 'a sticky mess'. The optimistic forecasts called for £600,000 worth of business a year, which Taylor thought ludicrously high – especially as Walsh had appointed no staff to handle it. From now on, Taylor concluded, he would handle the agency and the ad campaign. Walsh would become an 'adviser'.

And Taylor himself was also becoming confused. The trouble, as he saw it, was that the paper could not explain its beliefs, so it could not discuss them with the agency. But the real trouble was that Taylor himself didn't understand the political background, hence his growing sense of confusion. Hayling's worry about 'Big Golly' had given him a glimpse behind the façade which he had ignored. And at the first agency meeting Walsh had leant over to Taylor and hissed conspiratorially to him about one of the women in the agency: "Ere, you see that girl – she's not on our side. She's not one of us.' Taylor, not being 'one of us' either, had dismissed the remark.

The growing crisis had not yet reached catastrophe proportions. But as Nokes and Brown started drifting towards the other tack, it was about to. The creative team was forgetting what the paper was going to be about, now that the rude, bold approach had been rejected. Instead they were interested in what it was not going to be. And the only point on which everyone agreed was it was going to be Page Threeless.

The creative group picked up the new thread.

Barbara Nokes knew a lot about writing advertising copy. Her skill had enabled her to clamber out of a large working–class family to her comfortable lifestyle and plum position as head of copy at the agency. Now she pondered the equation set by this intriguing client. *NoS* was irreverent/witty/anti-establishment/youthful/investigative/ campaigning/gutsy – it had balls. And it did not have naked ladies/ unclothed women/nipples/bums/breasts. No tits, in other words. Lots of guts but no breasts. Lots of balls but no tits. Start with the negative, end with the positive. And there it was: NO TITS, BUT A LOT OF BALLS. A Great Slogan had been born. 'Vorsprung durch Technik' again!

The agency was jubilant. NO TITS, with its back-up posters, went out for independent testing in discussion groups, where 'ordinary people' were paid to give their opinion. Led by NO TITS, the posters researched brilliantly across the groups. One or two people thought they were vulgar, but overall the reaction was stunningly positive. NO TITS was going to sell a lot of newspapers. Or at least it would grab the GBP and make it aware *NoS* was coming. At least one person could not wait. Among the people on the groups who had laughed, clapped and cheered in their enthusiasm for the slogan, someone had pledged to take out a lifetime's subscription on the back of NO TITS alone.

By now BBH were beginning to see a little more behind the façade. Astley had got somewhere on the political front, and had a vague grasp of some of the mysteries of Big Flame. But the agency still had a long way to go. The next leap was to the fact that most people in *NoS* had taken on sexual politics as part of their political agenda, and discrimination of any kind against minorities and women was barred. And the paper was going even further than that. The discrimination was to be positive. Each mention or picture of a woman in the paper was to be carefully scrutinized for sexism. Pictures would be monitored to cut ones showing women in traditional poses, such as with a child or standing by, or – even worse – behind, a man. This positive discrimination was to extend to other groups such as gays and lesbians, blacks and other oppressed minorities. *NoS*, and especially its feminist section, was what BBH had clashed with before – the golliwog people.

Walsh, who was one of the first to hear about NO TITS, understood the debate about anti-sexism. By this time he was immersed in the 'below the line' ghetto for Right-On readers, which was to parallel the 'above the line' mainstream advertising. The below-the-line campaign had dragged him back to the preoccupations of the Grumbly Brigade he was now leading, and he was acutely aware of their sensibilities. He had a horrible feeling they would not wear this. Walsh had always been suspicious of people like advertising executives for not understanding fundamentals. Now he felt these suspicions being confirmed. Gerry Taylor was also beginning to learn about Right-On preoccupations and the way Right-Ons conducted their affairs. He had tried a day working in the London office instead of his own, and found it hard going. He symbolically kept himself apart by refusing to drink his coffee out of a plastic beaker, and insisting on a china cup and saucer, but at the end of the day he staggered out crying: 'It's like the Mad Hatter's Tea Party in there!' and did not come back.

Taylor realized that another lesson in Right-On business methods was coming his way when Walsh rang him and started going on about NO TITS. He couldn't really grasp what Walsh was talking about. The man was using phrases like 'losing the debate', and words like 'vote'. These were not words Taylor understood in what he knew as business. It sounded more like politics to him. In all his years on the *Guardian* Board there had never been a vote on anything. He told Walsh to relax. The new campaign worried him a lot less than WE DON'T KISS ANYBODY'S . . . Walsh should wait until he saw the whole campaign. NO TITS was only a poster for one week, and the others would not be as obviously explosive. But Taylor sensed trouble. He sat down at his desk, adjusted the cuffs of his immaculate shirt and started working out a 'rationale' to defuse the crisis.

Walsh was still twitchy. With his libertarian approach and concept of the left as a market, he was dreadfully torn by conflicting emotions. He had always favoured the outrageous approach, and cackled with glee at the thought of all the free publicity. But now he was nervous about the core Grumbly Brigade readership, especially women. Still, as Taylor saw it, Walsh might be uneasy, but he was not actually saying no. And Taylor did have a staunch ally in Karen Needham, the newly arrived head of the advertising department. Needham had been head-hunted by Taylor, and had done nearly as well on the salary stakes. He had offered her £40,000 and a car, which had been reduced to £39,000 when she demanded a BMW. Now she had set up the ad department in London with a staff of six and two more BMWs for the senior members.

Before Needham's arrival responsibility for working out an advertising sales strategy had been dumped on the unpopular Ben Lowe. He had even proposed an 'advertising-free' newspaper, relying entirely on cover-price revenue. Lowe was worried that the ad agencies would blackmail the paper into changing its political stance, apparently unaware of the fact that buyers in big agencies would take space in a publication advocating the public disembowelling of their own mothers as long as the ad reached the right audience and the price was low enough. But the distaste for selling advertising space, or for that matter selling anything, lingered amongst the Right-Ons, who treated Needham's department as a repulsive, but necessary, satellite to the main operation.

Needham, a strong-minded woman, did not mind. On the contrary, she made it clear from the start that she would be operating semi-autonomously. With her renowned approach, which was direct even by adland standards, she simply chucked out weedy suggestions that her staff should be fully unionized and subjected to *NoS* meetings-style management. She was miles away from the *NoS* feminists, who treated her with a mixture of contempt and fear of her legendary wrath.

Needham had been recruited from Haymarket and had been selling ads for years. She was a tough cookie with an extraordinary vocabulary of swear words, used copiously and at high volume in a strong Cockney accent. A magazine profile reported that the anecdotes about her past were invariably unprintable and she always said how she enjoyed being one of the boys. But although she was not a feminist, she was a socialist, and she was rivetingly unsentimental about the people *NoS* was trying to get through to. 'I know them,' she would say. 'Let's face it, they're white, bigoted and racist, a lot of them. Those people don't give a toss about half of what this paper's on about. Why do you think the *Sun* sells 4 million a day?'

At the *Guardian* Taylor would have gone ahead and approved the campaign without further consultation. Occasionally he used to show the latest Boase, Massimi, Pollitt effort to the editor Peter Preston, who would express mild interest. But the decision was his. *News on Sunday* was different, as Taylor knew, and he sensed he should have the decision approved by some sort of structure. He tried approaching Horsley, who was disdainful and told him it was unnecessary. But Taylor trusted his instincts, and was beginning to wonder slightly about what would happen to his reputation if things got out of hand, as they seemed to be doing in other departments around him. So he disguised the formal presentation, the point at which the client approves or disapproves a campaign, as a semi-social evening at Northern Foods' Clarges Street flat.

Before BBH arrived Taylor softened Horsley and Hayling up with a stern talk about creative people and how they reacted strongly to criticism. Everybody had to be very careful what they said, no matter what they thought.

Nigel Bogle, John Bartle and Brian Astley came early. The strain of such constant exposure to *NoS* was beginning to show. Time was getting short for booking poster sites and television time. And there was a lurking fear that Maxwell or Murdoch might mount a spoiling operation by booking them up themselves.

There was silence in the flat as Astley uncovered the roughs. The first board showed NO TITS, BUT A LOT OF BALLS in huge headline type on a screaming pink background. As the meeting reeled backwards it was hit by board two – a photograph of a naked woman on more howling pink, her breasts hidden by a scribbled cross, with the caption THE NAKED TRUTH NOT NAKED WOMEN. The third board was a stereotype old crone sporting a black eye, captioned: THE WOMEN ON OUR PAGE THREE WILL REALLY GET YOU STEAMED UP. And to round off this eye-smacking show there was a montage of the four party leaders naked to the waist. Thatcher's

head had been mounted on the body of a man with a hairy chest,
Kinnock was white and pimply, and Steel was a twelve-year-old
boy. The caption read: THESE ARE THE ONLY TITS YOU WILL SEE ON
OUR PAGE THREE. (The ads were very much a forerunner of the
Yellowhammer agency's series for *Today*, which earned the profes-
sional accolade: 'Nice ad. Pity about the paper.')

The presentation ended and the discussion began. The posters had
clearly not been an instant success. Hayling collapsed into emotional
indecision – he felt the campaign was provocative and would sell
papers, but he was very uncomfortable about it. Jill Armstrong was
quite clear – she was very much in support of NO TITS. Walsh was
obsessed with Scotland at this time and pointed out that the Scottish
papers did not have tits. He asked for something more Scottish.
Nigel Bogle, who was already close to breaking-point, felt his blood
pressure going up another notch.

Taylor stepped in. He had been preparing his 'rationale' for exactly
this moment. Using all his fluency and mental agility, he dealt with
the arguments one by one, building up to the conclusion that 'Page 3
girls' were trivia. The new campaign demonstrated that *NoS* was
'fun and powerful, and not obsessed with trivia'. He rested his case.
Even by Taylor's standards it was a virtuoso performance, but Hayling was still not reassured. He didn't see the campaign as standing
for substance. He thought NO TITS was 'salacious'. So it was left to
Horsley to decide. Bogle, stern, businesslike, and used to pitches for
such major clients as Audi cars and Asda, blinked at the Chair's
reaction. Sprawled uncomfortably in his armchair and with all eyes
on him, Horsley thrashed around for help. 'What do you think,
Ollie?' he asked, settling his gaze on his partner.

Olwen had been staring at the posters and the young chap, Brian
Astley, who had presented them. 'You certainly notice them, don't
you,' she replied helpfully. 'I think the kids would love them, Nick.'
(She was referring to her own children, who were in their early
twenties and perfect *NoS* material.)

'Well,' said Horsley, 'I don't know anything about advertising. If I
like an advert it's always no good and never sells anything. If I don't
like it it usually works.'

Taylor winced, and the atmosphere was tense until Olwen chimed
in lightheartedly: 'You can see them a mile off, can't you, Nick? I
think if I was driving along and turned a corner and saw one I might

have an accident. It's certainly shocking. You've got to see it from the amusing point of view, Nick – a bit tongue in cheek.'

Horsley actually thought the ads were 'bloody tasteless'. He modified his language, mindful of Taylor's warning about creative persons. 'Well, I find it pretty distasteful in some respects, but I suppose it's fine by me,' he finally concluded unenthusiastically.

BBH left the meeting having established formally that the campaign had been accepted. But Astley nursed a lingering doubt.

The staff revolt

The trouble with NO TITS, BUT A LOT OF BALLS in the row that followed was that even its most fervent opponents had to admit that it was a brilliant slogan. But only if you liked that sort of thing. Some people thought it was too tasteless and vulgar even for a straight tabloid and suggested that a variation like LOTS OF TITS, AND PLENTY OF BALLS might be just right for the tits-and-bums *Sunday Sport*. And this was to be the second line of attack – NO TITS failed the Right-On style book, and was considered to be naff. It was this part of the argument that was to enrage BBH most. They saw a company which was trying to reach a downmarket audience, had the weapon, and which now prevented itself from getting there by imposing its own judgement of taste on the potential readers.

Even worse, in the eyes of BBH, the company's management had approved the slogan to fulfil the object of the exercise – launching a big-selling popular newspaper. Behind that objective was the ultimate responsibility to the shareholders who were paying for it. But the question of making a profit simply did not enter the thinking of many of the *NoS* staff, and the management was too cowardly to force it on them, even as an element to be included in discussions. Making it a first priority never came up. John Bartle considered in the end that the agency and the paper were on different planets. He thought the company's failure to recognize commercial reality made it like a kamikaze pilot, and the recklessness with which commercial considerations were ditched bordered on obscenity.

There were the first inklings of the trouble to come the next morning at another meeting at Clarges Street, which was to tidy up a few loose ends. Horsley always went on a three-week holiday to Barbados at this time of year, and was not changing his routine for

NoS. Hayling was to step into the chief executive's chair as well as filling his present post of editorial director while Horsley was away. By now Hayling's constant use of the telephone had developed into a series of jokes about 'telephone incontinence'. As he left the room to use it once again, Horsley mouthed at Taylor: 'Alan's very worried about the advertising.' And when he returned Hayling explained moodily: 'I am worried, very worried. I think it is sexist. I'd buy it all if we could only take the tits and balls out, but otherwise I'm very worried.'

Taylor blew up on him: 'For fuck's sake why didn't you say that last night when you had a chance?' he demanded.

Hayling replied sullenly that he had been told to keep his mouth shut so as not to offend the creative persons from BBH. Because of Taylor's warning he had felt unable to speak up. After more of his agonizing Taylor tried to calm things down. 'Look, fellas,' he said. 'Tits and balls is the linchpin of the campaign. All the others build on it. But I'll see the agency and try to rescue things. I promise you I'll do my best to get it changed.'

The next point was more tricky – the staff. *NoS* was an open organization running on consensus. The original plan in Ben Lowe's feasibility study had contained a long section about 'democracy in the newsroom'. The reporters and other staff were to have a say in the running of the company as an additional guarantee against sell-out. Now the staff ought to be told about the slogan and allowed to give their views. Taylor, sensing that the 'rationale' might not go down so well, was adamant. 'We've got to approve the campaign before we tell the payroll,' he insisted. 'We'll do it when Nick comes back from Barbados.' He bound them to an oath. 'We all approved it. None of us can afford to float away now. We must agree not to breathe a word until we have got it all sorted out. Are we all agreed on that?'

Walsh had had time to make up his mind by now and he had decided to support NO TITS. He had considered it in ideological terms, and thought he felt a bit like Tony Benn in Callaghan's Cabinet. He must resign or go along with the decision. He would go along.

All the hands dutifully went up.

After the weekend, as Horsley and Olwen settled down to the warm sun and expensive delights of the Treasure Beach Hotel in Barbados,

Taylor called on BBH and explained the NO TITS problem. They said they would see what they could do. The following day a letter from Hayling, faxed down from Manchester, was biked round to Taylor's office. Hayling had made up his mind. The slogan, he wrote, 'is a very, very serious mistake'. It would put off ABC1 readers, discourage male readers, and was open to misinterpretation by those with a sense of humour as '*News on Sunday* — what a load of old bollocks'. 'I've no doubt this could stick,' he whinged. He also had a personal viewpoint. 'I find the slogan both tasteless and very offensive. *NoS* was never planned as a tasteless newspaper. If it ever moves in that direction and I am unable to prevent it, I will, without hesitation, resign.' Taylor must use his influence with BBH to get the poster withdrawn. 'I might even be able to sleep at night again!' Hayling ended pitifully.

But the sleepless nights were to continue. Distraught phone calls began to pour in to Taylor's office from *NoS*. The slogan had leaked, and Manchester was in uproar. Furious, Taylor rang up Hayling. Had he told anyone? Hayling explained that he had felt so worried about it he had told his partner, Noni, who had promptly informed him she and all their friends would not buy a paper with a slogan like that. What Noni said had worried Hayling even more. When he went to Liverpool that weekend he had confided in his mother, who, as mothers usually do, told him he must do what he thought was right.

Taylor ground his teeth. 'Anyone else?' he asked. Oh, yes — he told Joan Bohanna because she lived just down the road from his mother and was a fellow Director as well as being a Founder. She had found the slogan quite loathsome.

Taylor went berserk. He accused Hayling of trying to wreck the company by deliberately stirring up more trouble and dragging out another crisis. Did he have a vested interest in destroying everything?

Hayling was nearly in tears. 'Can't you see,' he wailed. 'I'm not well. I haven't slept.'

But even if Hayling had not told anyone, it would have been too late. NO TITS had already begun to spread round the staff in other ways. Jill Armstrong had shown some of the roughs to Marisa Casares-Roach, who now looked after special projects in the marketing department. Marisa had said no to the slogan immediately. She thought it was outrageous, and she was furious. She was also a woman who believed in action, and her behind-the-scenes lobbying to have NO TITS stopped was spreading the words. Now the whole thing blew.

Although the staff had not seen the actual poster, the slogan scored just as heavily as it had with market-research groups. Starting in Manchester, and spreading to London, the words got round. The reaction was mixed to start with, though. Many people were not at all sure what was wrong with the slogan and had to have it explained, and others were rather enjoying seeing Right-Ons struggling to come to terms with something for the masses. But there was no doubting the reaction of the feminists. Mayhem broke out. They reacted at first with shocked disbelief, then moved to the anger of the betrayed. Who could have done this? It was horrible, revolting! It was all part of the male takeover plot! Work stopped and the meetings started. The strength of feeling was enormous. At least one woman was in tears. Everyone, of course, felt entitled to weigh in and was positively encouraged to do so. The revolt was substantially led by the feminist brigade, but Matthew Nugent, the blue-eyed NUJ Father of Chapel who acted like a stereotype of the Irishman he was, was always looking for a fight. Many of the men had loaded in the feminist thinking by then, and some were fed up with the whole place anyway. Nugent led the official charge. The ad was declared blatantly sexist, vulgar, and, worst of all, naff. Those who approved of it felt obliged to keep quiet in public. There were some dissenting views muttered in the corridors, but officially the front was virtually unanimous. There were more meetings. The staff demanded that the ad be withdrawn.

Horsley came on the line to Taylor from Barbados. 'I'm very worried about the ad campaign,' he boomed across the Atlantic. 'Alan's been on the phone to me continuously. The office is up in arms and there's a near riot going on. We're going to lose people. I think the campaign is all right. You've got to do something.' Horsley's worries had been increased by bumping into Martin Boase of the other agency, Boase, Massimi, Pollitt, on the hotel beach. Horsley had been at Oxford with Boase, so he told him the whole story. Boase's laid-back attitude did nothing to calm his fears.

Taylor brusquely told Horsley to stay out of it. When a Chairman went on holiday he went on holiday, he shouted back at him. He should go away and enjoy himself and forget about bloody *News on*

Sunday – Hayling was running the place. By now Taylor's nerves were getting frayed as well.

But Horsley, who had just smeared on his sun-tan lotion when the phone started to ring, ignored Taylor and started interfering in an attempt to solve the crisis. Trying not to think about his soaring transatlantic telephone bill, he got on to Bogle, who quickly organized an emergency summit with Taylor. They met at Taylor's once-a-month dining club in the Hyde Park Hotel. Back in Manchester the uproar from the staff had escalated and turned on the subsidiary posters, which were now being savaged. The two men decided there was nothing they could do until after the weekend. A crisis meeting was called for 4pm at Great Pulteney Street on Monday.

Hayling got his instructions from Taylor. They were very definite: Hayling, as chief executive, was going to tell BBH at the meeting whether NO TITS was to go ahead or not. He must think about it very carefully over the weekend and be absolutely clear in his mind what he was going to say.

On the Monday Taylor, Hayling, and Jill Armstrong met up at BBH. The meeting, following the agreement between Bogle and Taylor at the Hyde Park Hotel, was to be solely to decide the fate of NO TITS. That was the only item on the agenda.

Hayling started the meeting off. He spent a long time telling the gathering how unhappy he was. He was very unhappy himself, and very unhappy about the rest of the world. He looked at them sorrowfully. 'Do you know what I care about most in the world?' he asked in a quiet and theatrically passionate voice. 'I care most about AIDS in Africa and the plight of the homeless in Britain.' Jill Armstrong snorted witheringly at this show of moral rectitude, and the others ground their teeth. Hayling was moved on to the point of the meeting. The NO TITS poster came first, then the others, one by one. As each was put up Hayling started picking at it. He dithered, complained, agonized and then finally rejected it. And before anyone fully realized what was happening, the whole campaign began to go down just like Walsh's domino theory. Bartle and Astley sat transfixed as their team's work fell to pieces. In the end there was no campaign left.

The meeting sat stunned.

Advertising campaigns may be commercial, but they are as fragile as any creative process, and just as vulnerable to a collective loss of confidence. BBH was a small, tight-knit organization and the ripples from *NoS* were already filtering across to other accounts and upsetting the whole structure. This was suddenly very serious. At that point BBH consider, with hindsight, that they should have resigned. John Bartle, Brian Astley, Barbara Nokes, Warren Brown and all the people involved had suddenly understood how much more there was to the paper than met the eye. Behind the façade which they had mistakenly thought was their client there lay a whole world which they had completely failed to grasp.

Until Hayling had first mentioned it, the word 'sexist' had never been used in the context of NO TITS or THE NAKED TRUTH. Throughout the agency, in the discussion groups, among the dozens of people the slogans had been tried on – including *News on Sunday*'s 'official' representatives, Taylor and Armstrong – the dreaded word had never been mentioned. And to this day many of the people who heard about the row cannot understand why NO TITS was pronounced to be sexist. Olwen's viewpoint was: 'I didn't think it was sexist because I am not sexist.' But for the Right-Ons the context of any mention of naked women, tits, or 'Page 3 girls' is irrelevant. It is sexist because of the automatic response it engenders in men, and because women's bodies are being used to sell a product. This deep, fundamental view was most clearly understood by Cynthia Cockburn, who was paid by Manchester City Council to monitor the paper for discrimination. Cockburn, a well-known expert, summarized the feminist point of view in a paper entitled 'Marketing News on Sunday – Sex Made Central', written after *NoS* had collapsed. (Cockburn normally publishes her work, but on this occasion decided not to.) 'At bottom [*sic*], the advertisers were looking for their mark', she wrote. 'And the mark was a man. The campaign thus became one that addressed men rather than women. It said (boldly) "You must be weaned from your obsession with soft porn." At the same time it said (sotto voce) "Never fear. We understand your game and speak your language."'

BBH discussed resignation, and came very close to it. But they realized that if they did pull out the disaster for the paper would be absolute. It would be their reputation against the paper's and, following the Pilger débâcle on the editorial side, it was obvious who would win. The paper would be dealt another body-blow which would cripple it completely. The little confidence it had managed to drum up in the advertising world would collapse, and the chances of Needham getting any companies to buy adverts would be zero. Anyhow, by now the high-minded principles which had guided each side were beginning to falter. BBH were looking not just at the embarrassment of losing a client – however much they would have been glad to see the back of this one – but also their fee for the £1.3 million spend. And once again *NoS* was finding its theoretical high-mindedness swept away by the speed of events.

The agency tried to pick up the pieces. The creative group which had been working on the campaign was exhausted. Bartle said he would put new people on and give them a week to come up with something. Three new creative teams tore into the paper simultaneously. The television campaign, which had not been mentioned, escaped unscathed.

And time might be getting very short for the main campaign, but there was an even more immediate problem. Ads were urgently needed for the trade press to pull advertising for the paper. Needham grabbed the opportunity. She thought they were bloody good posters. NO TITS and THE NAKED TRUTH NOT NAKED WOMEN – the 'Page 3 girl' with her breasts crossed out – could be used for the trade. They would pull in her punters. And because they were trade ads, they would only be in trade papers such as *Campaign* and *Marketing Week*, which the GBP did not read. Officially the public image of the paper would not suffer. Hayling authorized the decision.

The new creative teams failed to come up with anything very exciting. There was a stab at a replacement for NO TITS in the shape of THE PAPER WITH FIRE IN ITS BELLY, but nobody thought much of that, and it was feared in the new atmosphere of terror that it could even be animalist. The only other idea was a four-sheet designed for Adshels, the display units at bus stops, which had been thought up to cater for Walsh's Scottish campaign. The four-sheets showed a roll of lavatory paper with the front page of the 'Daily Smut' printed on the sheet hanging off the edge of the roll. The copyline read AT LAST THERE'S AN ALTERNATIVE. There were two different editions of the Smut, one with the headline SEX-MAD COLONEL SPANKED MY PRIVATES! and the other reading KINKY VICAR EATS GERBIL KEBAB! When these posters leaked out the attack was a more muted one, and this time it came from the journalists. Sutton, along with many of the hacks, felt that stories like this were irresistible to punters, and fondly remembered one of his great favourites, FREDDY STARR ATE MY HAMSTER. The feminist lobby, which by now was almost as exhausted as the agency by the emotional excitement, expressed disgust at the women on the front pages, one of whom had SIZZLING SONYA SHOWS ALL emblazoned across her breasts. Again the cry went up that the ads were tasteless, vulgar and naff. But the workers' revolt had almost run out of steam.

The row about NO TITS and the other posters now set off on its noisy progress round the labyrinthine committee structure, ending up with undiminished volume at the Board. Although NO TITS itself had gone, BBH were still trying to hang on to NAKED WOMEN and the ONLY TITS YOU WILL SEE ON PAGE THREE poster of the four party leaders, which entered a rarefied stratosphere of feminist thinking. The montage of Thatcher, it was claimed, was sexist because the man's chest was hairy, which was sexual stereotyping of men. Nobody was quite sure whether the debate had become a wind-up.

But the semantics were swept aside when the Needham trade press bombshell hit the news-stands without warning. NO TITS, BUT A LOT OF BALLS appeared splashed in two-inch-high white lettering on the lurid pink background across the centre-page spread of *Marketing Week*. Even worse, a small strapline added: 'For vital statistics contact Karen Needham.' The idea that the trade press was somehow a closed circle to the rest of the GBP was quickly dispelled. *Marketing Week* was on display in most big newsagents. Marisa Casares-Roach, energetically plugging *NoS* at the Women's TUC Conference in Blackpool, had her work unravelled in a second. An indignant delegate rushed up to her quivering with rage and brandishing the copy of *Marketing Week* she had just bought at the news-stand outside the conference hall. Casares-Roach, like the rest of the staff, was thunderstruck, not only at the ignominy, but at the duplicity of the company. It had been as economical with the truth as the government it was supposed to be about to expose, and had led the staff to believe the slogan had been totally scrapped.

This time the revolt, now the staff had been hit by the full visual impact, was more serious. Sutton furtively rang Taylor to say he thought the slogan was great, but there were other calls. Production manager Tony Hodgson rang at 1am almost in tears, pleading: 'It's killing us! It's killing us! Call it off, call it off, for God's sake call it off!' Taylor's 'rationale' was powerless in the face of such emotion.

The mandatory meetings started again, and other newspapers began to pick up the story. Horsley, back from Barbados and still not understanding the 'sexist' argument, rushed to Manchester and was amazed at the strength of feeling. Although he had known Christine Jackson for thirty years, he blew his top with her for not handling the staff better, failing to realize that she was central to the revolt.

As Horsley and Hayling tried to quell the riots there was fresh excitement when the Father of the NUJ Chapel, Matthew Nugent, got into an argument in a wine bar with the *NoS* press officer, Kevin Mousley. Mousley, recruited from the co-operative Headline News agency in Manchester, was unwisely making a half-hearted attempt to defend the slogan when Nugent's notorious temper flared. With a cry of 'This is from the working class!' he leapt up and flattened Mousley with one punch, giving him a large black eye which Mousley subsequently tried to hide behind a pair of sunglasses. Instead they merely made him look like a Mafia bagman. Attempts by the company to discipline Nugent were sidestepped on the grounds that the dispute had taken place outside office premises.

The following week there was a fresh horror. This time it was THE NAKED TRUTH NOT NAKED WOMEN slapped across *Campaign*, with more pink and the photograph of the pin-up with her breasts scribbled out. Christine Jackson, guardian of Equal Opportunities, had had enough. She sat down and wrote a quivering formal protest to Horsley as Chairman of the Board. 'The picture of the naked woman was blown up and copies posted round this office this morning until they were torn down by staff', she reported. Abandoning all pretence at dignity, she went on: 'I am writing to plead with you . . .' The new ad must be withdrawn – it was worse than tits and balls and used 'the most puerile kind of sexist imagery'. Reaching a crescendo, she added: 'Some people thought the tits and balls ad was "raunchy", whatever that means. This ad is straight pornography. Please, for the sake of our principles, for the sake of our staff, can you stop it now?'

It was no longer a question of stopping something – but it was a question of starting something. The deadline for the poster sites was rapidly looming, and as they had been pre-booked at a cost of £350,000, BBH were close to panic. Confidence all round had plummeted to zero, and it was now just a question of getting anything approved to cover the space. Jill Armstrong had despaired of trying to get home and had taken her sleeping bag down to Great Pulteney Street, where £30,000 of posters were waiting to go out the second the go-ahead was received. Taylor had given up and was backing away rapidly, washing his hands of the whole business. He told them helplessly that it was no longer anything to do with him – nobody could retrieve the decision from the bowels of the committee structure. Even by its own standards *NoS* was cutting it finer than usual. The executive committee meeting which would make the final decision was being held only twenty-four hours before the final poster deadline. If they could not make their minds up, the hoardings would be blank.

As the crunch meeting was to be in Manchester, Jill Armstrong, Taylor, Bartle and Astley arranged for an open line from the committee room to Great Pulteney Street. They gathered round on tenterhooks as the meeting began and an embattled Horsley started putting the posters up for judgement one by one. A series of uproars echoed down the line, each followed by Horsley coming to the phone and reporting in an exasperated fashion that yet another poster had been rejected. At the London end astonishment began to give way to fits of the giggles, which rapidly degenerated into hysterical laughter. Horsley, doing the nearest he would ever come to James Cameron's war reporting, stage-whispered down the phone above the din: 'The buggers disagree with everything we want. They're turning down everything. I can't do anything with them. I just don't know what to say any more!' The hysterics in London increased.

When the line from Manchester was finally closed down, still wiping their eyes, BBH took stock. The laughter at their end had died rapidly. For them the last fortnight while the posters were endlessly discussed in Manchester, and meetings and phone calls came day and night, had been a horrible experience which had completely destabilized the whole agency. Everybody had become so involved that work on other accounts had been wrecked. It took the place weeks to settle and regain its poise, and the wounds only really began to heal months later, when the agency pulled the prize of the account for the *Independent*.

But the AT LAST THERE'S AN ALTERNATIVE toilet roll posters were rescued by the determination of Chris Walsh. Realizing that there was nothing left, he reconvened the executive meeting and persuaded it to change its mind about them. Astley grabbed the posters before anyone could change their minds again and altered them from four-sheet to forty-eight sheet to go on the big hoardings. Desperate for anything to go with them, he seized what artwork he had, wrote OUT ON APRIL 26TH on the now familiar shocking pink, and finished off with a picture of a rolled-up copy of *News on Sunday* salvaged from one of the rejects. It was sent out as a back-up to the bog-roll.

As they lived near each other, Taylor went home with Bartle, who told him that this time the agency was going to resign the account. Taylor sympathized, but said they would have to go their separate ways. Taylor had to hang on. He still had his fee at stake. BBH were as good as Bartle's word. They were about to put out a press release announcing their decision to resign when Horsley intervened and persuaded them to withhold it until after launch. They agreed, but only on condition that if it was leaked to the papers they would have to confirm it. But it was rumours about Taylor that came up first. Ten days later he was on the front page of *Media Week*. The story said he was on the point of resigning. A furious phone call from Kevin Mousley in Manchester threatened the magazine with a writ for libel, and the editor rang Taylor. He confirmed the story, rang Horsley and told him he wanted to leave as quickly as possible, preferably without acrimony.

Taylor went to dinner the next night at the Meridiana restaurant on Fulham Road with Horsley, Karen Needham and Olwen. He was under the impression they were going to discuss how he could best leave without doing more damage to the paper. But instead, as the Frascati flowed, Karen and Olwen started a long discussion about men and Taylor found he couldn't get Horsley round to the matter in hand. Eventually he gave up, went home, and at 4am sat down at the kitchen table in Beaconsfield and wrote a press release announcing his own resignation.

It went out the next day. *News on Sunday* had fallen at yet another hurdle. Taylor's departure was quiet, and almost unnoticed by the outside world, in sharp contrast to the noisy exit of John Pilger. Pilger, who was now just a distant memory, had publicly announced the demise of the editorial side of the paper before the crisis over the advertising campaign had even begun.

6 · MI5 stole my bicycle pump

The journalists arrive

Ten days after Hayling's Canute-like Christmas announcement: 'The trauma is now over,' Pilger unleashed a tidal wave of bad publicity from which *News on Sunday* was never going to recover. On 2 January a double-page spread entitled 'The Birth of a New *Sun*?' was slapped across the erudite pages of the *New Statesman*, the forum for academic left-wing discussions on popular newspapers. Pilger laid bare the horrible spectre of what he foresaw and compared his alternative to Sutton's with devastating clarity.

The *NoS* press officer, Kevin Mousley, tried to stem the tide. But Pilger was determined to write the project off in public. Horsley lamely counter-attacked with a letter saying it was 'pretty disgraceful' of Pilger to go on like this. He was 'obviously trying to undermine' the paper by 'washing dirty linen in public'. Pilger promptly revealed that just before Christmas Horsley had rung him and read out a memo in which he called for Sutton's dismissal as 'crucial to the paper's survival'. He added that four of the five people who had appointed Sutton now admitted they had made a mistake. Horsley went quiet.

Worse still, Pilger exposed the convoluted committee structure and muddled decision-making process which had finally driven him out. The Founders were horrified. One of their main reasons for not dismissing Sutton had been to keep the bust-up quiet. In the words of one of them, Mike Power, they had been trying to avoid 'blood on the floor'. Now it was spattered all over the place for the public to see.

The paper was granted a right of reply in the *New Statesman*, where a jumbled version of the marketing brief was printed unsigned. It was an unconvincing stringing-together of the familiar buzzwords:

'*NoS* will be a popular Sunday tabloid of the non-sectarian left to be read with pleasure and interest by over three million ordinary working people, with entertainment second to none.' It affirmed that the paper would certainly not be a radical *Sun* as Pilger had charged. It would be 'itself'. The committee structure was even more fiercely defended. It had arrived at a 'clear, unequivocal decision', and anyhow Pilger himself had called the structures 'the fairest possible' in *UK Press Gazette* the previous year.

Sutton had been doubly infuriated by Pilger's *New Statesman* attack and became more and more convinced that he was one of the few people on the paper who actually knew what he was doing. This middle-class pontification was also giving him a lot of trouble on the paper itself. The *New Statesman* sold less than 30,000 copies a week, and they wanted him to sell a million. In fact *News on Sunday*, as the NO TITS, BUT A LOT OF BALLS fiasco would reveal, had no idea where it was going. The lack of clear direction now brought development on the editorial side to a standstill. Pilger's articles caused a loss of interest from good journalists. Rumours about the application-forms disaster were circulating outside the paper, and many of the more talented, rather than just enthusiastic, people fell away.

'Below the line', in the twilight world of the committed, *NoS* explained away the argument as a personality clash. For committed lefties, used to the bitter faction-fighting of their own organizations, this was familiar. And those who knew Pilger found it plausible. Even Horsley had gently complained about the way he rubbed people up. 'John is the Geoffrey Boycott of newspapers,' he would say, 'a brilliant individualist, but not a team player.' Pilger instantly torpedoed the disinformation exercise. In *Marxism Today* he revealed that the paper had been conducting Stalinist training sessions in which employees and supporters were encouraged to parrot the 'personality clash' line. The reasons for hiring Pilger as a journalist were rapidly becoming apparent, and the paper gave up the unequal struggle. From then on Pilger ignored *NoS*, and remained forever as a ghost on the sidelines, with a group of supporters who yearned daily for his return.

The dispute was a personality clash, but not between people. It was over the personality of the paper – an uncomfortable fact for the comrades who could understand it, and a contradiction which had not even occurred to some of them. The paper had been deliberately structured to avoid sell-out by involving as many people as possible in decision-making, and ensuring managers were as 'accountable' as possible to the Founders and to each other. All decisions were to be made by consensus and committee.

Unfortunately, this is not how papers work. They are shaped by strong individuals – either editors given a free hand or interventionist proprietors who instal puppets to carry out their instructions and work on a clear chain of command. At the very least, somebody has to have the authority to shout: 'Hold the front page!' At *NoS*, where no individual – employer or employee – was to be allowed to gain too much power and influence, the Founders had thought they could avoid a strong personality taking over by creating a two-man mini-committee – Pilger and Sutton. The two would cancel each other out.

By demanding to be in charge, Pilger had broken the rules, so it had been natural to pick Sutton, who went through the motions of consulting them and whom they thought they could control. There were other reasons as well. Whatever opinion people had of him as an editor, he gained respect over the months for his kind manner, dignity and innate modesty. He thrived in Manchester and formed personal friendships with many of the Founders. And Sutton also looked the part. Although he was forty-one, he appeared if anything slightly older, and in his suit, with his thinning silver hair, he had a distinguished appearance which impressed the worthies who visited him. When required to, he could exude an aura of *gravitas* quite out of proportion with his depth of thinking; off-duty his relaxed manner and sense of fun endeared him to people.

The *Wapping Post* had prepared Sutton for the committee mine-field. The strike committee had produced a paper of studied dullness which he transformed into an inky riot, horribly rude about Murdoch, and never taking itself too seriously. He described the *Post* as 'a humorous parody of the *Sun*' on his application form. The *Post* mortified union officials and committee people because they could not control it. The 'lads' loved its anarchic muck-raking and calculated offensiveness, and demanded ever more outrageous material. Sutton gave them a policewoman in riot gear as a 'page 3 girl', double-page spreads of people being beaten up by the police and haunting pictures of strike-breakers being escorted into work. (Sutton's editorship cropped up after he had joined *NoS* with a letter from Gavin Laird, leader of the right-wing Amalgamated Engineering Union, which had unexpectedly invested £250,000 in the paper. The *Wapping Post* had printed a front-page story and picture describing his colleague Eric Hammond of the Electricians' Union as 'a rat'. Was this the work of the new editor of *News on Sunday*? Walsh assured him that Sutton had left by then.)

Sutton planned to use the Wapping strategy at *NoS*. He knew some people would hate his sort of paper. But they hated all pop papers anyway – it was nothing personal. And some would be appalled by its vulgarity. It wasn't going to be the sort of thing they could show to their friends, but their friends were trendies and intellectuals. He had already seen Hayling being sickened at the Beechwood conference. But if the punters thought it was great and it sold like the *Wapping Post*, he would be in an unshakeable position.

With Pilger gone, according to *NoS* structure Sutton should have been supervised first by Hayling as editorial director, but ultimately by the Founders, wrapped into their watchdog, the product development committee. The PDC, chaired by Board member Hilary Wainwright, was a mixture of Founders and people on the staff of the paper, designed to give editorial direction and (although such positive activity was rare at *NoS*), support and encouragement. But the PDC, the Board and the Founders were helpless. Most of them simply did not know what instructions to give, and certainly could not show what they wanted. They were like people who enjoy art, but can only describe what they like by pointing to specific paintings. When they were shown sample pages or editions of the paper, they could only say what they didn't like, and often they couldn't be specific about what exactly was wrong. Throughout its history *NoS* was entrusted to people essentially ignorant about journalism. Not a single member of the Founders, the management team or the Board had even earned a regular living from national print journalism. None had anything like enough experience to help Sutton. Instead of giving an active lead, they were reduced to endless complaints; they became a Super-Grumbly Brigade. Sutton, in turn, became increasingly outraged at their ill-informed comments, which included one instruction that rounded edges on the borders of pages were 'politically Tory'.

By the end of January 1986 Sutton knew the paper had to sell a million copies a week, if it made it to launch at all. The original business plan had been abandoned and the paper was now operating on 'Plan B', drawn up by Gerry Taylor during his two-week stint as chief executive. The break-even sales figure had been increased from 800,000 to 948,000 and then 967,000 to whistle up the extra £3 million a year needed to cover mounting costs. The financial goal-posts kept moving about as yet more costs were uncovered and fed into finance analyst Henry Stewart's IBM. A new break-even sale of more than one million a week came up on the screen. Meanwhile overheads were building up to £100,000 a week. But instead of cutting costs, the Board and management, now fearful that the paper might not come out at all, went for a simple approach, summarized by Stewart as 'shit or bust'. As it happened, the paper was to be both.

Hayling was dreadfully aware of how the paper of his dreams had disappeared with Pilger, who never forgave him for not resigning at the same time. The two men did not speak again. As Hayling showed over the NO TITS episode, he had the surest theoretical instincts, but the trouble came with the practice. Throughout his terms in various posts he was constantly unable to assert his authority. Torn by his vision and instinct, he watched the paper steering a course he knew would lead to disaster. But because of the company structure and his own inability to grasp the nettle, he could never bring himself to use his power to any effect. Instead he moved from crisis to crisis, adrift on a sea of emotion, constantly clashing with Sutton over the paper that was being produced and causing more damage by demoralizing the editorial staff. He said afterwards that his trouble had been that he was never prepared to commit the ultimate 'sell-out' of firing somebody.

Increasingly isolated, loathed by most of the management team, Hayling mounted coup attempts against Sutton, inciting journalists into open revolt and gathering any scraps of criticism to hurl at the editor. On the verge of tears, he would plead with them to get in some of the hard-hitting material he and Pilger had wanted, and he would rage at Sutton, both in meetings and outside. Some people were convinced he was cracking up. He worried constantly and would pace the floor in his flat through the early hours, appearing in the office in the morning with deep bags under his eyes and shoulders hunched. He started chain-smoking, and his hands would visibly tremble as he fumbled with his matches. He ended up going to a health farm for a week just before launch.

Events had in any case moved *NoS* away from Hayling. At the beginning of the year the two new offices opened. The Manchester headquarters was in Bridgewater House, a huge recently converted open-plan office on the eighth floor of a Victorian cotton warehouse. It was conveniently situated five minutes from the lifeline to civilization, Piccadilly station. From the sloping attic-type windows the newly arriving staff could admire the Edwardian Gothic spires of the Refuge Assurance company, a clone of the Pru in London, but now closed down, like so much of the city. Walsh proposed buying the place and converting it into Yuppy-style flats.

The London office was another new conversion, but not so grand – a three-storey terraced building just north of the City in Corsham Street, an area being redeveloped after the Big Bang. The building was bought freehold on the advice of new director Owen Oyston. London was seen as very much a back-up. The main departments – editorial, production, distribution and management – were all in the north. London was left with the advertising department, Walsh's marketing headquarters, the picture desk and the remnants of the 'heavyweight' journalistic team planned by Pilger.

The Manchester office was a brilliantly convincing façade disguising the chaos that engulfed nearly every department of the organization. The showpiece was deeply reassuring to the trade-union functionaries and other investors shepherded round to see what their money had bought. It was acoustically engineered and tastefully colour co-ordinated round the boiled-mushroom-grey carpet. Copies of the Charter were plastered on available vertical surfaces. All the trappings of new technology and modern business efficiency were on display. Blankly glowing computer screens assembled in neat rows in the editorial area connected the reporters and sub-editors directly to the machinery, under the terms of the new direct-input agreement. Modern telephones trilled discreetly, and the latest line in photocopiers dealt smoothly with the thousands of memos which descended like confetti. The traditional clippings library had been renamed the 'information unit' and instead of old-fashioned cuttings dispensed reams of computer print-out which reporters waded through hopelessly in a hapless search for nuggets of information.

The production department, tucked round the side of editorial, was a sight to behold. Coach parties of trade-union officials would be shown around, nodding sagely as the technical jargon went straight over their heads. They would leave mightily cheered up by the massive number of hi-tech machines bought with their share money, blithely unaware of the mounting hysteria behind them. What they did not know was that the whole operation bore a strong resemblance to some Spanish hotels of the early 1970s. The money had run out before all the equipment had been installed, so various relatively cheap, but crucial, items of equipment were missing. There was no proofing machine for the colour scanner, which was like having slides but no projector to view them through; the £1 million computer system had no spelling checker; and the air-conditioning was inadequate. The latter was vital for the computer, which had to be kept at a stable temperature. When there was a sudden heatwave in the early spring, rows of cheap electric fans, originally brought in to cool down the staff, were commandeered and pointed at the central processing units to try to stop them scrambling themselves and 'crashing'.

The inner production area, where the central processing units lived, was like a cross between the Starship *Enterprise* and a hospital intensive care unit, complete with men in white coats. There was even a Clive Sinclair look-alike, production consultant Rick Anderson, who was rushed in to cope with the frequent emergencies.

The only obvious link with the past was a mug-shot of Eddie Shah, the pioneer of the new wave, stuck on a dartboard. The compositors, known as the Black Hand Gang, were now reduced to pasting up the pages for the contract-hire presses after the sub-editors had mucked about with them. Many of them had worked for Shah before being made redundant from his nearby Warrington plant. They used the main tool of their trade these days, a surgical scalpel, for target practice on their old boss. Although they were still members of the once all-powerful National Graphical Association, they had bowed to the inevitable at *NoS* and agreed direct typing-in by journalists, but only those on the staff. The agreement had saved them some face.

The editorial selection process which now proceeded apace to fill these new headquarters was complicated by the twin lists of Hayling, who had taken up Pilger's mantle as editorial director, and Sutton.

They horse-traded staff between them, sounding out potential re-cruits with wildly differing accounts of what the paper was supposed to be. But the fast-approaching launch deadline and the increasing air of panic played into Sutton's hands. Hayling's last stand was to try to entice the award-winning team of David Leigh and Paul Lashmar from the *Observer* with a direct headhunt that had Christine Jackson reeling on the ropes. Leigh, who has a strong sense of journalistic commitment, was enormously torn, but smelt a rat, and hesitated, and was lost to the counter-offer of a salary hike, the title of editor and a company car to solve his endless motoring problems. Instead he recommended Peter Chippindale, who was stuck on a book at the time. Like others, he sympathized with the aims of the paper, though he had never been involved in it. He joined as Special Projects Editor.

Attention naturally focused on the glamour end – the news-gathering team. It ended up a mixed bag. The Pilger fall-out, along with the salary levels, had ruled out many first-class Fleet Street reporters, but Sutton persevered with the overall plan. The London office was stocked with older, more experienced hacks such as Lew Chester, Sylvia Collier (the editorial co-ordinator from the early days), Ole Hansen, who was a solicitor with a background of radical lawyering and part-time journalism, and Malcolm Boughen, the Parliamentary correspondent, who had been made redundant by Westminster Press.

In Manchester Sutton and Whitaker assembled a team of reporters, the core of which were young 'gopher' (go for it) reporters in their mid-twenties, mostly pulled off local papers. They ranged from Malcolm Evans, an aspiring heavyweight from the *Daily Mail*, through William Flatau, a Yuppy Old Harrovian whom Sutton, with his working-class background, was enormously tickled by, to Mike Taylor, a straightforward, enthusiastic young reporter from south London. Two young women reporters, Kate Muir and Margaret Rooke, balanced the team out.

Not everybody fitted the Right-On mould, particularly the older reporters. David Anderson, who applied after twenty years' bashing round papers in the north-east, found it too much. One day, like Oates in the Antarctic, he went out on a story and never came back. But David Wickham, with a lifetime of service at the seamier end of Fleet Street and recruited by Sutton as 'a dirty vicar chaser', was not so easily intimidated. He cheerfully brought in his battered portable typewriter to sidestep the baffling new technology and, pebble glasses gleaming, rattled away to the shudders of the feminist element on his two favourite topics – Frank Sinatra and Samantha Fox. 'I'm not a sexist,' he would say. 'But those boobs . . . Cor!'

The recruitment of the vital sub-editors, regarded by Sutton as the heart of the paper, was solved by pulling in the entire team from the *Daily Mail* office in Manchester, which had conveniently closed down. The subs, led by the amiable pipe-smoking Jon Whitaker, took some time to get adjusted to the new atmosphere. Apart from the Right-On handicap of being all men, they were initially suspected of right-wing leanings inherited from their previous employer. But within weeks they were judged to have adjusted to the correct attitude and joined the comrades.

The paper got its columnists. Attila the Stockbroker, an old Wapping friend of Sutton's, started a political column or a 'social-surrealist stream of vitriol' as he put it. Things went well until Sutton pronounced the column 'over the top' and Attila was dispatched to the sports pages to provide a Right-On hooligan commentary on the noble game of football, signed off 'the fan on the terraces'. Melanie McFadyean, a well-known figure on the left, started up 'Help!', an alternative Agony Aunt column. In a genuinely original approach, she gave practical, forthright advice which encouraged people not to be afraid to discuss frankly the most intimate and personal of problems. As part of her punchy style, she played with concepts like printing the word 'c*nt' and pushing back the barriers on such taboo subjects as incest. The Founders, and even Karen Needham, despite her own colourful language, were shocked, and McFadyean toned the column down.

The big-gun columnist was Anna Coote, a committed feminist and *Beyond the Fragments* enthusiast with a newspaper background. Her father was John Coote, a former managing director of Beaverbrook newspapers. One of her many claims to Right-On fame was leading a feminist protest against El Vino's wine bar in Fleet Street. El Vino's had been strictly men-only until falling foul of sex-discrimination laws. It was now illegal to ban them altogether, but women were made as unwelcome as possible by the management insisting that they could only be served if sitting down. In 1982 Coote and radical lawyer Tess Gill challenged the rule by standing up, were refused service, and took El Vino's to court, where they won a famous anti-discrimination case. Coote had worked for the *New Statesman* where she and other staff feminists would light-heartedly block out the 'man' suffix from 'Statesman', by manipulating the cover picture, for as many weeks as possible. She came to *NoS* from *Diverse Reports*, the eclectic Channel 4 current affairs programme. Coote was totally committed to the feminist cause, but found communication with the masses a difficult business, and grew increasingly distressed about her column. Sutton, who had little or no time for politics, which he was always trying to banish from the paper, gratefully let her organize the editorials.

But there were curious gaps in the operation, which partly explained the lack of decent news stories for which the paper was to be panned. Apart from getting Boughen to cover Parliament, Sutton appointed no specialists. There was no housing correspondent, City correspondent, local government correspondent, environment or energy correspondent, and, most extraordinary of all for a union-backed paper, no labour correspondent. These specialists are vital to any paper, no matter how downmarket. They gain the trust of personal contacts in the various fields who give them stories and keep them informed about what is going on behind the scenes. The only specialist, Boughen, showed how effective they are. Because his parliamentary beat was narrower than the rest of the reporters', he always had a couple of stories, even if they often followed the tired old formula of 'Labour MPs are to protest . . .' Sutton's answer was that there weren't enough reporters to waste on specialisms.

The great hopes for international journalism using Pilger's contacts were cut down to one foreign editor, Barbara Altounyan, recruited from Granada Television in Liverpool. She shamelessly introduced a novel element to the non-sexist office with a nice line in 1950s uplift bras and innocent flirtations with male staff. Like Pilger she had her worldwide 'pals' to draw on, and she importantly installed five clocks behind her desk showing the time in Delhi, Cyprus, Moscow, Sydney and New York. But she was told when she arrived that the budget meant she couldn't go anywhere. Sutton loved her boundless enthusiasm and multifarious story ideas, but she never recovered from an interview with the *Guardian* in which she announced breezily that the paper did not have a stance on Chile, Cuba, Israel and Gibraltar. It was not a paper for 'muesli eaters', she explained.

And missing right up to launch was the most important appointment of all, the oddly named Assistant Editor (News), who would run the news-gathering operation. Sutton complained in an exasperated fashion that he couldn't find anyone to fill the job, and persuaded Chippindale to try it. But after three weeks in Manchester, baffled by the lack of organization and rowing with Sutton about the nature of the paper, Chippindale retired back to London and his original job of Special Projects Editor, which he had carefully negotiated to skirt the various rocks on the paper. Brian Whitaker stepped into the breach, but the Assistant Editor (News) job was still being advertised after the paper had launched.

Instead the onus to get the news fell on Kolton Lee, a twenty-five-year-old black journalist who was cynically exploited by the paper for the Right-On points. Lee was one of Sutton's first appointments. Pilger had thought that he was only experienced enough to be a reporter. But he fitted the Equal Opportunities policy of giving important and responsible jobs to black journalists, and his arrival produced a burst of positive PR. The marketing department specifically told regional activists to stress this appointment to counter the Pilger bad news. Lee was pushed on to current-affairs and specialist black television programmes such as *Ebony*, where he made it clear that he was reserving judgement about how he was being treated by the paper. He was a star turn at the first conference for black journalists organized by the NUJ, but was given a mixed reception. There was much embarrassment at *News on Sunday* when it was discovered he didn't hold a current NUJ card.

Lee's appointment showed how far *NoS* was from understanding the minorities it was supposed to be fighting for. His journalistic credentials were limited. Thanks to his height, way over six feet, he had been a professional basketball player with four England caps. But a damaged cartilage put him out of the game, and he moved into sports journalism and general news before becoming editor of the London black paper, the *Voice*. Although this title is commercially successful, with large amounts of local-authority Equal Opportunities advertising, it has its critics, and Lee was not seen by many other black journalists as representing the real voice of their community. He was in any case hopelessly inexperienced for the load put on his broad shoulders, and eventually he came to the conclusion that he had been a token black.

After headlines, Sutton's major enthusiasm, which he shared with Pilger, was 'picture power'. Pilger envisaged this as a return to powerful photo-journalism with strong black-and-whites which would drive home the type of misery, exploitation and cruelty which the paper was exposing. Sutton, on the other hand, saw pictures as illustrations with short captions – strong pictures, but without any real story attached to them. He kept in his office a huge blow-up of a policeman walking by rolls of barbed wire at Greenham Common which smacked home the image of a creeping police state. But although he showed it to many people, he never actually printed it in the paper. He was really much more taken by a moody print of a Mersey tugboat given to him by Founders' secretary John Bohanna, which he hung on the wall.

News on Sunday only had one staff photographer, Tom Picton, who had been with the paper before capitalization and was based in London. Picton worked alongside a battery of left-wing freelances imported by Carlos Guarita, a Portuguese photographer who had worked at Fords in Dagenham and met Hayling on the network. Guarita had been mesmerized by Pilger, who he daily hoped would return to rescue the paper from Sutton. His real dream was exciting foreign coverage like Vietnam and Mozambique. With the *NoS* budget he was lucky if he got as far as Penge.

Running the picture show was Colin Jacobson, another import from the *Observer*, who was immensely experienced and excited by the commitment to photo-journalism the paper espoused. Jacobson, an angular, wiry man who never stood still, would leap from his cubicle in the London office tearing his hair at the latest impossible flood of picture requests from Manchester. More than anyone, he was strapped by the immense difficulties of coping with the twin-site operation and became a virtual Inter-City commuter as he dashed backwards and forwards to and from Manchester trying to sort it all out.

Getting to work

Both offices were, of course, enormously egalitarian. Everybody was on Christian-name terms, and encouraged to participate in all aspects of office life. But the grandiose plans for VDU-screen restrooms and relaxation areas soon crumbled. Such tribulations only increased the sacred rite of meetings, which dominated office life and produced piles of resolutions varying in importance from smoking in the office to the whole design of the paper. A distinct rift emerged between the meetings people, who had mostly been involved before capitalization, and the newcomers. Many of these showed open contempt or exasperation at the constant interruptions and were accused of the *NoS* crimes of being 'difficult' and 'demanding'. They in turn found their eyes glazing as meetings erupted into long-standing catfights and rivalries whose complexities were beyond them.

Although Cynthia Cockburn assiduously rooted about in the bedlam for evidence of sexism, the Equal Opportunities commitment was reduced to shreds. At one stage a statement came to the alarming conclusion that 'qualifications and previous experience are called for only when these are really necessary to do the job' and one recruitment ad said people should apply 'regardless of ability'. It was a typographical error; the ad should have read 'regardless of disability'. There were mutterings that it made no difference.

The plans to give all employees training in 'Equal Opportunities awareness' were somehow salvaged. New recruits were treated to 'induction courses' presided over by the training officer, Kieran Williams, provided for by the EEC training grant arranged through Manchester City Council. Kieran, a cheerful woman with purple hair and baggy sweaters who sent memos warning of 'hobgoblins and frogs in your lunch-box' if various forms were not returned, commèred these events with enormous gusto. Embarrassed cleaners were jollied along to give their comments on the paper, and would wriggle uncomfortably until they were released. A series of workshops gave employees awareness of disabilities and minorities. There was a 'deafness awareness' course and an all-day seminar on the problems of the disabled, which unfortunately had to be held outside the Manchester office when it was realized there was no disabled access. A women's self-defence class took over the Manchester boardroom once a week, clashing with the soaring number of committee meetings. The premature crash of the paper left the women stranded halfway through various groin-crunching manœuvres. The men, determined to uphold their side of the bargain, policed themselves for sexist remarks and behaviour, although they were puzzled to find the women had assembled a 'toy-boy' league table featuring the dishier members of staff.

After Equal Opportunities, the second great political objective in *News on Sunday*'s employment plans – basing the paper in Manchester to bring journalists into closer contact with 'the people' – also ran into problems. The reporters in Manchester were totally disorientated. Separated from their familiar haunts and contacts, they turned inwards as their lives revolved round the office. They became an émigré community, locked in their own circle away from the outside world – a disastrous frame of mind for any journalist. The newcomers headed for the districts south of the University, such as Chorlton and Didsbury, similar to London but with rents a fraction of the price. Not that they spent much time at home. The extraordinary intensity of the paper, where social and professional life merged into one, meant that it soon became a twenty-four-hour-a-day job, adding to the faction-ridden air and fuelling the conspiracies and petty plots. There was talk about the delights of the nearby Pennines and Derbyshire Peak District, but expeditions were few and far between. Instead, some time before midnight, and occasionally afterwards, the hacks would fall out of the office exhausted and crash into taxis. Some would head for the cheap-restaurant district of Rusholme, where they could gorge themselves for a fiver, but usually they slumped in the office local, which was a gay pub. Less Right-On members of staff complained it was full of 'shirt-lifters'.

There was one consolation in Manchester for those who had rejected the fat life of Fleet Street – the end of expense-account lunches. For people like Pattullo, tired of them after years on the *Observer*, it was a welcome relief. Breakfast favourite was the 'Coming and Going' near by. Lunch revolved round sandwich bars, cheap Chinese restaurants and more 'greasy spoons', with Horsley joining in the egalitarian sport and tracking down steamy dives in the Jaguar.

Lunchbreaks were carefully monitored. Sutton used to say only half-jokingly that people were disappearing for 'shoot the editor' discussions. Great suspicion attached to people who were out of the office for too long. It was an unhealthy, introspective, hothouse atmosphere where the premium was on being in the office, rather than getting out and chasing stories. The young reporting team was given little help or encouragement to get out of the office-centred swamp. They knew few people locally and had few contacts on the national scene. And the army of freelances and informants, the door-to-door salespeople of journalism who wander London, rarely ventured to Manchester, where the lack of tip-offs and 'walk-in' stories was remarkable.

The provincial freelances who sell to the nationals on a regular basis also avoided *NoS* in the main. Many of those who thought their material was suitable for the paper had applied for staff jobs or regular freelance contracts back in October. Their applications, more often than not, had been lost in the great recruitment-forms disaster and they assumed the paper wasn't interested in them. In addition, *NoS* refused to touch anybody who had worked for Murdoch during the Wapping dispute – either as staff or an outside contributor – which ruled out the majority of the country's freelance network. The ban was lifted at the last minute, but too late, and even then freelances were not impressed by the rates the paper paid.

The launch of any new newspaper is a red-letter day for the numerous cranks who hang around the edges of the newspaper industry. Many of them now made a bee-line for *NoS*, its London office in particular. A newspaper can be judged by the standard of informants it attracts; a letter from someone calling themselves 'No name, No pack drill' was fairly typical of the tip-offs *NoS* began to receive. In un-joined-up handwriting, the informant disclosed: 'Has you can see by the post mark that I live in a very HIGH "blue" area. Rumours are very few and far between. But there are two that seem very explosive. 1. no treatment at hospitals or doctors for unemployed. 2. no unemployed person of a certain CATORGORY will be allowed to vote. These two items are only heresay.'

Another nutter phoned from Nottingham, explaining he had some dynamite material about a huge scandal in the Conservative Party. He was invited down to London on the off-chance. He then produced a video of *Casablanca* and insisted, quite calmly, that the film contained a secret message that revealed everything. When told to go away, he became nervous and claimed that Carmel Bedford, the London office researcher detailed to look after him, was part of the conspiracy, ending with a final demand that *NoS* pay his train fare back to Nottingham. The paper obliged to get rid of him.

The 'leads' offered by regional-group activists were scarcely any better. The germ of a good story would sometimes bubble up through Ben Lowe's convoluted local-regional-national committee system over a period of months. Lowe would triumphantly hand the story over to a reporter who would then try and track it down.

Suddenly, faced with the prospect of having to offer the proof needed to get the story into print, rather than have it chattered about excitedly in a committee meeting, the informants would become evasive, saying that it was more than their job was worth to deliver the evidence.

The London office, the rump of the operation, was a straightforward disaster area. It did have cane chairs and bone china, bought by office manager Anne Diamond in the Harrods sale. But on a more mundane level there was a lot missing. The building had been chosen for a staff of twenty-five, but the complement grew to sixty-four and it simply burst at the seams. Huge arguments and meetings about whether the Roboserve coffee machine should be free, and fierce memos about the danger of bringing in kettles, were submerged in the mounting horror of everyday existence. The tie-lines connecting the machinery to Manchester were months late, and the floor was littered with trailing wires and snaking cables. There would be periodic crashes as people tripped and went flying, wrenching phone sockets out of the wall and abruptly terminating conversations. Reporters trying to keep their feet in the chaos had to share desks, and found themselves two or even three to a telephone. The building, housing the marketing and advertising departments as well as the investigative reporters, had only eight outside lines, which were continuously jammed. Anybody grabbing a free line was constantly interrupted by desperate colleagues scrabbling for an extension. Hundreds of outsiders reported the number as out of order.

Lew Chester, after twenty-five years on the *Sunday Times* obeying the No. 1 rule of keeping your lines of communication open, found himself, like the others, marooned in the office and cut off from the outside world. Sylvia Collier, now a reporter, took one look and decided to work from home. Sutton wasn't interested. The rift with Hayling had hardened his determination to cut London out, and he warned reporters working there that it was 'a branch line'. Regarding the place as a hornets' nest of Haylingite plotters, he seldom visited and instead sent Whitaker down once a week to field the barrage of complaints. Worse still, the remains of Pilger's 'investigative team', the part of the paper which needed the back-up of strong editor, lawyer and control over the finished result, was left stranded.

While journalists adjusted to the problem of communicating with the outside world, progress – if it could be called that – towards the finished product was charted by 'live' dummies which started appearing at the beginning of March. The dummies were real papers, produced weekly to proper schedules, and, as the paper geared up to launch, printed in increasingly large numbers to test the other parts of the system. But the only public they reached were market-research groups, who provided feedback from 'real people'.

The dummies were behind schedule because of an accumulation of delays, and the first was not until 7 March, when Sutton had a stroke of luck in newspaper terms. It was the weekend of the Zeebrugge ferry disaster, the best Sunday story for decades and every editor's dream. A reporting team was thrown together amid great excitement and the whole news section was cleared for the coverage, which was extraordinarily competent. Sutton and Packford were very proud of the result, which they thought was the best of any of the papers. The headline – WHEN WILL THEY EVER LEARN – was pure Sutton, straight out of the culture of the 1960s.

The front page was made up of two pictures – a German girl survivor wrapped refugee-like in a blanket, and the ship lying on its side. There was, however, a serious editorial error. In cropping the picture, the bow doors of the ferry – by then suspected but not proved to have been the cause of the tragedy – had been carelessly chopped off. When this was pointed out, Sutton shrugged. It didn't mean anything to him that the paper had basically missed the story – it was a detail. In contrast to Pilger, who believed people were desperate for correct information, Sutton was more interested in the emotional impact of any headlines, pictures or words. He never tired of saying that the appeal of the paper had to be emotional and not intellectual. A notice went up on the wall in Manchester, saying: WHO THE HELL READS THE SECOND PARAGRAPH?

Apart from this minor detail, the 7 March dummy got the team off to a flying start, and Hayling congratulated the staff. 'A great improvement,' he told them in a memo, 'and much better than the first dummy produced by the *Independent*.' But a potential million-selling news event like that was not going to fall into Sutton's lap every week. The market research he had seen showed that the 'likely-to-buys', the paper's potential audience, wanted gossip, scandal and, above all else, cheerful and heartwarming stuff. The paper plunged into the Great Right-On Debate.

There were two problems. First there was the split audience needed to sell the magic million, and then there were the consequences of aiming the paper at Right-On obsessions. Pattullo grappled personfully with the multitude of contradictions cropping up on the features pages. Did the readers want health and beauty, or was that not allowed? Should the motoring page be aimed at Lada owners like reporter Sylvia Collier, the XR3i readers identified by BBH, or just stick to bicycles on the grounds that cars were environmentally unsound? It ended up in a classic *NoS* fudge as 'Wheels'. The title was tried out in a dummy before the feature was dropped altogether for the live editions. Did the readers have big gardens or were they stuck with miserable little yards? Brown-rice cookery or Lancashire Hotpot? and what sort of money advice did they want? Were they on the dole, getting their local-authority salaries, or dabbling in the new game of share ownership? And if they were doing the latter, as the paper supported Labour should they be discouraged? The other pops were consulted for guidance and it was noted that the *Sun* carried the top seven shares. A wag pointed out unhelpfully that many readers would probably turn to the racing pages for investment advice.

Sport was a particular problem. Apart from the nightmare of co-ordinating the Saturday afternoon soccer reports, Sports Editor Bob Edwell had other things to chew on. Hunting was no problem – after all it was officially banned in Islington, with less green space than any other borough in the country. But what about fishing? It was the biggest participant sport in Britain, but some people maintained it was cruel. Then there was boxing, which Hackney was proposing to ban. Should the paper support this? The arguments went on late into the night.

What about 'advertorial' – the thinly disguised consumer articles designed round the ads which are the sole reason for their existence. Were they to be in *NoS* and, if so, at what level? The same with fashion – Right-On designer clothing, or good value Richards Shops? The male fashion editor, an upper-class Indian, put in an expense claim for a book on the history of men's underwear as part of his research into the dilemma. Then the books page – the latest offering from Virago, or Catherine Cookson? That was if there were book reviews at all. Astonished publishers attending a reception in London were ranted at by Mousley, who slagged off traditional reviews and told them *NoS* was not having a book reviewer. An hour later he shot back to correct himself. There was going to be one after all, but the reviews would be 'different'. He did not know in what way.

The continuous search for 'something completely different' spilt over into the music and TV pages. Hoyland sent furious memos about the music coverage, entrusted to Sheryl Garratt, a Right-On recruited from *City Limits*. The *NoS* music tour was being ignored by the paper itself, and she in turn was reeling from Beastie Boys to Tom Jones under the bewildering influx of contradictory suggestions. A lot of the Right-Ons were distinctly past it, and interested in bands which made anybody under twenty-five yawn with boredom. TV was simpler on the face of it. The paper had decided from the beginning to have lots of coverage, in line with Walsh-style promises of more of everything. But at the same time it wasn't going to carry stories about soap operas dressed up as news. So what instead? Sutton produced his secret weapon – a series called 'Psyching the Soaps' which amateurishly psychoanalysed leading stars. The market-research groups gave it the thumbs down.

There was one positive way forward – minorities. They were definitely being ignored by the opposition, presumably on the sensible grounds that there were not very many of them. But *NoS* could plug the gap. Features started appearing designed to cover as many as possible in one go – like a woman speedway rider and a black man from Toxteth trying to be a Formula One racing driver. Toni Williamson joined as a female sports columnist.

On the general features, as opposed to news, front there were the outside contributors and a host of would-be columnists. Blithely unaware of the iron disciplines of the pops, some sent in screeds of copy littered with three-syllable words and obscure phrases. Others tried with an audible clash of gears to move into what they thought ordinary people wanted, even though they were completely out of touch. Pattullo hired a re-write man, Andrew McKenna, who had worked for the tit-and-bum paper *Sunday Sport*, to hack the stuff down to the paper's length and style, which was muddling its way towards standard pop cliché language, helped by the subs and Sutton's punning headlines. The paper's reading age eventually emerged as nine, one year above the *Daily Star*. Labour Party figures such as Ken Livingstone were pulled in to plug the politics gap, but Sutton was more interested in printing a picture of Livingstone with his pet newts than the article. He would sit at his desk, staring hopelessly at the blank computer screen whose mysteries still eluded him, surrounded by screeds of earnest, concerned writing. 'What are we going to do with this crap?' he would say to people who wandered in.

The sub-editors minced it all up for him. Being literal-minded folk, they were often slightly bemused by some of the copy which came their way, including a comment in one article that the writer was sick of having heterosexuality 'thrust down her throat'. But after a time they got into the fun of it. A story about Namibia (which Sutton could not place on the map), featured the Bushmen. The subs, trying to get into Right-On sensibilities, but determined not to appear idiots in the eyes of their colleagues on other papers, had a great debate about whether it should be Bushperson or Bushdweller. Exasperated, one of them suggested: 'Let's just call them wogs, at least it's not sexist.'

The agenda

The real problem was emerging on the news pages. Here Sutton was in deep trouble. He had never been a reporter; the stories on the *Wapping Post* had walked into the office, which was next to the strike HQ. At *NoS* the burden fell instead on Brian Whitaker, who carried around a dog-eared document known as the 'long-term story list', occasionally reprinted from the Norsk Data to freshen it up. Reporters breaking the security code and hacking into his filing system gazed with wonderment at the curious mixture of old chestnuts, unprintable or untrue allegations, mega-conspiracy theories and stories so boring they had already been printed elsewhere without anyone noticing.

Tackling the Page Three problem, Sutton replaced the customary pin-up with different picture power. He tried a shot of a hermit in Cobham, Surrey but the photographer grumbled that the man was a filthy old racist. The next week, page 3 featured a daunting picture of a fifty-foot-long Iranian missile being hauled through the streets of Tehran to the ecstatic cheers of Kalashnikov-toting revolutionary guards. Coote complained it was a phallic symbol. He just couldn't win.

The Royals, that other great staple of the tabloids, caused endless debate. It was decided to attack from the Grumble angle. The Sut-tonesque headline RIGHT ROYAL MEANIES appeared above a story complaining that staff at the Royal households were paid only £5,000 a year, putting them below the Euro-poverty line. But the Grumble business was beginning to be monotonous. Dave Wickham heroically tried to roll back the frontiers with stories like one on a group of 'exotic dancers' who had been ripped off by an entrepreneur in Italy, but this merely plunged the paper into a debate about how much leg should be shown in the picture.

What was needed, thought Sutton, were animal stories. Peculiar items began to brighten up Kolton Lee's newslist, otherwise a cata-logue of minor grumbles generally involving black people and the police. Two notables were: 'A cat in a hospital has been taught to wee in the toilet' and 'A budgie in the same hospital has been taught to swear'. These were beyond the journalistic team, but they had more luck with the story of Mutley the Alsatian dog which had been elected as treasurer of Liverpool University Students' Union. The student press beat them to it by six months. The dog appeared wearing a mortar-board and the reporters erupted in outrage.

News on Sunday, of course, was not Loony Left and this was no longer a subject for discussion. But it was recognized that the paper had a duty to fight back against such a slur on its principal backers. *News on Sunday* would turn the tables with its own catchphrase – the Raving Right. Or the Rabid Right, the Rancid Right, the Rotten Right or something. Secretaries weighed in with helpful suggestions as the debate continued. But whatever the name, what was needed was some material. The hacks turned up a front-page story about a beauty queen whose career as a model was being sponsored by a Tory council on the grounds of small business enterprise. A pic of the pouting lovely duly appeared in the office, showing her qualifi-cations. Up went the chorus of 'Sexist!' and the story disappeared. The column never got sorted out.

Sutton then turned his hand to brightening up serious issues. He chose A NAZI PIECE OF WORK as the headline for a dismal exposé of a grubby-looking Manchester fascist who was threatening a Sri Lankan refugee. The fascist had been pursued by photographer Tom Picton but had given in and agreed to a picture on condition he was allowed to comb his hair first. There was fresh uproar over the headline at the weekly London meeting; Whitaker explained that the headline must have been the work of the subs, with smirking references to their *Daily Mail* background. Subsequent detective work uncovered a large sheet of tracing paper behind Sutton's desk, with the incriminating words painstakingly drawn out in his own hand in heavy pencil.

Inept though Sutton's efforts might have been, he was quite right in thinking the paper needed brightening. The concentration on Right-On obsessions and the subjects which would appeal to the Grumbly Brigade produced an unrelieved diet of misery. The paper found to its horror that it was producing an equally negative reaction from the people sampling the dummies in the market-research groups, who were observed through two-way mirrors.

The pattern that emerged was called the 'victim thesis'. Right-Ons wanted to read about problems suffered by the people at the bottom of the social ladder. But the victims of society's ills, who were constantly portrayed as suffering, did not want to read about how helpless they were. The reactions were a re-run of GLC politics, when the concerned moved in on the local population to give them what they were sure they needed, without actually asking them first. At that time they had often been dismayed to find their obsessions were not shared but instead rejected by the masses, and the dummies proved that nothing had changed. The people in the lower social groups knew about the problems only too well. They had to put up with them every day. They showed interest in simple matters, like trying to get prams on and off driver-only buses, but they didn't want depressing tracts about subjects like housing which merely pointed out the problems without being able to do anything to relieve them. Instead, as the other papers had realized, they wanted to escape from their own world, and read things that would cheer them up.

The market-research groups tried to get some fun out of the dummies by singing little songs like 'If you're loony, daft or bent, get a job in happy Brent!' when they saw the pages of local-authority recruitment advertising drummed up by Walsh, or by speculating that the paper might sell well in Cuba. (The pages of jobs came up again and again with the lower socio-economic groups as one of the most cheerful things in the paper. Sadly it seemed that simply reading lists of jobs on offer, which most of them were not interested in or qualified for, was counted as 'good news'. Actual response to the ads was to be minuscule.)

Many of the people in the lower market-research groups were
overtly racist. When a travel article was printed on Tunisia a Birmingham man made a typical comment: 'Who wants to go to Tunisia?
– you can see enough blacks in Handsworth.' It was an uphill task for
both sides. Fierce attempts to hit leading Tory party figures such as
Cecil Parkinson, described in the Coote column as 'Mr Sneaky',
produced cries of 'unfair', and the groups showed little interest in
reading the alternative versions of political life on earth by people
like Livingstone. It seemed Sutton was right when he said they didn't
want to read about politics.

The most difficulties were encountered over the 'investigations'.
Chippindale, in his short tenure as Assistant Editor (News), tried a
couple of heavy dummies guaranteed to appeal to the Right-Ons
about the plight of people in prison, where the population was rising
faster than the Stock Market and going over 50,000, with consequent
dreadful overcrowding. The paper zeroed in on the current row
about people being jailed for non-payment of fines, which was
making the problem worse. A screaming front page demanded SET
THEM FREE NOW! Inside under the head PRISONERS OF POVERTY
there was sordid details of prison life which are not often printed,
such as men gathering up shit on their socks and hurling it out of
their cell windows in what are known as 'parcels', rather than facing
the stink all night if they use the bucket.

The reaction among the lower social groups was summed up by a
woman who said that she felt sorry for these people, and wouldn't
mind watching a programme on television about them. But she did
not want such a depressing paper hanging round the house all day.
Other group members commented that *NoS* looked like the
Undertakers' Gazette. The dummies missed out just as much at the
top end of the social scale, where ABC1s thought the coverage
cheap sensationalism. The poorest reaction was among ABC1
women, who were disgusted by much of the paper, thought it vulgar,
ostentatiously wiped black ink off their hands, and were distinctly
sniffy about Right-On concerns which do not feature so much in
normal suburban life.

Other depressing facts did nothing to cheer up the editorial team.
The lower groups all said they would have thrown the paper in the
dustbin by Monday morning. One group of twelve women, sampling *NoS* on Monday evening, could not remember one story they

had read in their usual papers the previous day. Anyhow, they added breezily, they did not expect to believe a word of them. Some *News of the World* readers were particularly adamant that they expected their paper to be all lies, and would be disappointed if the stories turned out to be true. It emerged that the choice of paper was usually made by the member of the household who walked the dog in the morning, and that the front page was crucial. People wanted sex, scandal, the Royals and smiling faces to persuade them to pick the paper up. Otherwise they would not bother. Back in Manchester the gloom deepened.

In another attempt to brighten things up, the 'investigations' degenerated into farce. One dealt with the theft of traffic cones from the Lancashire police by the Yorkshire police. Another was proposed on the back of a story Brian Whitaker had heard that most television sets sent in for repair had nothing wrong except a blown fuse in the plug. Whitaker suggested using the regional group activists. They would spray the back of their sets with mystery chemicals, put blown fuses in the plugs and take the sets to their local repair shops. When they came back with the expected huge bill they could be examined under ultra-violet light by the fearless investigators to see if the claimed repairs had been carried out. The proposal was eventually dropped. Then it was suggested that a copy of the first edition of the paper be sent to the Queen, in the hope of getting a polite standard reply which the paper could print as some kind of spurious endorsement. Sutton had pulled the same stunt at the *Wapping Post*. The reporters killed the project by ignoring it.

The prison obsession gave way to AIDS, and then to spy stories. Long voyages through the entrails of the intelligence world are an old stand-by, more favoured by the 'quality press' than the tabloids. Sutton's interest in the subject was limited. Spy stories sometimes yielded good headlines, but he would sneeringly describe them as '*Observer*-type' material. The reporters persevered, knowing that their great attraction is that they can make a paper appear to be in the know, whilst the security services cannot reply if they are wrong. The paper fell on spook-spotting with relish for a couple of weeks, moving in on some of the early Peter Wright material and allegations by Colin Wallace, a former Army intelligence officer in Northern Ireland. An entire edition of a tiny circulation spook enthusiast's magazine called the *Lobster* was gutted by deputy editor Brian

Whitaker and spread across the middle pages of the paper in an impressive wodge. Sutton waved the *Lobster* re-write about as evidence of the serious 'investigative' work that was now coming on-stream.

Spurred on by this triumph, reporters searched for more half-baked spy stories. The obvious place to look was at *News on Sunday* itself. Rumours began to fly about that the paper had been infiltrated. Half the reporters were convinced their phones were tapped. In London there was a witch-hunt for the Special Branch person who reporters were told in great secrecy was actually on the staff. The size of people's footwear was examined for clues. There was great paranoia when photographer Tom Picton was ordered to take everybody's picture for new security passes. In Manchester any peculiar incident was minutely examined for leads. Spook-spotter in chief Whitaker often used to bring his bicycle into work, and on quiet Sunday afternoons would put it on his desk and do a spot of maintenance. One day he discovered the pump was missing. Such was the paranoia and dearth of stories that one jaded hack commented: 'I can see next week's front page – MI5 STOLE MY BICYCLE PUMP.' He added: 'At least it would be a better story than WAS THE PRIME MINISTER A SPY?' (A reference to Sutton's uninspired first dummy.) A freelance reporter excitedly rang up offering to sweep the office for bugs, using a gizmo obtained from the columns of *Exchange and Mart*. When it turned out he wanted the paper to buy the machine for him the offer was declined.

Underneath this harmless activity there was a real problem, based round what became known as 'the agenda'. The original concept, way back in the mists of time, had been that the paper would weld the 'fragments' together. But now they were sent spinning further and further apart. The ideas that flooded in were often impractical or even illegal, but they would at least have made a 'different' paper. Because the 'agenda' was never tackled, though, there was no clear direction from the top about what the paper was trying to do. And, more seriously, no attempt was made to try some of the ideas in the dummies to see how they went down with the punters.

One section of *NoS* wanted to load the readers with information and analysis, designed to be easily understood and to give them facts and figures to back their opinions. But Sutton was opposed to this approach, preferring to go for a gut reaction. It was only just before launch that he succumbed to the pressure and circulated a memo to the staff asking for suggestions for a five-part series called 'The Wastelands'. First would be on the unemployed, followed by the old, sick, and poor; housing; education; and privatization. 'I already have ideas of how to pursue some of these subjects, but would very much welcome further ideas in these areas,' he added.

The 'Wastelands' project, which was a Right-On Lowest Common Denominator of spongy grumbles, was Sutton's first real attempt to tackle the 'agenda'. And whatever his ideas were, they were never revealed. By then it was only three weeks to launch, and frighteningly late to embark on such a major project with the other worries that were cropping up. 'The Wastelands' was ignored by the majority of the reporters and in-house writers, and never got off the ground.

Other ideas, with the odd exception, foundered in the growing realization that the paper was heading straight for instant mediocrity by simply trying to ape its rivals. Everybody connected with it, from the Founders through the Board and the reporters' room, and right down to the most junior level of staff, had been completely de-moralized by the endless petty squabbles and the indecisiveness and lack of leadership that ran right through the organization. People became totally confused about what could and could not be done and the atmosphere of bullish confidence that was needed to get innovations off the ground evaporated. From being daring, people reverted to timid rehashes of the features that made other papers successful.

In any case, the sub-editors were preoccupied with the mind-bending complexities of learning how to use the new Norsk Data computer, whose central processing units had been given the folksy names of Winken, Blinken and Nod by their Norwegian manu-facturers. The £1 million system had been chosen as cheaper than ATEX, the one normally favoured by newspapers, and because of the manufacturer's 'image'.

As a relatively small Scandinavian company, Norsk Data treated its workers well and was free from commercial links with South Africa. The system was also said to be easy to use and maintain. There was one snag – it did have to be thoroughly programmed. Programming could not start until Sutton had fixed a standard layout and chosen the range of typefaces and sizes he intended to use. But he never did this, and so the computer could never be formatted. Instead, partly as a result of continuous battles over design with Hayling and the product development committee, he demanded total flexibility, sending the production department into what the consultant Anderson described as 'a neurotic spin'. Sutton and Packford finally chose a *Sun*-like main typeface called Holsatia Compressed. The suppliers warned *NoS* that there would be problems with this typeface. There was a long delay before it arrived, and when it did, half-English, half-Icelandic type would sometimes pour out of the typesetting machine in a peculiar gibberish. Eventually a Norwegian engineer was flown in to sort it out. News of her arrival planted a last glimmer of hope in people's minds. The wishful thinking quickly turned into a rumour that the launch was definitely off. This was excellent news, and it spread like wildfire. Could it be some sort of divine intervention? If the computer wasn't working in time, the launch would have to be cancelled. They would be able to sue the manufacturers, get the money back and start again!

On 1 April the engineer emerged from the bowels of the computer and announced cheerfully that everything was OK and ready for launch. She was puzzled by the response. Most of her customers would have been delighted to get the repair job done so quickly. But this lot seemed depressed by her efficiency. Still, she thought after spending a couple of days in the place, it was a strange sort of newspaper anyway.

7 · The Death Valley Curve

The countdown

Horsley began to get worried. The latest panic was the most basic of all – the paper might even not come out. The various tangled problems dogging the progress of every department were dragging on and on. The managers were at each other's throats and would keep passing the buck. What was needed was someone who had sufficient authority and experience to sort them all out. But who was it to be? They had resisted Gerry Taylor, brought in briefly as chief executive to replace Hayling, whom most of them loathed. Taylor had only lasted three weeks in the £67,000 a year job before he had resigned after drawing up his 'Plan B'. Now, Horsley thought bitterly, the buck had stopped with him, not just as Chair but as chief executive. This was not what it had said in the company's prospectus.

Taylor's strategy, in desperation, had been to bypass all the committees by setting up his own shadow management system in London in a room in the expensive Portman Hotel. There *NoS*'s time-wasters and purveyors of disinformation could not get at him. Taylor was relying heavily on Henry Stewart, who would struggle down from Manchester with his IBM to work out a series of mutating business plans with him. In Stewart, Taylor had finally found someone combining both ability and reliability in the *NoS* management morass. But even with him around the position was hopeless, and Taylor had decided to leave at the earliest possible opportunity.

Horsley was distraught. With the man who was 'going to teach us how to run a newspaper' on the way out, it looked as if it was going to be up to him to stamp some semblance of leadership on the place. The snag was that he was a chairman, not a chief executive. He knew nothing about newspapers, and while this was not unusual for people in positions of high authority at *NoS*, he, unlike others, had repeatedly and cheerfully admitted it. He had even told reporters assembled for the official opening of the Manchester office that he still had a lot to learn.

Horsley's answer was to bring in a professional – an 'adjutant', as he put it. The managers were summoned to hear about the plan. 'We've gone from one crisis to another,' he complained, 'but failing to launch would be the worst crisis of all.' Referring to the endless power struggles, he talked of 'terrible misunderstandings' and 'dissatisfactions which have been rampant'. The management structure had 'clearly failed'. He pleaded that the paper 'must not go on to the Death Valley Curve' and told them to stop making executive decisions. The 'management team' committee meetings were to be relegated to 'forums for information and co-operation', leaving strategic decisions to the Board. The experiments with 'consensus management' had brought the company to the brink of collapse. It had to stop, and normal methods of management were to be introduced.

But *NoS* was ready for him. Christine Jackson led the counter-attack, point by point. 'There is no reason why the managment team cannot act together to run this company and make day to day decisions,' she stated. What was needed, if anything, was more, not less, 'participatory democracy'. The fiasco over NO TITS, BUT A LOT OF BALLS had been because not enough people had been involved in decision-making. Jackson agreed with Horsley when he said there had been 'misunderstandings', and had already tried to get the managers to understand each other better. Instead of a business expert, Jackson had given the job of pulling the paper off the 'Death Valley Curve' to a representative of the Right-On 'therapy' industry. A clinical psychologist she knew, Maye Taylor, led off a series of sessions in which the managers explored their feelings about each other.

Maye Taylor, who specializes in management consultancy, saw the managers individually as a first step. Her report fuelled the paranoia and mistrust still further. She incisively pinpointed one of the main problems for the members of management who had taken their jobs when the company was capitalized. 'The widely held belief that some posts were either "given" to friends or were a reward for service rendered to the original project (jobs for people regardless of skills) led to not inconsiderable distrust and insecurity,' she explained.

There was another problem. 'Organisational hierarchical ambiguities were startlingly obvious, which allowed for the privatising of information as an exercise of power rather than as an exercise of management skill.' Which led in turn to Interpersonal Management Style, where 'I am direct and honest' became seen as 'You are aggressive and rude'. Maye Taylor suggested some group training activities, but these were abandoned at an early stage after opposition from Hayling.

Horsley's attempt to stamp some authority on the committee system did not get far. The management team's only concession to his demand for more power for the Board and the proposed 'adjutant' was a sulky counter-proposal to set up two extra committees. The operations committee and the organization committee, both chaired by Hayling and a mixture of Founders and managers, were established. The company was now being run by six separate and sometimes overlapping committees, including the management team with its new sub-group, 'Women in Management'; the Board; the already existing product development committee; and the Founders, with their power to block the firing of Sutton.

Hayling eventually retired to a health farm for a week to pull himself together. But three weeks before launch, refreshed and looking considerably better, he bounced back more determined than ever to get rid of Sutton. His line of attack was the design of the paper. Sutton had been using the frequent computer and typesetting breakdowns as excuses for the paper looking so awful. His designer, Bill Packford, had been baffled by the whole place. Not only was he not used to the new technology, but he found it impossible to get any feedback. He rowed bitterly with Sutton and Whitaker about how downmarket the paper was going. When he had been first appointed he had put in a series of innovative designs with devices such as blue colour washes. But although they had gone into the system, they had just disappeared. He had no idea what happened to them, or even to Pilger's expensive pages. Packford had looked at Pilger's pages with some interest, but dismissed them as hopelessly impractical. He thought they looked like *The Times' Educational Supplement*. They were not flexible enough for a newspaper where there might be a good strong story one week, and a ragbag of bits and pieces the next, with both having to be accommodated in the same layout.

Packford had become a victim of the *NoS* lack of direction. Whenever he tried to grab something, it slipped out of his hands and floated away, so, like others, he gave up innovative ideas and reverted to more mundane ground. But then he found that nobody had actually worked out what a paper between the *Mail on Sunday* and the *Sunday Mirror* actually looked like. On top of which, Sutton seemed to want *NoS* to look like the *Sun*. With these contradictory briefs, Packford found himself in the same position as the ad agency, BBH, and the result for him was a design he was very unhappy with. Instead of tackling the whole subject of design, Sutton would only pick at little bits and pieces. His reviews of the dummy papers would come back with instructions for 'Heavier underscores, more WOBs', 'desperate shortage of WOBs WOTs etc', 'should have exploding WOB here', but nothing that cut through the muddled look of the paper.

Hayling decided at least to try and make sure the paper's design improved. There was a huge outcry about how bad it looked. Sutton had been sent copies of other papers such as *Libération*, bombarded with names of designers, and slagged off throughout *NoS*. The market-research groups had joined in. Some had likened the logo to the *News of the World* in the 1950s, and many had said *NoS* looked like a local paper or a freesheet, was dull and lacked sparkle. Hayling made little direct progress, ranting away that if Sutton was not sacked he would go public and expose the plight of the paper to bring him down.

Just before launch, Hayling insisted on bringing in an outside company, Information Design Workshop, at a weekly fee of £4,000. The new designers took the train up to Manchester and went to work producing parallel pages. Hayling duly pronounced them superior, but Sutton fired back that the new designers were too slow. Packford, who agreed that his and Sutton's pages were shoddy but blamed (with some justice) the production shambles, was publicly humiliated when the minutes of the product development committee, which endorsed Hayling's opinion, were posted on the editorial noticeboard.

But with Sutton still – if only just – in the driving seat, it was time for *NoS* to prepare its editor for the big day. Two weeks before the paper was due to launch, Gerry Taylor went to the send-off – a Board meeting. Horsley had asked him to come to give the impression of a united front, even though he had already resigned. Taylor decided he ought to go, but resolved beforehand not to get involved, and not say anything.

The meeting started and Sutton was sent for, as Taylor described it, 'like a schoolboy'. He was told to sit down and explain how he felt about the progress of the paper. 'Well,' he shrugged. 'What can I say?'

Packford had just left and gone home to Cornwall for good. After months of constant and brutal criticism, he had taken the arrival of the new designers as his chance to clear off. He could take that sort of stick – after all, he had worked for the old *Daily Express* – but there were other problems. He was commuting from Cornwall to Manchester every weekend and by working at *NoS* he risked losing the steady clients upon whom his freelance business depended. He packed up his battered briefcase and quietly walked out. It was a couple of days before people believed that he had really gone.

Sutton wearily reported the news of Packford's departure to the Board. It would cause enormous problems. The members grunted half-heartedly; he was dismissed to go back to his pencils. The second the door closed they began to tear him to pieces. With growing astonishment, Taylor watched detestation run round the table like a forest fire. It was so fast he could hardly believe it. He sensed wave after wave of sheer hatred for Sutton in some of the voices. Nobody had a good word for him. Behind the scenes Hayling had been privately insisting to Horsley that Sutton be sacked immediately. He underlined the demand in a letter which described the dummies as 'drab and mediocre – a curious mixture between *Militant* and the old *Evening News*', and suggested he should be made temporary editor until launch.

Hayling showed his feelings in front of the Board. He for one was delighted Packford had gone. Then he vented his spleen on Sutton. He had to go. Horsley nearly forgot his lines and was on the point of ineptly giving the game away about the inner sanctum, where the real discussions were now being held. 'But, Alan, you don't want me to sack him now, do you?' he spluttered.

Taylor was so appalled by the denigrating of Sutton that he broke his vow of silence. He told the Board it was a simple matter with Sutton – they should back him or sack him. He asked if it was a universal feeling round the table that Sutton should go. 'Yes,' came the answer. 'But not until immediately after launch.' Taylor, flabbergasted, warned that if one word of the conversation got out, it would all be over and they could forget the launch. He walked out

of Bridgewater House for the last time, poured himself a large gin
and tonic on the Pullman back to London, and, like Packford, began
to readjust to the normal world.

Taylor left behind a host of problems which had been fudged by the
NoS committees. The paper's print contract was not the one it wanted
and was to cost more than had been budgeted for. Originally the
paper was to have been printed on the ultra-modern *Daily Telegraph*
presses in London's Docklands and Trafford Park, Manchester. But
the *Telegraph* realized that another steady customer, Rupert Murdoch, was looking at Trafford Park as a potential contract printer for
northern editions of the *News of the World*. They put their price up
by £470,000. And shortly after that Murdoch grabbed the capacity
for good by actually buying the factory, causing a minor blip on
the News International financial graph and a mini-catastrophe for
NoS.

Just one month before the launch, NoS finally clinched the deal to
print the southern edition in Docklands. Now the hunt was on for an
alternative northern printer. They were in the position of having
announced the launch date before settling the print contract, which
meant the printers had them over a barrel. In the crevices of the
printing industry there are people known as 'print farmers', who hire
themselves out on a consultancy basis to find print capacity for their
clients. NoS chose not to use the services of print farmers, even
though it had to find two or more smaller plants for the mammoth
1.6 million print run of the first edition. They looked at printers in
Wigan, Stoke, Derby, Carlisle, and Leeds. They almost struck a deal
with printers in Sunderland as an auxiliary for the first edition. The
problem was that the printers had no fax equipment to receive the
pages from Manchester. Undaunted, production manager Tony
Hodgson turned to the air. The pages could be flown by helicopter.
More problems. 'There are night-time flying restrictions for smaller
helicopters,' Hodgson reported. 'But it is rumoured that Granada
TV now have a large helicopter, and it may be possible to come to
some arrangement with them for using the machine.' The project
never got off the ground. NoS was gazumped again, this time by the
Observer which bought up the Sunderland capacity at a higher price.
In the end the paper signed with Central Lancashire Printers in
Wigan. But there was a snag. Wigan, like Sunderland, had no fax

machine and *NoS* had to pay an extra £140,000 to have it quickly installed.

All the managers had contributed their two-ha'pence to the great helicopter print-contract debate, as they did about everything, regardless of their experience or responsibility for the matter in hand. Christine Jackson thought she had spotted an unmissable 'promotional opportunity' in the Wigan deal. She put her brainwave in a memo addressed: 'To anyone interested'. (This did not supersede an earlier memo which had been sent to everyone in the office to tell them it was a waste of money to send a memo to everyone in the office.) Jackson pointed out, incorrectly, that 'The first ever railway ran near Wigan. *News on Sunday* could be carried on that track.' (The first railway was actually at Stockton.) There was a second amazing thing about Wigan – it had Municipal Swimming Baths, which were 'Olympic standard'. 'Should we throw Keith Sutton in on the launch night?' she asked. It was a publicity idea which had already been used by a successful local estate agent.

Circulation manager Liz Cooper also had railways on her mind. There had been a budgeting error. The cost of getting the papers from the printers to the railway stations to catch the trains – approximately £250,000 a year – had been left out of the budget. The comrades had been muddled about the mundane business of getting the paper into the hands of its readers and had simply forgotten to include it as a separate item. The problem was 'solved' by increasing the break-even circulation by a few more thousand. But there was a bigger worry. If the paper was printed it might now not get through the shops. Guarding the gate was the National Federation of Retail Newsagents, infuriated by the way it had been handled. The problem revolved around the expensively printed glossy colour section, which had to be printed a week in advance and then inserted separately. ('Inserting' is the trade word for placing a section of a paper inside the main body.)

The colour section was the last link with Hayling's original dummy. But as he had lost interest in it, and it simply didn't figure in the Sutton scheme of things, no thought had been given to it for months. With launch approaching, it began to float away, turning into an entirely separate publication, aimed at a totally different market and without even a passing resemblance to the main body of the paper, spinning round it like a small bright planet in orbit. It nearly perished at one stage in the desperate search for savings, but was saved by the 'loss of profits' clause in the three-year contract negotiated with its printers, Hunterprint at Peterlee, which would be invoked if *NoS* reneged on the agreement. The cost of breaking the contract was estimated at up to £300,000.

The original plan had been to get the printers to insert the section before it went into the distribution system. But the *Daily Telegraph* did not have the machinery. Tony Hodgson was dispatched on a futile mission to Germany to find the relevant machine, order it and pay for half the cost of installing it. But the *Telegraph* refused to agree to pay for half, and the scheme foundered. Instead the inserting was going to have to be done by the newsagents. The National Federation of Retail Newsagents demanded a bigger percentage of the cover price for their members in return. Circulation manager Liz Cooper held out for a lower percentage, believing the Federation was not important and did not represent ordinary newsagents. It was much more important, she said, to make sure the wholesale distributors got it to the newsagents in the first place. Though Cooper eventually offered more, the Federation did not get the figure they wanted, and reacted by telling newsagents to 'withdraw goodwill' for the launch, the strongest sanction they could take within the law on restrictive trade practices.

'Below the line'

And so the paper lumbered towards the starting post. By this time it was correctly on financial target, and therefore broke. The management structure had dissolved into six overlapping committees. The advertising agency and advertising consultant (and former chief executive) had resigned and wanted nothing to do with it. Huge meaningless pink signs saying OUT ON 26 APRIL and AT LAST THERE'S AN ALTERNATIVE! were being pasted up on billboards all over the country. It had a printer, just. The newsagents' national federation was not co-operating. The design of the paper had not been sorted out, and the computer kept crashing. The journalists were exhausted from working twelve- or fourteen-hour days and two had suffered nervous breakdowns. There were no good stories, and the news-gathering operation was shot full of holes. The Founders were wandering about swearing under their breath. The management were at each other's throats – and not even a therapist could sort them out. The only hard indicator of the paper's financial position was the raw bank balance. Most of the Board of Directors wanted to sack the editor, and it seemed the editorial director was doing everything possible to enlist the support of journalists for his efforts to achieve this. On top of this, the Founders were waiting for the journalists to move against Sutton as well.

The last hope was Chris Walsh and his 'below the line' marketing strategy designed to deliver the 'committed' readership. Walsh had no doubts. He reached high peaks of excitement and shortly before launch ran through the editorial floor excitedly proclaiming that the paper could expect to sell up to seven million copies.

'Do you really believe that, Chris?' a sceptic asked.

'Yes, I fucking well do,' he snapped back and ran off.

Walsh had thrown himself into the 'below the line' strategy with characteristic energy, and rapidly earned a new reputation in the office for his management style, which he summed up cheerfully for one person who did some work for him: 'I exploit people. Prepare to be exploited.' The person considered afterwards that he was.

Walsh's marketing department had grown apace. He had kept office manager Anne Diamond busy with his long list of requests for desks and furniture. The well-stocked drinks cabinet in the 'presentation room' of the London office stood waiting for the long line of famous persons, who rarely appeared. Instead, harassed members of staff attempted to raid it, on the rare occasions when the area had not been commandeered for another meeting. Walsh now had somebody in charge of merchandising the special offers about which Taylor had complained. More staff had been drafted in to cope with the numerous mailing lists being built up on newly installed computers. And John Hoyland, who had originally been recruited to bring some order into the fund-raising, had now joined the department as one of Walsh's lieutenants after failing to get the features job he wanted. Hoyland was particularly bitter that he had not even been interviewed, and his grudge against outside professionals, which he shared with others from the early days, had deepened.

Hoyland had been put in charge of a music tour in conjunction with Anti-Apartheid which was one of the major planks of the below-the-line strategy, and was designed to make the paper a lot of friends. He was able to devote more energy to it than he had expected because of the scrapping of the plan to raise extra money through a Business Expansion Scheme share issue. Hoyland and others, including Ben Lowe with his regional structure, spent an enormous amount of time and energy on the BES share issue, which was supposed to be the next stage of the paper's expansion. It had been canned in January by Taylor as part of 'Plan B'.

Hoyland was a gaunt man with a Quaker background who resembled a nineteenth-century undertaker, and took his pop concerts seriously. He clashed furiously with Sutton, who took scant notice of his many thousand-word memos and refused to give more than a couple of inches in the paper to plug the gigs. There were twelve of them, organized under the slogan of '*NoS* hates racism, loves good music', and they were now reaching a climax with the Communards at the Royal Albert Hall, which had been sold out.

Rick 'Rambo' Nelmes, an itinerant Australian whom Walsh had met whilst he was doing some casual driving for BBH, had been recruited to put together the numerous complex competitions which were another marketing-department contribution to the paper. 'Rambo', a heavy, lumbering man with a typically Australian attitude to life, had been learning as he went along, and spent much of his time hassling manufacturers for free goods to give away. He was zeroing in on washing machines and cameras. (A plan by Kevin Mousley to give away a yellow 1926 Citroën motor car, which was to be sold to *NoS* by a friend at trade price, had fallen through when the friend also demanded a job.)

Walsh's numerous activities included a running commentary on the editorial side of the paper, expressed in undated memos called 'Positioning Papers' and 'Who Are You Writing For?', coupled with a stream of story ideas of varying quality. The various strands came together under what he called his 'integrated marketing strategy', with a budget of £200,000. The main 'strategy' was the old stand-by of leaflets. 'Below the line' members of the marketing department felt on familiar ground, and they were convinced that this traditional left-wing method of communication was the answer. The result had been a huge operation to print more than three million A4 leaflets, using the unions, political organizations and the faithful from the regional groups to help distribute them. With the leaflets had gone 100,000 posters, backed up by a series of adverts and articles in local-authority and trade-union magazines and freesheets.

According to its advertising-rate card, *NoS* had reached a total of 15 million people as a result of this and the above-the-line activity. The below the line was enormously thorough. By launch the marketing department was claiming to have reached 'directly' every CND supporter, every Labour Party branch and member, every Labour local authority, every trades council, every unemployed centre and an extraordinary series of organizations ranging from Accountants Against the Bomb to housewives' registers, Age Concern committees, student unions, Community Development Associations, widows' social clubs, housing associations, over 400 women's committees, the Council for Voluntary Service, Anti-Apartheid, Greenpeace and thousands of community groups, women's and black organizations, pressure groups, and single-issue groups. And that was before you started on the unions.

The leafleting had gone well except for a bad moment when Walsh was caught in the fall-out from the BBH fiasco, and a meeting of regional groups refused point-blank to hand out THE NAKED TRUTH NOT NAKED WOMEN. After agonizing debates while the presses waited to roll, the offending slogan was replaced by THE PAPER THAT BITES BACK. Various GOOD NEWS! messages were attached – good news for youth, students, pensioners, women, trade unionists. All promised them the paper they had been waiting for. The GOOD NEWS slogan was a misnomer, as the paper was going to be full of bad news, but that would be GOOD NEWS FOR GRUMBLERS!

A heroic trawl for anyone remotely famous who would endorse the product had largely ended up as a *Who's Who* of rejection letters. But cartoonist Ralph Steadman came round for a riotous afternoon at Corsham Street. Walsh used the occasion to try out some slogans he had dreamt up himself, like: WHAT'S THE POINT OF POLICE CHIEFS IF THEY BREAK THE LAW? and WHAT'S THE POINT OF A LABOUR GOVERNMENT IF IT DOESN'T CHANGE ANYTHING? Other suggestions thrown about in the brain-storming session included FUCK YOU, I'M RICH (SAID IN THE NICEST POSSIBLE WAY) and WE MAY SELL ONE COPY OF NEWS ON SUNDAY – YOU'RE THE ONE. The upshot was three typically savage Steadman cartoons based on BITES BACK which were an instant hit with Right-Ons. One of them, which showed City businessmen suckling on Thatcher drawn as an Ethiopianlooking cow, ran into minor difficulties, which were recorded by Cynthia Cockburn. The comment in her report was: 'Objectionable really. There seemed to be some negative reference there to breast feeding. There were undertones of fellatio. It was racist probably – because Hindus are unlikely to see sacred cows as funny.'

For once, though, Cockburn was in a minority, and Steadman's spattery signature was transferred on to badges, stickers and T-shirts and formed a successful cottage industry for Greg, the office junior, who tirelessly flogged items to the other staff. They were charged full price.

The 'below-the-line' publicity was, it was hoped, going to compensate for the 'above-the-line', which was spluttering badly. The television campaign limped off on a glorious Bank Holiday evening with John Blunt, trendyperson, appearing in arty-farty black and white against the house-style shocking pink, bouncing a large variety of balls – meaningless activity without the scrapped NO TITS posters. Blunt then pranced about bursting balloons and playing hockey. At one point his spiel changed into Serbo-Croat, a language spoken in Communist Yugoslavia, which subtitles revealed the paper would not be written in. Blunt then opened his jacket to reveal a tasselled bra-like arrangement – the last shrunken vestige of the NO TITS theme. A group of target 'above the line' early-evening boozers, gathered round the TV in a Manchester pub waiting for the Bank Holiday sports results, immediately pronounced Blunt 'a poof'. 'Nobody's going to touch that,' they jeered about the paper. 'It'll give you AIDS.'

Other viewers assumed that Blunt was the editor. Encouraged by the fact he only looked about twenty-two, many wrote congratulating him on reaching such a responsible position at so young an age. An attempt was made to keep him going with a column in the paper, 'John Blunt's hot-line', a sort of written phone-in page. It was quietly dropped shortly after launch.

With the advertising campaign in tatters, the main publicity burden had fallen on Kevin Mousley, the PR person. He devoted much of his time trying to get *NoS* spokespersons on to as many local radio drone-in phone-ins as possible. As a former hand in the Piccadilly Radio newsroom in Manchester, he had a messianic belief in the power of the medium. News editor Kolton Lee was whisked away from his desk in launch week for a lightning tour of local stations. Walsh and Hoyland rushed off to fill the air with the manic 'Good News!' message, adapting it slightly when the particular grumble of each drone-in participant was ascertained.

But apart from big chunks on *Newsnight*, Channel Four News and local Granada TV, the mainstream coverage was much less than had been hoped for. The best exposure was on the trendy Right-On *Media Show* on Channel Four. A special printing had to be arranged at huge cost just for the cameras. Following *Today* and the *Independent*, television interest in newspaper launches was dropping.

The advertising trade press had been adopting a sceptical tone, but at the same time acknowledging that the ad rates were not unreasonable. 'Could be cheap' was the overall message. Various commentators, such as Paul Johnson in the *Spectator*, were intellectually monitoring the paper's progress. The quality papers were giving the story some space, and trying not to be too patronizing. The *NoS* rivals in the marketplace were publicly ignoring it, but they were taking steps behind the scenes. The *Sunday Mirror*, the most obvious competitor, had suddenly become harder, less of the 'ladies' paper' Thornton had complained of. It was running lengthy 'campaigns' and 'investigations' into *NoS*-type subjects, such as escaped Nazis hiding in Scotland and lack of screening facilities for breast cancer.

But there was, as they already suspected, no real need. It is an old adage that there is no news on Saturday, but at Bridgewater House it was rapidly becoming No News on Sunday. Sunday journalism is nerve-racking, even for hardened professionals. During the week the dailies have a constant stream of events to fill the pages. But there is often nothing on the Saturday diary except sport, and much of the paper has to be filled with real stories, rather than the flammed-up 'news' events organized for the papers during the week. The gap can be filled by tracking stories which develop over the week so they can be summarized on the Sunday. But often a story which starts out big on Monday is dead by Friday, and something has to be found to put in its place. The only real answer for a Sunday paper is to be bold, and strike out for a big story of its own, which could be anything from a bought-in Hollywood Joan Collins-type to a major security scandal. But *News on Sunday* was missing any material like this.

Throughout the whole organization nobody seemed to know anything that a journalist would call a really good story – including the journalists themselves. And despite the hundreds of thousands of pounds spent on marketing, and the £1.5 million on advertising and promotion, nobody had had the wit to solve the problem by buying a story in, which could have been done on a minute fraction of the promotional budget.

Whitaker's 'long-term' story list had proved to be just that. Also never making it to launch was an extraordinary riddle involving a British Cabinet Minister, Spanish tenants, assault, safe housing, the CIA, an Italian taxi driver, two firms of builders, a meat tenderizer, P2 (current underground rulers of the world: based in Italy, operating worldwide and specializing in laundering money, terrorism, drug-dealing, assassination, kidnapping, Neo-Fascism and gun-running), a plot to sell Exocets to the Argentinians during the Falklands war, and international freemasonry. This story was Hayling's secret weapon. But reporters trying to investigate it were never given the pages of documentation which *NoS* was said to hold exclusively, but which had been taken to the house of a well-known TV current-affairs broadcaster for safekeeping. The pundit was never home long enough to find them, journalists were told.

Moving to the next source, they walked into a dispute between two rival penniless freelance conspiracy theorists, one of whom had been investigating the story for two years, and had evolved a complicated wallchart with spidery lines which 'proved' the connections. The other had been side-tracked into studying ancient Egyptian moon-worshipping cults in an attempt to trace the story down to its roots. He was still working on it.

(Later a fragment of the story, which goes on a regular round of conspiracy circles, spun into the lap of Foreign Editor Barbara Altounyan while she was watching a late-night TV chat show. The mention of the salient facts relating to a key part of the story had caused horror among the country's journalists, who waited breathlessly for a shower of writs to descend on the programme makers, who were experimenting with an 'upfront' new show, broadcast live. Everybody looked to Peter Carter-Ruck, London's most feared libel lawyer. He would have a field day! But although hacks who missed the show swapped videos and endlessly replayed extracts for snippets of information, nothing happened to the programme makers. Altounyan managed to land the story on her desk, but fortunately *NoS* never printed it.)

The launch

Even now, there was still hope left. In launch week Sutton crossed the same tracks as the executive had done and became a real editor, finally throwing out the committees and insisting that he was in charge. Though his mean streak came out as he lost his temper once or twice in the next few days, he never descended to the style of his arch-enemy, Kelvin Mackenzie, the editor of the *Sun*. Mackenzie is renowned for his bullying manner and the vitriol he pours over the majority of his staff. Sutton was different. He was a quiet person with a knack of sidling away, nodding, if you tried to pin him down. He would retreat into his cubicle, where, towards the end of the week, he would spend more and more time with his pencils and pencil-sharpener, tracing layouts and trying out headlines and pictures. The rest of the operation dealt with the words that would fill in the gaps. He would saunter out to grab someone he trusted, with a conspiratorially whispered 'Gorra minute?', usher them back to his cubicle, and furtively produce his drawing from under the desk for an opinion.

Hilda Holden, his patient secretary, would attempt to keep him in touch with the various meetings he grew to dread and which played havoc with the production schedules. Most started at 'News on Sunday time', which was basically when everybody turned up. Now Sutton went one further and also scrapped all editorial conferences – the regular meetings editors always have with their senior journalists. The senior editorial staff, enraged, finally crowded into his cubicle and forced an impromptu meeting. As they discussed things, Sutton dreamily pulled out a piece of paper. It was a quote from *Ragged Trousered Philanthropists* by Robert Tressell – the text that meant so much to him and Bill Packford. He was toying with the idea of using it on the front page of the first edition, alongside an exposé of the plight of bed-and-breakfast children, housed in terrible conditions at huge expense by councils in London. The research for the piece had effectively been done by Sutton's girlfriend Stephanie. Attempts by *NoS* to get pictures and stories to beef it up had collapsed in the normal muddle. Sutton mustered as much dignity as possible and began to read from the scrap of paper to his hushed and startled audience:

Every little child that is born into the world, no matter whether he is clever or dull, whether he is physically perfect or lame, or blind; no matter how much he may excel or fall short of his fellows in other respects, in one thing at least he is their equal – he is one of the heirs of all the ages that have gone before.

Sutton finished the reading and looked up. A voice piped up from the corner: 'I think it's sexist. What about the little girls?' The Robert Tressell approach to the first edition, originally written in 1910, fell to the ground, killed by the new wave of feminism.

With Tressell gone, the gap on the front page of issue one still yawned. The male regression to spook-spotting was instant. Two reporters had been offered some hair-raisingly secret material, which if published would breach not only the weedy and discredited Section Two of the Official Secrets Act, but the infinitely more serious Section One. It would also be contempt of court, adding up to penalties estimated as a six-figure fine and gaol for the editor. The only defence would be 'public interest', which does not go far these days.

Sutton was delighted and wanted to publish the documents, which were being referred to in coded messages between Manchester and London as 'the crown jewels'. But the decision had to go to Horsley who, as proprietor, was given his first opportunity to thunder '*Publish and be damned!*' Horsley chose instead to bottle out after taking legal advice. He said there was no money in the bank to pay any court costs. And he also revealed the paper had no libel insurance or fund. Christine Jackson was partly responsible for this amazing state of affairs. Noting that there was a libel budget of £25,000, she suggested employing a full-time lawyer, Peter Smith from Thames Television, at the cost of £15,000. Since Smith would read the paper and suggest changes, there would be no libel and the fund would not be needed. She had missed the point that libel actions are often caused by simple errors with no malice attached, or brought by rich people on the off-chance, and the up-front cost is enormous, even if the case is eventually won.

The incredulous investigative team was told libel insurance had been looked at, but rejected as too expensive. With no libel insurance or fund, the hacks could be sued personally without the paper being committed to backing them – an extraordinary position for a paper telling its journalists to rip into the establishment at every available opportunity. The protesting journalists were fobbed off until Horsley wrote a personal assurance that the company would back them. But enthusiasm for upsetting the rich and powerful – the only people really in a position to bring a libel action – wilted.

The next idea for the front page was the anniversary of the Chernobyl nuclear accident, which conveniently fell on launch date. There was a big CND march in London on the Saturday afternoon, at which the marketing department was going to be distributing showers of leaflets. Sutton set to work with his pencils and produced a page liberally decorated with radiation symbols. The page was to be tied in with the release of 5,000 black balloons from Hinkley Point nuclear power station, on the edge of the Bristol Channel south-west of Bristol. Chippindale, the organizer of the stunt, believed the balloons would look like a sinister black mushroom cloud and could go on the coveted page 3 spot to dramatize the front-page article with a simulated nuclear accident. The picture would also draw attention to Hinkley Point, being highlighted by campaigners for the decrepit state of its two existing reactors and for the fact that a third was being planned. Anyway, it was something he had always wanted to do, and he had persuaded the Marketing Department and Greenpeace to finance the operation jointly.

The balloon party rendezvoused in a field on the edge of the power-station complex at 6am on Saturday 25 April – the day the launch issue was going to press. They unloaded their equipment and set to work filling the 5,000 balloons with hydrogen inside a giant sack which gradually bulged as the number built up. By 10am all the balloons were inflated and the sack was heaving. So far the operation had attracted little attention, apart from a once-over by the security men with their binoculars and the owner of the field, who had arrived with his wife and daughter for the free show. There was a two-man television crew from BBC Bristol. The only other witnesses were a flock of peacefully grazing sheep.

Chippindale gave the signal, the ripcord was pulled, and the balloons started emerging. But instead of rising in a clump to form a nuclear mushroom, they dribbled out of the sack, creating a passable imitation of a tornado. As they went up into the sky they started to resemble a flock of giant wingless birds. The higher they got, the more bird-like they became, until at 4,000 feet they wheeled gracefully round and, by now mere specks, set off across the Channel to Wales. The balloon team jumped into Chippindale's ex-police car and set off on the 200-mile race with the pictures to Manchester. They walked into the office at 2.30pm to be greeted by an atmosphere of subdued hysteria. The film was shot into the darkroom. Page 3 had arrived.

But meanwhile there had been fresh developments. Sutton had abandoned the Chernobyl front-page idea. Instead of a simulated nuclear disaster, the readers were to be treated to a real journalistic disaster. Barbara Altounyan, the gung-ho foreign editor, steamed into the cubicle to re-offer her story about a man who had put a classified ad in the papers offering his kidney for sale. He said he wanted $100,000. The story was exactly the sort of stunt the Manchester news team had been hunting for in the classifieds. Kolton Lee had sent them all a memo telling them to buy the local paper wherever they lived (which was mainly in the same part of the city) and read it carefully. That was where a lot of the paper's stories were expected to come from, he said. But, he had warned them, they were not to let on that they were from *News on Sunday* in case the local paper cottoned on to the fact that its stories were being pinched. (The reporters on the local papers were, of course, flogging themselves to death trying to sell anything they could to the nationals on the side, and freelances regularly combed their columns for crumbs.)

There was only one snag with Altounyan's story. Instead of coming from Chorlton, Manchester, it came from Rio de Janeiro, Brazil. The story had been used in the previous week's dummy, and universally rubbished by the product development committee, which was by this time getting even more hysterically critical. Altounyan is good at her job, which is to get hold of as many stories as she can and put a rocket behind each of them. It is up to the editor to enquire about their veracity and sort out the wheat from the chaff. And as far as the front page of the first edition was concerned, this was chaff in spades. Committee chair Hilary Wainwright said later: 'We never actually forbade Sutton using it in the first edition, because it never occurred to us he would.' But Sutton was ignoring the committee by now, and even though Altounyan thought it was an inside-page story, he had decided it should go on the front. What difference did it make that it was in Brazil? He thought it was a bloody good story. At least it was about a person and therefore in the true tradition of pop journalism.

But the front page still needed something else. Something, as Walsh might have said, 'irreverent and witty'. Chippindale had got hold of the canteen menu from the Ministry of Defence, which is technically an Official Secret, and suggested printing it to emphasize the absurdity of the law. Sutton thought that would give the Establishment the required two fingers. To satisfy the Right-Ons he would have to run it with a worthy article by Duncan Campbell, the country's leading spook-spotter and a cycling enthusiast to boot, but it was still worth it. He set to work chopping up Campbell's copy.

Unfortunately the menu was not a story but a stunt, and it couldn't really carry a headline. So instead a sign like one on a supermarket product was slapped across the top of the front page. It read: 'WARNING! – This newspaper is dangerous. If you read page 11 you are liable to two years in prison – OFFICIAL'. The menu was printed inside, revealing that cream of mushroom soup cost 22p. The warning sat above a picture of Altounyan's Brazilian, stripped to the waist. THIS MAN'S KIDNEY IS FOR SALE, the headline said, above three reporters' bylines. The picture had had to be wired from Rio via New York at a cost of £2,000. The accompanying six column inches tucked away on page 2 failed to inform the reader whether the Brazilian had had any takers. After a couple of paragraphs it veered off into a separate story about a murder in Uruguay, the only connection being that it took place in the same continent. The reason for both incidents, the article concluded, was the world debt crisis. (Nobody ever found out if the classified ad came to anything, because the story was never followed up in later editions.)

Few people had seen the results of Sutton's thinking about the front page until staff, Founders and well-wishers turned up at Central Lancashire Printers in Wigan for a ceremonial viewing of the first copies off the press. When the presses started rolling at precisely 7.30pm, a delighted print manager yelled: 'We were ready, Eddie!' – a dig at the huge printing disasters which had engulfed Shah's *Today* on its launch night. For once something was going right. But down in Docklands it was a different matter. The *Telegraph* plant was causing endless trouble to its various users and breakdowns led to *NoS* losing 83,000 copies. Despite this, 1,524,000 copies of Edition One of *News on Sunday*, price 35p, went out on the distribution network. Horsley's 'worst crisis of all' had been averted. The paper was out and ink had managed to cling loosely to all of its forty-eight black-and-white pages. The tremendous feeling of relief soon turned to euphoria as the party piled into the large quantities of booze laid on by the printers. Somebody remarked that *NoS* should get the Newspaper of the Year award for coming out at all.

But as people began to read it, the feeling was already building up that Sutton had bombed. The paper existed, but it was nothing to get excited about. Horsley chatted to reporter Mike Taylor. 'I wonder what John Pilger would have made of it?' he asked himself out loud.

The best story was on the sports pages. Headed THE KILLER FENCES, a well-laid-out double-page spread explained how 342 horses had been killed in British racing in the last two years. The article pinpointed certain fences with an abnormally high death toll, and kicked off a *News on Sunday campaign*. The strapline bellowed: ACT NOW TO KEEP DEATH OFF THE TRACK, without actually telling you what to do. Pundits later praised the story, and some said it should have been the front page. One of the paper's great boasts was that the story was repeated almost word for word in the *Sunday Mirror* a few weeks later.

The paper carried a front-page logo line of 'Britain's bravest and brightest' and the editorial inside, penned by Sutton and Coote, was headed WE HAVE A DREAM. In direct contrast to the marketing department's approach, it stated: 'We're a small outfit with a fraction of the budget of our competitors. We're brand new and learning every day. We'll make mistakes, we'll infuriate you, but we'll keep on getting better.'

This modest statement was rammed home with the message: 'We're not owned by a Murdoch or a Maxwell. No-one here wants a knighthood or a peerage. We don't have to kow-tow to anyone. That makes us unique among national Sunday newspapers in Britain today . . . A dream cherished by women and men, young and old, all over the country. A dream of a radical, independent, popular newspaper that stands up against the privileged and the powerful. A paper committed to equality, justice and freedom.'

Continuing the dream theme, Coote also had a hand in setting up the main feature article, 'The Dream Machine', based on a tract about the subconscious by feminist writer Brenda Mallon. There had been a terrible row when Sutton wanted to spice it up with the headline I DREAMT I SLEPT WITH HITLER AND ENJOYED IT, but the headline had been shouted down by the feminists. A limp substitute had been found: I WAS TOLD TO KILL HITLER – I STABBED HIM IN THE BACK. Later market research reported that 1 per cent of readers found the article 'liberating' and 2 per cent 'interesting'.

On the facing page a disparate group of people wished the paper well under the words WELCOME TO THE WORLD. Tony Benn told readers they would be getting 'news that is not censored, and opinions that are widely shared but have been deliberately marginalised by the establishment'. Neil Kinnock said it would 'provide real news about real issues'. David Steel wished it success. The only other notables were the remnants of the celebrity trawl – actors Bob Hoskins, Glenda Jackson, Ed Asner, who plays Lou Grant in the American television newspaper series, Ricky Tomlinson of *Brookside*, and two reggae performers, Smiley Culture and Linton Kwesi Johnson. The gaps were filled by standard left-wing figures such as Harriet Harman, MP, radical lawyer Paul Boateng and Merle Amory, leader of Brent Council. The only comment that was not 100 per cent predictable was from Nicholas Winterton, Tory MP for Macclesfield, who wished the paper well despite its politics.

Chippindale's balloon picture had been junked by Sutton as useless and page 3 was now a punk who had been elected a town councillor for Buckingham. Dismal items of news were broken up by 'The Secret Diary of Margaret Hilda Roberts aged 14¼' by Sue Townsend, author of the *Adrian Mole* books. There was speculation in the Coote column that there might be no kissing in the latest James Bond movie because of AIDS. Heroically disregarding the market-research groups, Coote had also dusted off the Cecil Parkinson article, and he appeared again as 'Mr Sneaky'. Chippindale's 'Not the News on Sunday', one of the few original ideas which had survived the dummy process, gave an opportunity to run a conventional diary under the pretence that this was 'not news' as the paper saw it. A large and dated article on the real 'Rambo' dominated the television section. The back end of the paper was a graveyard of eight consecutive pages of job ads, mostly from London councils, including Brent (just under two full pages) and Southwark. The only article floating in this sea of Right-On opportunities was 'Working Week' – a ghetto slot for trade-union coverage promised by Walsh during the fund-raising drive.

The launch party moved on from the printers to a seedy Manchester nightclub and continued until dawn. Partners of staff were charged £10 to get in, after which they could drink as much as they liked. The captive audience was harangued for hours above screeching microphone feedback by Sutton's mate Attila the Stockbroker and assorted 'ranting poets'. Sutton went round praising everyone and accepted polite and timidly offered congratulations.

The following morning Walsh and 'Rambo' Nelmes met up at a Manchester version of a Right-On pub, where there were punters to be seen leafing through the paper. Mousley turned up optimistic from a tour of local newsagents he knew, and reports from his friends and relatives indicated that sales were buoyant. Walsh and Nelmes accepted a lift back to London in Chippindale's car. The night before Walsh had been over the moon, declaring *NoS* was 'the biggest launch since the *Sun*', and confidently predicting sales of well over a million. He was chuckling about the articles that would appear in the trade magazines as they were forced to eat their words.

But his mood was beginning to sober, and it worsened when the party stopped at a motorway service station. Walsh dived into the Shoperama, where there was a huge pile of unsold *News on Sundays* next to the disconcertingly small heaps of its rivals. He headed off to the Country Kitchen, snapping at Nelmes to see how many there were. Nelmes reported back mournfully that there were probably forty. Walsh spluttered on his burger and went to investigate. Nelmes was right. Glaring at the assorted families peacefully chewing on their junk food, the two decided the service station was a rogue sales blackspot. They debated buying up thirty copies, but the car boot was already stuffed with first editions pinched from the printers as priceless souvenirs, and the cost was daunting, so they left it.

Monday was the calm before the storm. The verdict in the morning papers was scornful. The *Independent*'s resident media pundit Maggie Brown reviewed the paper, describing it as 'weak and tee-total' and lacking in hard news. The problem was editorial content. The *NoS* 'had promised hard-hitting regional stories, dug up by the Manchester-based team. Where were they?' she asked. She added a sympathetic comment from Mike Molloy, the editor of the *Sunday Mirror*, who explained the difficulties of digging out a good Saturday story. And there was revenge for Hayling: 'The lay-out was a muddle: sad to say, but it looked in parts like a provincial free-sheet – apart from the splendid colour section . . . The accent is on up-grading the look, feel, and in some cases, the content of papers to keep readers sweet . . . Britain's national press is going through a re-think which a new newspaper cannot ignore.'

Sutton shrugged off the *Independent* article. It was a posh paper for Yuppies, and if it slagged *NoS* off that was fine by him. Anyway, nobody ever says pop papers are good. They weren't supposed to be some sort of work of art for snooty reviewers to witter on about. The only pop journalist who had passed comment really liked it. Derek Jameson, former editor of the *Daily Star* turned radio pre-senter, and the original 'Sid Yobbo' in *Private Eye*, had already weighed into the *NoS* debate when Pilger had been appointed editor in chief, commenting at a Communist Party/*Marxism Today* seminar: 'No way in two million years is Pilger a man of the people; he's as much related to the people as my arse.' Now he went on breakfast television to support Sutton and declare the paper a success. 'It's fantastic,' he said, 'the best newspaper launch for years – a great paper.'

Market-research fieldwork began on the same day. Over the next three days 2,500 people were phoned to ask what they thought of the paper. Only 12 per cent could remember its name unprompted. When they were told what it was called, 44 per cent of them (1,100 people) remembered they had heard of it, but a third of these did not know it had come out. Only sixty-five people had actually bought it. 'The *NoS* 65' turned out to be the hardest of the hard-core Grumbly Brigade. Only two of them had bought it because of the front page, and all of them were pretty unenthusiastic. They rub-bished the TV and entertainment section, and had only glanced at the sports coverage. They agreed with the *Independent* that the paper's colour section was the best part, probably because they were *Independent* readers during the week. What they wanted was highly political campaigning material on unemployment, nuclear issues, the health service and state education.

On Tuesday journalists struggled back into the office to start work on issue two. A stupid sign screaming 'U HAD THREE MONTHS FOR

FIRST ISSUE. U GOT FIVE DAYS FOR NEXT' appeared on a pillar in the middle of the editorial floor. There was only one topic of conversation – the sales figures. Speculation varied widely. A press release was written claiming 'just under a million sales', then changed to 'around 700,000'. New releases were being drafted almost hourly. As the figure dropped, the tone moved from triumph to 'It wasn't our fault.' One release blamed BBH for their 'inappropriate and uninspiring campaign' which had failed to 'relate to Northern working class people's interests and aspirations'. The press release was withdrawn at the last minute. In the end, with all the returns in, the circulation figure was 518,300, less than half the required number to make the paper viable in a normal week. But this was launch week, and 60,000 of the sales had been guaranteed by pre-orders from the below-the-line leafleting. The total number of chance buyers was 458,000 – an unmitigated disaster. And sales were set to decline by half again, down to 230,000, by issue four.

Horsley issued a statement: 'We have a beach-head in the market and we shall now go on to produce an excellent newspaper which will be read by millions every week.' He had to say it, but he did not believe it. Like everybody, he was shocked that the worst fears had been justified. With those sorts of figures there was no hope. Financial graphs had not even been calculated for such a low figure, but they didn't need to be. The paper had gone down the launch slipway and, instead of floating, carried on straight down. It was still heading for the bottom, and was finished unless a financial rescue package could be put together quickly.

And there was only one man remotely interested in baling it out – *News on Sunday*'s biggest single private investor, Owen Oyston, the man who had put in £100,000 for a seat on the Board. That evening Horsley drove up to Claughton Hall to fulfil the dinner engagement Oyston had arranged five days previously. The multi-millionaire estate agent murmured sympathetically as Horsley poured out the long tale of woe. Oyston had only attended a couple of early Board meetings, and although he had been tracking the paper and keeping in touch with developments, his interest had been diverted by the much bigger deal of selling his estate agency business to the Royal Insurance company for a reputed £30 million. With building-society deregulation, and the rapid changes in the field, the innovations he had pioneered had now become standard practice, and he had decided to move across to the new future he saw in cable television.

Selling up gave Oyston the finance and cleared his desk to enable him to concentrate on his rapidly developing cable interests, where he needed to be able to move quickly to maintain a competitive advantage over his rivals. But the sale of the business had been an enormous wrench. He had negotiated an Oyston Foundation and a share scheme for the 1,000 employees as part of the package with the Royal, but he was becoming acutely aware of how the business had been his whole life. Now that it had dropped away, he was feeling curiously empty and depressed – almost, he realized, as if he had had a bereavement. As a workaholic, needing only three or four hours' sleep a night, by his standards he had plenty of time on his hands.

Horsley told Oyston that he was going round all the directors and explaining that he wanted to do the honourable thing and wind the company up while it still had assets to pay off all its creditors. Oyston thought closing the paper then and there was premature. Not only was his money at stake, but here was a worthwhile challenge – something which might be therapeutic for him. He felt strongly about the right-wing bias in the press, and thought *NoS* was a paper with something to say, which reflected many of his ideas. He was also very supportive of any project which brought business and jobs to the north. He had been aware that the company was not going well, but like others had not expected the instant disaster which had now taken place. He quizzed Horsley gently about the company's position. Just how bad was it?

That was the trouble, Horsley confessed – nobody actually knew.

8 · Well, I'll be gobsmacked!

The crash

In his drive to make *NoS* a pop paper, Sutton had invented his own version of 'Sunspots' – snippets of way-out trivia such as break-dancing parrots or assaults on the world razor-blade-eating record. These 'gobbits', he enthused at one editorial conference, would 'save the paper'. He struggled for days to find a suitably zappy title for the feature. It ended up limply in the paper as 'Sunday Bizarre'. Sutton's first choice had been 'Well, I'll be gobsmacked!' – perfect for hooking the attention tabloid-style, graphically implying that the material would leave you speechless with wonderment, and suitably northern. But after dancing about with delight at the phrase, he had reluctantly rejected it as too over the top.

The correct place for the slogan was not, however, in the paper, but above the door to the Manchester office. In the weeks following launch almost all the people involved were to find themselves well and truly 'gobsmacked' as the scale of the débâcle emerged.

The paper, it was agreed, had only had one chance to get it right in the first place. The £6.5 million capital raised by the share issue had been earmarked for the period leading up to launch, and the paper was scheduled to hit the streets virtually broke. According to the plans, the launch would trigger loan facilities of £3 million arranged with a consortium of banks including the Midland. Although banks had been reluctant to co-operate in the early stages, Horsley had gently reminded the Midland that Northern Foods had been banking with them for fifty years. The bank had taken the point and granted the facility.

The pattern of newspaper launches is invariably that the highest sale comes on issue one, partly through novelty value, followed by a dip until sales bottom out and the graph, it is hoped, begins to climb again. According to the projections, the loan would see the paper through the interim period. But what many people at *NoS* did not know was that the Midland had attached a condition. The paper had to sell at least 600,000 copies a week, otherwise no money would be available. The bank had examined the figures in the prospectus, and noted how delicately the paper was treading the line. For the investors to get anything like a decent return on their money – 34 per cent – the paper needed a launch circulation of 800,000, building up to 1.1 million over three years. If it started at 700,000 and ended up at only a modest 1 million, the return would be nearly halved at 18 per cent. Of course if *NoS* was phenomenally successful, and sales soared to the market-research possibility of 1.5 million, profits would be huge. But if they dipped below the 700,000 the graph was just as abrupt the other way. Anything under 600,000 and it wasn't worth thinking about. The first issue had already made it clear – as Horsley had told Oyston – that the position was bleak. Week two had horribly confirmed that the paper was effectively dead. The buying public, unimpressed by the first issue, was already turning away, and it was obvious that the various excuses for the initial poor sale, which included such considerations as the warm weather on launch weekend, did not run.

Bombarded by feminist complaints that the paper was dominated by 'boy's stories', Sutton led the second issue with a freelance story about child abuse. He used his headline skills to come up with FEAR OF LOVING above a depressing bleached-out picture of a father walking with his arm round his young daughter. The story was a half-scoop, pointing out that parents were being wrongly accused of molesting their children and suggesting, in typically exaggerated *NoS* style, that 'the age of innocence for family relationships may be coming to an end'. Although the story didn't come from Cleveland, it did presage the row that was about to break out there. Inside the paper various stories were served up from old dummies, but things hadn't cheered up much. The stripping of the ozone layer was going to lead to the end of the world, children were being bullied at school, and David Wickham had popped in his favourite 'chimney of death' story, likening a vivisection laboratory in Harrogate to Colditz. A lonelyhearts dating agency could turn out to be a 'death trap' because of AIDS. The sports page led on one Manchester MP promising to pursue the 'Killer Fences' campaign.

One of the interested customers for the first two issues had been Paul Beber, a smart young accountant with the firm of H. W. Fisher in trendy Right-On Covent Garden, the company's auditors. Beber, who helped set up *City Limits* magazine, had last worked closely with *NoS* verifying the business plan in the prospectus. He had approved the figures, now long since abandoned, but carefully noted that they were based on assumptions yet to be put to the test – notably the pre-launch advertising campaign and the quality of the first edition. Since then Beber had stayed in the background. He had visited the Manchester office in February and been struck by the lack of financial controls but not unduly worried. He knew the pre-launch accounting was bound to be a bit hit-or-miss, and the system would only settle down after the paper had started publishing regularly. But when he picked up the first edition his heart sank as he saw THIS MAN'S KIDNEY IS FOR SALE and heard the disparaging comments of his friends.

Beber was not surprised to get a call from Henry Stewart on 5 May – the Tuesday after the second issue, which had only deepened his pessimism. There had been a dramatic drop-off in sales. The early returns had shown slump to around 370,000 – down nearly 150,000, and worse than many had feared.

'Paul, we're fucked,' said Stewart in a resigned and matter-of-fact tone. He rattled off the figures from his computer print-outs. On his models and future predictions, the paper now had no prospect of survival. He was not even sure if it could publish that week. He had chewed many biros trying to work it out. Confirmation came the next day for the staff. The unions were meeting the management to negotiate the house agreement covering wages and conditions – which had still not been sorted out – and Horsley told them that there was no chance of any improvements as the company was in a serious financial position and needed a substantial injection of cash. The rumours started flying, and Hayling asked Horsley if he could address the staff. Horsley said that Hayling could, and in line with the company policy, that he should also tell them the truth.

The decision was to have fatal consequences for the company. The next day there it was in black and white – or rather pink – in the papers. A highly accurate and detailed report on their precarious financial position by the authoritative reporter Ray Snoddy appeared in the *Financial Times*, headed: NEWS ON SUNDAY FACES CASH CRISIS

AS SALES DECLINE. It reported that the paper might run out of money within three weeks. The *FT* article caused consternation both inside and outside the paper. Those outside knew the launch had been a disaster, but most people expected the paper to stagger on for six months or so, during which time there was a chance it might get better. There was deep shock at the revelation that it was about to fold before it had even begun. And inside the paper there was equal disbelief. Few staff had any inkling of the true financial situation, and there was immediate suspicion that this was some sort of devious plot. This was natural enough, as the leak to Snoddy was from a person in an extremely senior position. And although *NoS* was notorious for leaks, they were usually low-grade, harmless and fed to Right-On outfits such as *City Limits*. But the purpose was obvious enough. The *FT* was the right place to advertise as a damsel in distress – the paper needed a white knight who read pink pages. But the more immediate effect was an avalanche of phone calls as alarmed creditors, equally caught on the hop, rushed to demand payment. The *FT* report virtually put the company out of business, by destroying the normal cash-flow balance. Companies rely on a balance between money owed and money owing; a sudden increase in demands from creditors can close them down, even if they are fundamentally sound. And *NoS* was not. The accounts department was besieged by creditors, many of whom demanded to be paid in cash. At one stage the company literally ran out of money, and had to make emergency arrangements with the harassed local bank. And, of course, credit was stopped all the way down the line.

The journalists, fearing the paper might go down on the spot, added to the panic by holding an emergency chapel meeting which demanded weekly rather than monthly pay. Horsley acceded, but was overruled because it would be too costly and difficult to organize. Now more suspicious than ever, the journalists decided to call in their own accountant for an unbiased look at the books. William Flatau, the Old Harrovian reporter who was now on the chapel committee, arranged for his man to come up from Golders Green at the weekend. The company surlily agreed to let him inspect the figures. The accountant reported that the cash crisis was not as bad as was being made out; there was no need to panic. There was only one snag – *NoS* was losing £100,000 a week. The accountant's view was that a chief executive with financial experience was urgently needed.

The journalists dug into their pockets for a fiver each to pay his fee and thanked him. Their suspicions had been confirmed. The information was passed on to the Founders, who held a crisis meeting on the Sunday. They too were suspicious.

Takeover rumours had instantly thrown up the name of Eddie Shah, the local equivalent of Rupert Murdoch, who was now back home in Warrington after his unfortunate expedition to London to start up *Today*. The whisper was that he was going to be part of a consortium – far worse than just him on his own, as it conjured up the image of a group of capitalists plotting together and ganging up on the paper. The NGA compositors were mortified. A second picture of Shah arrived next to the mug-shot on the dartboard. This time the union-buster was in a montage on a field of sheep. The caption read: 'Eddie Shah with the New Board of News on Sunday'.

The Paper That Tells the Truth attempted to roll back the clouds of gloom with an editorial which blandly assured the world that 'although last week there were reports that News on Sunday wasn't selling enough copies and was running out of money' the paper had 'a bright future'. The creditors weren't fooled – they kept coming. Security had to be stepped up on the doors of Bridgewater House after one marched in and tried to snatch the headphones off copy-taker Melvyn Hackney's head.

The fact was that no figures reliable enough to make a sound judgement of the paper's financial position existed. When Paul Beber arrived from London at the beginning of the following week, he discovered the only accurate guide to the financial state of the company was not in the accounts department, but on Henry Stewart's IBM PC/AT computer. Stewart had carried the machine down to London to meet Gerry Taylor in January when the 'shit or bust' approach was adopted. Since then it had rapidly grown to become the financial heart of the paper.

Stewart spent countless nervous hours crouched in front of the screen, flicking a biro top from one side of his mouth to another in a fast-forward imitation of Humphrey Bogart. He had bought a baggy pinstriped business suit during the fund-raising drive, and though he had sworn on capitalization day it would never be worn again, he had become used to it. Stewart had found his vocation. He had been feeling his way in the early days when he got his first Filofax and began to face up to the new league he was finding himself in. After the Beechwood conference he had sent a memo to the marketing department in which he recommended that they read *Everything is Negotiable* – a classic of the new genre of junk business books sold at railway stations. The memo explained how John Bohanna had negotiated 20 per cent off the price of his meal at Beechwood on the grounds that he did not want the starter of melon. 'This is an inspiration to us all,' Stewart wrote.

For three months Stewart effectively ran the financial affairs of the company by wandering round the different departments in his suit, crumpled from being worn under a tracksuit for his timed bicycle journey to work (it varied around the eighteen-minute mark), gathering figures which he jotted down on his clipboard. He would break into a nervous, infectious giggle every time he was told of new and vital, but unforeseen, spending. His friendly manner enabled him to pull off the ticklish exercise with remarkable panache. People like Polly Pattullo, the Features Editor, had already started running their own accounts, and simply handed over their figures. As his responsibility grew, Stewart became part of an inner sanctum formed to bypass the committee swamp, and the oracle to whom they turned for advice in the constant search for savings and for any permutation of the figures which would show the way ahead. Because he was in his mid-twenties they patronized him, and he was known to everyone as Henry.

The inner sanctum needed Henry because the official accounts department had broken down. It was a sorry story, which had started with Horsley bringing in Vince Luck, a Guyanese accountant who had spent his life supervising the financial affairs of Northern Dairies milk rounds. Luck had taken early retirement and was now Horsley's choice as financial controller. But he had a bad clash of style with the comrades, who passed motions at meetings condemning his 'authoritarianism'. And although he had worked successfully for many years in the dairy business, he had no experience of newspapers, and was unfamiliar with the computer technology into which the accounting system was to be loaded.

Anna Bennett had been found as Luck's successor through a local employment agency. She was qualified and came with good references. But like Luck she quickly found herself bogged down in the computer morass, and for weeks was unable to give the Board or the various committees up-to-date figures on the state of the company's affairs. Instead of saying what was happening, she had continually stalled, promising repeatedly that figures would be ready the following week. They seldom were, so the management fell back on Stewart's spending estimates, backed by the raw bank balance.

Beber went to Manchester and started to prepare some figures for the next Board meeting. He was appalled by what he found in the accounts department. The system had been falling steadily behind over the weeks, but in the final fortnight before launch, bills had poured into a torrent as everything built up to a climax, and what system there was had collapsed under the strain. Beber gave up and went to talk to Stewart.

The Founders, though they didn't know the exact position, now faced their first real crisis – the long-awaited hour of the sell-out had arrived. Their Golden Share, which limited any outside shareholder to a maximum 15 per cent of the total holding, had been incorporated into the company structure to prevent a takeover when the paper was a success, not a rescue when it was going down. But the Founders were still the key. Nobody was going to pump money into the company while they still had control. If they refused to give up – or literally sell out – the Golden Share, no rescue would be possible.

It was the responsibility of the Board to ensure that a saviour was found. The Board had now settled down. It was wholly made up of non-executive directors, except for Hayling during his period as chief executive, and composed mainly of people who, like Horsley, knew nothing about newspapers. The exceptions were the three worker-directors, one from each of the unions, who had just arrived. They in turn knew little about being on a Board. The Founders had three seats, occupied by Joan Bohanna, Joe Farrag and Steve Riley, and there were three men from the money side – Anthony Everett from Guinness Mahon, Owen Oyston and Vella Pillay, a South African Asian in origin, who had been in the City for thirty years and now worked for the Bank of China. Pillay had been involved with *NoS* since the early days and was Vice Chair of Anti-Apartheid in Britain. The last three seats were filled by Ron Todd from the T and G (who seldom came in person, although an *NoS* press release had quoted him as looking forward to 'playing an active role on the Board'), Hilary Wainwright, and Verity Lambert of Euston Films, who played little part in events. The unorthodox make-up of the Board, and its unusual proportion of inexperienced business people, had ensured so far that all the arguments in the company were repeated at this highest level.

On the eve of the Board meeting, after a long and agonizing debate, the Founders grandly issued a statement to the workforce, a copy of which was placed on each employee's desk. The statement condemned 'scaremongering' which had resulted in 'an unnecessary lack of confidence in the paper's financial viability'. The Founders had heard rumours of a takeover bid, but they were determined to explore other options. They would not be 'railroaded' into making a decision detrimental to the principles enshrined in the Charter. They were confident that there was a future for 'an independant [*sic*], socialist, national newspaper.'

There was still an irrational hope that more money could be raised by the company itself without having to rely on outsiders. For many people the shock had still not worn off, and they refused to accept that it was so cut and dried. The Founders had followed the lead of the journalists' accountant and were thinking about a new share issue – not a very likely prospect, given that Guinness Mahon still had 260,000 of the old old shares to get rid of. A bank loan was obviously impossible. The Midland, even with its strong ties to Horsley, had abandoned the paper to its fate. And the early figures for issue three showed no signs that the rapid decline in sales was slowing. The front-page story, a re-hash of a year-old *City Limits* article about secret MI5 action against the Labour Party during the 1983 election, was calculated to appeal to the paper's hard-core politicized readership.

The third *News on Sunday* was reviewed in the advertising industry magazine *Campaign* by ex-*Express* editor Christopher Ward, under the headline 'NoS: Out of the cradle with one foot already in the grave'. Ward described his time on the *Daily Mirror* at the height of the circulation war with the *Sun*. The biggest weapon, Ward said, was not tits, but 'the smile count'. Readers had deserted the 'well intentioned gloom' of the *Mirror* for the more cheerful *Sun*. 'I applied the smile count test to the popular tabloids this Sunday,' he wrote. 'The score was as follows: News of the World 37; Sunday People 24; Sunday Mirror 12; Sunday Today 8; News on Sunday 5 – and four of the five smiles were in one picture.

'For reasons that defy rational explanation,' Ward continued, 'Britain's newest newspaper has decided to trade in human misery.'

NoS, it was becoming apparent, had made a fatal error in catering for the Grumbly Brigade. They were by their very nature un-appreciative folk, and now they began to grumble about the paper as well. Sales of issue three were down to 306,600; if the paper continued to lose readers at this rate, the projected figure would be exactly zero by issue six.

Oyston arrives

The Board meeting on the Tuesday following publication of issue three started late as usual, but the drama was instant. Horsley tendered his resignation on the spot. He blamed the Founders and the re-solution which they had given the workforce, blocking any chance of the company being rescued. Horsley was quite definite. He had in fact resigned the second he heard about the Founders' statement, but been persuaded after much lobbying to hold the resignation back to the meeting. Now, he told the shocked Board members, he felt it was likely that it would be proposed that the company be kept going for political reasons in breach of Company Law. He was going to be no part of that.

Horsley had good reason for saying what he did. The day before the Board meeting, Margaret Thatcher had announced that the gen-eral election would take place in one month's time, on 11 June. The announcement had not been surprising, but the timing had elevated the crisis at *News on Sunday* to vital importance. Until now the other newspapers had tracked the progress of *NoS*, which was increasingly described in press reports by the standard epithet 'troubled', as a minor news item. After it had failed to emerge as a serious com-petitor, it was a story which had never really happened – 'Small accident in Manchester – nobody killed.'

But now, for those in the know, a ghastly and deeply worrying spectre had arisen. The paper was obviously nearly insolvent, and would probably have to fold as soon as the accounts were sorted out and brought up to date. That would be next week. It would no longer be a question of how the paper was going to implant the message 'Vote Labour' in ordinary people's heads. Labour would have to go to the polls without it. That it could live with. Un-fortunately the responsibility did not stop there – the people involved could not just apologize to the shareholders for having blown their money and walk away. At this stage, with the campaign just opening, Labour's chances were not being written off. Although few people thought Labour was going to win, it looked highly likely that the Tory majority could be slashed, leaving Thatcher with a 'lame-duck' third term. But Labour was worried, expecting the Tories' opening shots to concentrate on the 'Loony Left' councils issue, cranked up for more than a year by the *Sun*. And if the paper folded, the Tories would grab the news to spotlight *NoS*'s 'Loony Left' council investors and the large sums they and the unions would be writing off in the disaster.

At this moment though, back in the boardroom, the directors had other things on their minds. Robin Bynoe, the company secretary from Jacques and Lewis, was giving them a brisk summary of the law about insolvent trading, and the words 'personally liable' began to ring round the room. This was a new horror. What Bynoe was saying was that if directors acted in an irresponsible way, they could actually be pursued as individuals by irate creditors, and forced to pay up out of their own pockets – even to the extent of having their houses taken away. Hayling was particularly interested in this aspect of directorship. Bynoe suggested attention be given to Section 142 of the Companies Act. The words 'liquidation', 'receiver', and 'administrator' were mentioned. But at the same time Bynoe reminded them that the company's main asset was its continuing business and that the directors should think very seriously before allowing that continuity to be broken. There were nods round the table.

Beber was then asked to report, and he explained that bills worth hundreds of thousands of pounds had not gone through the accounts department. As a result, he could only guess at the financial state of the company. He was asked to get a statement of affairs together for the next meeting in a week's time. Stewart added that whatever the company's state, it was losing at least £130,000 a week.

There was a general round-up of the state of play. Liz Cooper reported that the paper was selling to middle-class radicals, rather than the working-class audience it had hoped for and aimed at. Market research on the live editions of the paper was beginning to show a pattern of the remnants of the 'below the line' committed hanging on, though not in sufficient numbers to make any difference. One of the successes claimed by Walsh's marketing department was the 60,000 people who had taken out advance orders, usually for the first month – the kind of commitment they had been looking for. Ben Lowe disagreed with Cooper and claimed that the paper had more working-class readers, but it was already becoming clear that the major market was going to be *Observer* readers taking it as a second paper – part of a market known as 'caring professionals', another name for the Grumbly Brigade. One of the fond hopes in the early days had been that *NoS* would be the tabloid with 'street cred', a Right-On badge in the pub on Sunday lunchtime or casually discarded on the Habitat sofa at home.

Karen Needham reported that advertisers had reacted in their normal world-weary way. She was finding the ball she had been so vigorously pushing uphill was rapidly rolling down again. More than any other sector of the paper, her business depended on a general air of confidence. She told the Board that although £100,000 worth of advertising had been sold, there was considerable cynicism about the paper, many advertisers had not yet paid, and there were no ads whatsoever booked beyond the next two weeks.

The discussion to this point, though, was desultory. The Board was really waiting for Owen Oyston, who had now surfaced in the media as the paper's only hope – dubbed tabloid-style a 'Red Knight'.

Oyston's name was nothing new at *NoS*. One of the reasons his estate agency was so successful was his name's distinctiveness, though people often did not remember it exactly. Taxi drivers would ask, if *News on Sunday* was mentioned: 'Who's that bloke with the funny name who's tied up with your place?' When you grunted 'Owen Oyston', they would nod sagely and promptly forget it again. Several of the staff had taken up his earlier offer of using his estate-agency facilities to find flats. But over the months his name had come to the fore as more than just an estate agent. The sub-editors, who arrived at the paper from the *Daily Mail* in early March, knew the local scene well, and already thought Oyston was interested in the paper. When they discovered how shaky it was, their suspicions grew stronger. And before launch Sutton, who seemed to know a lot of what was going on, had pulled people aside conspiratorially and told them he knew Oyston was going to buy the paper.

Oyston soon overtook Shah as front runner on the rumour machine. The compositor's montage of Shah leading the sheep was replaced with a picture of Oyston's typically ostentatious gold-painted Rolls Royce (complete with 'OO' personalized registration plate) with the caption: 'The new company car'. The latest rumour was that they were in partnership or, even more wild, that Oyston was acting as front man. The only other possibility, put up by Brian Whitaker, was the *Toronto Star* from Canada, which was apparently roaming the country looking for a new-technology set-up. The source of Whitaker's rumour was tracked down to a gawping American with whom Oyston was dealing over his cable-TV interests, and who had been brought round the office for the standard tour. Stewart rang Toronto on the off-chance, but they weren't interested.

So far Oyston had stayed away from *NoS*, and had not appeared formally at the paper to explain where he stood. But behind the scenes he had been getting more and more involved. What had started as a challenge for a few days was now developing and sucking him in more and more. With the announcement of the election, everybody was looking to him to keep the paper going.

Now he walked quietly and unannounced into the boardroom, bowing slightly in greeting. He was perfectly relaxed, smiling and unhurried. The only thing that jarred slightly was the bilious colour of his jacket. Oyston took a seat slightly back from the crowd round the table, now swelled by the three worker-directors trying to find their bearings in this unfamiliar and obviously crisis-torn world. Accompanying Oyston was his lawyer and adviser, Michael Connolly, in his regulation dark suit and sporting a thin-lipped version of the Oyston smile. And there was another money man, Derek Zizman from City accountants Peat, Marwick. Oyston had employed him to look through the accounts, and he had got a rough picture, but because there were no up-to-date books, he had told Oyston that so far he could not give any figures that could be absolutely relied on.

Horsley welcomed them, and Oyston waited politely for a suitable break in the proceedings before he made a little speech. The directors relaxed noticeably as he told them that he was there to help and thought the paper should definitely publish that week. His smile became broader and he chuckled slightly as he told the meeting he had not discouraged speculation that he might be a 'Red Knight' as he thought that any publicity was good for the paper. He had considered his position, and he wanted to make it quite clear that he did not want to get involved personally unless there was a common purpose among everybody involved. He had laid out his feelings in a letter to Horsley, a copy of which he suggested should be read to the Board. He handed it across to Everett, excused himself politely, gave another smile and left.

Everett read out the letter, which was distributed the next morning to every member of staff. It stated that Oyston was prepared to 'give a substantial financial lead' in helping the newspaper over the next few weeks past the election. But if things were to go further than that, nobody on the paper could afford to adopt 'rigid positions'. Then he added, 'If asked to do so, I shall be pleased to place myself at the Company's disposal, but I must have the support of all concerned, the staff, the chapels, the Board of Directors and the Founders, in order for me to do so.' The gist of the letter was simple – Oyston was only prepared to do anything if he was given a free hand, with backing from everybody. He was looking to them all to help him in his joint enterprise of saving the paper.

The silence after Everett had finished reading was broken by Harry Timpson, the executive finance secretary of the company's biggest shareholder, the Transport and General Workers' Union. He pointed out exactly what Labour feared – that the paper would fold during the election campaign. This, he said, would be like 'shooting yourself in both feet'. (The T and G was a virtual branch of the Labour Party, and therefore had the most to lose, quite apart from the wrath of the members, if NoS went down.)

Timpson, a heavily set man whose battered briefcase was a veteran of many a long union meeting, seldom spoke – and when he did it was invariably as a diplomat. He now quietly suggested he adjourn with the three Founder-directors, Steve Riley, Joan Bohanna and Joe Farrag, to discuss the question of the Founders' statement and Horsley's resignation.

The Timpson formula worked. Riley came back and explained there had been a misunderstanding. The Founders knew they might have to give up a degree of control and were prepared to negotiate. Would Horsley please not resign? Horsley grumpily warned them that it would probably mean their Golden Share would have to be sacrificed to allow new financial backers, led by Oyston, to take the paper over. But he agreed to stay on. Walsh was told to polish up the press release, and it was agreed that the only person who should talk to the media in future should be Horsley as Chairman. The paper was battening down the hatches against its erstwhile competitors, who might now at last see it as a real story.

But, still trying to avoid the inevitable, some of the directors were clamouring for an appraisal of the paper by a senior newspaper expert. There were two objects to the exercise: to see whether it would produce anything that would interest another 'Red Knight', and – if the paper was to go to Oyston – to give an idea of what cuts could be tolerated from a newspaper, rather than an entrepreneurial, point of view.

A sub-committee was set up and tracked down Charles Wintour, who was relaxing at his Islington home after an exhausting few months supervising the launch of Robert Maxwell's *London Daily News*. Now in his sixties, Wintour was an experienced and well-known figure on Fleet Street, mainly because of his editorship of the *Evening Standard* from 1959, with one short break, until 1980. Since leaving the *Standard*, Wintour had worked for the *Express* and spent a year as editor of *UK Press Gazette*, apart from his work for the *London Daily News* launch. He said he would be delighted to help any newspaper that was in trouble, and furthermore would not even charge a fee. He started work the next day, leading to a fresh spate of rumours that the Board, by now regarded as a hornets' nest of capitalist intrigue, was preparing yet another sell-out.

Wintour worked with characteristic brisk style, interrogating the different heads of department in turn, and had his report finished in five days. It was the first time an experienced editor and newspaper manager had examined *NoS*, and the verdict was a damning indictment of incompetence. He described the state of the paper as 'worse than critical: it is desperate'. The absence of a chief executive or managing director had led to 'an appalling vacuum of authority'. Horsley could not fill the gap as executive chairman, partly because 'he is perhaps almost too sympathetic to the dreams and ideals of the Founders'. The Board, with its lack of media expertise, 'cannot be expected to give strategic direction to the enterprise'; the lack of a financial controller was 'another glaring deficiency'.

Wintour formed a poor opinion of Walsh's marketing department. 'For reasons which are obscure to me the Marketing Department appear to have played a major role in determining the editorial strategy as well as the launch strategy,' he reported. 'There is almost an excess of enthusiasm in this area, not always backed by large scale experience . . . It is not absolutely clear that the money being spent in this department is being wisely used.' He recommended the canning of Walsh and the entire London end of the operation. The printing arrangements were 'grossly extravagant', the word most used to describe the management structure was 'shambolic', and at the present rate the paper would lose £6.5 million in its first year – doubling what it had cost to get to this point.

But while cuts were urgently needed, Wintour said they could only be mild in the editorial department, though the London building should be sold and replaced by smaller leased premises. The paper could afford to loose ten journalists at most out of a total of sixty. As a seasoned newspaperman, Wintour had noted how slender the staff was in comparison with the other papers. If it was to retain any pretensions to being decent, no more could be shorn 'without destroying the paper'. Sutton, he said, had 'done well in difficult circumstances', and should stay, but Wintour did note that there was a 'serious divergence of views' about what sort of audience the paper was trying to attract.

'Left to itself the enterprise will founder within days,' he concluded. 'Too many unsuitable appointments have been made, silly decisions taken, and personal log-rolling allowed.' The paper needed an immediate injection of £4 million, £3 million of which should be spent immediately on direct promotion, cashing in on the election when people's minds were focused on politics. But even with this and the cuts, he still only estimated a fifty-fifty chance of survival. He summed up: 'It is quite a gamble.'

Wintour's report was treated like an MI6 file when it was presented at the following week's Board meeting. By now the Board was totally paranoid about leaks, and the doors were locked when the meeting started. Copies of the report, each numbered, were issued to each member, and withdrawn before the end of the meeting. Demands that it be given out to the staff were refused point-blank. Horsley moved quickly to have it effectively suppressed by pointing out that it was 'extremely sensitive' – not least in comments about certain individual members of staff. He added that there was no point in discussing it unless more financial resources were available. (The report never really saw the light of day officially again, although it was later stolen from a filing cabinet and leaked to the staff, who read it with mixed feelings.)

After that bombshell it was time for the next – the Fisher report,
Paul Beber had unleashed the first of a long line of Men in Suits into
the accounts department. Solar-powered calculators at the ready,
they loosened their ties, rolled up their sleeves and waded into the
morass. They made some headway and uncovered various horrible
financial skeletons lurking among the heaps of paper. Nearly £1
million was unaccounted for. Some bills appeared to have been paid
twice. A neglected piece of paper informed them that the company
had never filled in a VAT return, and was owed as much as £850,000
in back payments. Tony Cook, the national regional manager, whose
job had been abolished when the *NoS* 'regionalization' empire constructed by Ben Lowe collapsed, was ordered in, and had the return
filled in within thirty-six hours. It was shot off to Customs and
Excise, only to disappear in the similar morass caused by industrial
action taken by the Civil and Public Services Association, one of the
few large unions not to invest in *NoS*.

Beber summarized a nightmare position in the accounts department. Apart from the neglected VAT returns, the paper had had no
proper financial control over the ordering system, so the accounts
department had not been notified of debits which were pending, and
as a result they had kept popping up unexpectedly. Statements had
got mixed up with original invoices, so there was a duplication
amounting to at least £80,000 going through what books there
were. The invoices which had flooded in during the final weeks up
to launch had not been processed, and his original estimate of nearly
£1 million which had not gone through the system had to be increased by another £250,000. Advertising revenue was being written
off as nil, because the vast majority of the advertisers had simply not
paid.

The point was not that the money had disappeared, but simply
that the accounts had not been processed properly. The net result,
put simply, was that the company was to all intents and purposes
broke. Two weeks after launch the paper only had a surplus
£157,000 of assets over liabilities, barely enough for another week.
The official verdict in the report was 'a complete absence of financial
controls and a general very poor state of the accounting records'.
Any short-term plan to rescue it would realistically need an injection
of £2 million. In the long term it would need another £6 million.
But, as Beber pointed out, £6 million was a cheap way for anybody

to acquire a national newspaper voice. Chris Walsh was asked if anybody had contributed to the 'fighting fund' he had proposed to keep the paper going through the election campaign. The answer was no, though councils and trade unions had been canvassed. Now, with some firm financial information to hand, for the first time Oyston was in a position to decide what to do.

Oyston was absent from the meeting, away in the South of France on a mixture of business and plans to buy a yacht, and already it was obvious that the paper was relying on him more and more. The news that he was missing had spread round the staff like wildfire, fuelling a crop of inaccurate rumours that he had lost interest. Now his lawyer Michael Connolly spoke for him. Connolly was starting to be bitten by the newspaper bug and the peculiar attraction of the nävety of *NoS*. Previously he had joined with Oyston's other money-men, when they had been to see Oyston 'mob-handed' and forcefully tried to talk him out of getting involved, insisting that, as he knew himself, if he wanted to invest in a new project they could think of hundreds of other opportunities infinitely more attractive financially.

By now Connolly had spent a lot of time at the paper on Oyston's behalf. Although he was a lawyer at an established practice in Preston, he was also an extremely skilled accountant, and Oyston relied heavily on his judgement. The staff had been somewhat bemused by Connolly's inscrutable smile and quiet manner as he went round politely asking questions and building up a picture of the paper for his employer, but they had appreciated the way he listened to what they had to say.

Connolly explained the position. Oyston was prepared to put in £100,000, providing the paper was published the following weekend. He told the meeting Oyston was very enthusiastic about being involved in the fighting fund. Discussions had been set up for the following weekend which might even lead to a rescue package.

Harry Timpson had also brought along some good news, though the T and G was seeing things in a slightly different light. The union was prepared to put £150,000 into the fighting fund to see the paper through the election period. But it was less sympathetic to the idea of participating in a longer-term survival plan.

There was a problem even now. How was this money to be put in? If the company simply borrowed it, even if it came from 'friendly' sources rather than normal trade credit, this would be acting wrongly, as it would increase the number of debtors to be paid from the company's dwindling assets. The dreadful spectre of 'personal liability', which worried Hayling so much, might crop up again. The prospect of Men in Wigs following on the heels of the Men in Suits had floated into a few minds. But there was a way out. The money could be put in as a 'subordinated loan'. In theory it was loan which should be paid back, but in practice, because it was subordinate, it would be last in the line of creditors to be paid. The subordinated loan money would be used to pay all the expenses day by day, so the balance between the company's assets and liabilities would stay the same.

Though the election had given *News on Sunday* its reprieve, the actual election coverage in the paper was completely unprepared. Sutton had tried to get the paper moving along the lines of the Labour election campaign with his widely derided 'Wastelands' project. When that collapsed the paper had been left with no plans whatsoever. Now the campaign had started, Sutton and Whitaker struggled with a scrappy plan of subjects to be tackled, which changed from week to week and, at first, left out unemployment as an issue. But Sutton was not very interested in hard political 'issue' material. Instead he spent long hours concentrating on the logo, which started as YOUR VOTE FOR THE FUTURE above a picture of columnist Coote's baby daughter, Ruby, and then changed to BATTLE FOR BRITAIN '87 featuring cutouts of the four party leaders.

With the important bit done, it was now just a matter of throwing in a few stories to go under the logo. But where were they? From the editorial floor Sutton could be seen in his cubicle waving wildly at the progress chart on his wall, which would invariably be blank except for Altounyan offerings such as a story on the British people looking after monkeys rescued from Gibraltar or the slaughter of kangaroos in Australia. Meanwhile in London reporters attempting to communicate with Mission Control would be fobbed off with vagaries and the occasional incomprehensible newslist via the fax machine. They continued to load what stories they could into the void of the Norsk Data.

The paper launched into the election campaign with the story of Harvey Proctor, the Tory MP for Billericay, who was involved in a homosexual 'spanking' scandal with 'rent boy' prostitutes. Though the story had rumbled for weeks, *NoS* focused on it to indulge a new editorial interest in sexual perversion. Spanking was outrageous and deviant behaviour riddled with class connotations, Proctor was an extreme right-wing Tory and gay, and the story involved prostitution. Sutton was beside himself. This was the story that had everything. The news team was deployed to 'get Proctor', backed up by Lew Chester, deputed to write a feature on the history of the English spanking classes. Pattullo's deputy in the features department, Alison MacDonald, who complained that she had earned a reputation as an 'old tart' because she constantly went on about getting more sex in the paper, promised to follow up with another 'rent boy' scandal. This featured a well-known opposition politician and former Minister of State, though not one *NoS* particularly liked. Egged on by Sutton, she produced a trendy young gay man who resembled a 1930s Italian blackshirt and claimed to have intimate knowledge of the story. Macdonald, whose forte was not hard news, lost enthusiasm on hearing of the paper's shaky libel-defence arrangements.

Sutton was enormously tickled by the way spanking combined sex with class war and Tory-bashing, and did not care about the minefield in which it placed the paper. His opportunity came when Proctor resigned his Billericay candidacy at lunchtime on Saturday, 16 May, as edition four was closing up. The story, which had been widely expected, was on the wires by early afternoon and by the end of the day had been flogged to death by the television news bulletins, complete with film coverage and interviews with distraught Billericay Conservatives who had dim-wittedly supported Proctor. The vast majority of Sunday editors decided the story was over as a lead, and put it on page 2.

But Sutton had been waiting for this moment, and nothing was going to stop him. Ignoring fundamental news judgements, and niceties such as the fact that Proctor was to appear in court in four days' time, he led the paper with SPANKER PROCTOR RESIGNS. The office was deluged with letters and phone calls accusing the paper of picking on Proctor because he was gay, not just right-wing. The disgust was shared by the Founders and many of the staff, and the outrage was given an extra fillip by the BBH bog-roll advert, which had used SEX MAD COLONEL SPANKED MY PRIVATES! as one of the headlines on the Daily Smut. Sutton, in their eyes, had done exactly what *NoS* advertised it would not do. He didn't care. For him SPANKER was the equivalent of GOTCHA! There was no other headline for the paper to run.

The SPANKER front page was apparently a great sales plus. The rapid decline in the circulation graph was momentarily flattened out, only to be sent hurtling downwards again to just above the 200,000 mark the following week by TORY SALE OF THE CENTURY – LOOK WHAT THEY'VE DONE TO OUR HOMES and the paper's first WORLD EXCLUSIVE exposing THE MERCHANTS OF DEATH. The colour section did not help by devoting its front page to a lifesize picture of a rat crawling out of a dustbin. The inside pages were covered with gigantic vermin, house flies, flea eggs, oriental cockroaches and other household horrors, and the article told readers that their beds were full of microscopic insects. On seeing this, Oyston, already horrified at how the paper kept printing material which he regarded as amounting to sales suicide, became animated. 'They've got a death wish, a death wish!' he cried, waving the offending pages about as he stomped the echoing corridors of his castle.

Sutton took a perverse glee in the SPANKER row. He made no secret of his conviction that he was right, and that the Grumbly Brigade was wrong. He had managed to have his day after all. But from that moment on he was doomed. All eyes, once again, turned to the Founders. Surely this was the last straw? Would they act?

They would – but in their own peculiar way, assisted by Oyston, who, now he had put in more money, was introducing his own people to look after it. Starting with what the company had always lacked – an effective chief executive.

9 · Making it less sad

'Personally liable'

Roy Barber's appearance as *News on Sunday*'s interim chief executive added more people to the 'gobsmacked' total. He was introduced to the Board meeting by Michael Connolly, who smiled thinly as he asked the members if they were ready to receive him. Getting nods of assent, Connolly opened the door gingerly, and stepped back smartly. Barber bustled in like a little tank and went straight to the head of the table, opposite Horsley. He sat down and let his eyes travel clockwise round the table, making brief contact with all the others in the room. He adjusted his shirt sleeves. 'My name is Roy Barber and I am now the interim chief executive of this company . . .' he started in a broad Yorkshire accent. The smack of firm management had arrived.

Barber was a blunt man. He set out the position straight. From 9am the following morning there would be no payment for any goods or services whatsoever without his written authority. Did he make that clear? The Board members, open-mouthed at this sudden authoritarianism, nodded meekly. Right, said Barber. And when he said all spending, he meant every single item, right down to a paper clip. Was that also clear? There were dumbfounded nods and individuals exchanged uneasy smiles. Right, said Barber, there was one more thing. The Board members, and everyone else in the company, must understand that if they made any payment, no matter how small, they would be personally liable for the expenditure if it had been made without his authority. Was that absolutely clear as well? The Board members, now becoming haunted by 'personally liable', nodded glumly. 'Good,' said Barber. He briskly gathered up his papers and walked out.

Barber, of course, was an instant hate figure in the office. The staff

nicknamed him 'Klaus Barber – the Butcher of Manchester' after the
Nazi war criminal who was in court at the time. Many were confused
and thought he was one of Oyston's employees, but in fact he had
been hired in. Barber was a fireman, whose job was to go into
companies which had hit the rocks, prepare a short-term business
plan and get out. He had been doing it for thirty years, twenty-five
of them for a major company, before he took early retirement and
went freelance to give himself more time to enjoy his life in Cheshire.
His main client was Lonrho, and his last job had been in Kinshasa,
Zaïre, sorting out an African import-export company that had run
through $50 million in eighteen months.

Oyston, although he stressed to the end that he did not want to
control or chair the paper, was by now effectively running it with
Horsley's approval. The T and G, which was funding the exercise
jointly with him, was leaving the business decisions to him. Barber's
arrival was the first tangible sign of the strategy they were pursuing
in concert. Both had initially stepped in with the subordinated loan
money to keep the paper going through the election period. Behind
the scenes, agreement had been reached to increase the amount
from the original £250,000 which had prevented the paper from
closing on the spot. Another £600,000 had been committed on
paper, making a total of £850,000 in all. So even with its weekly loss
of £160,000, the paper could now relax slightly from its previous
week-by-week existence. The additional injection of funds had pulled
it back from the brink and given a virtual cast-iron guarantee that it
would continue to publish past the election. Duty could now be
done to the Labour Party.

But Barber's arrival was part of a bigger plan. One option facing
Oyston and the T and G was to retire after the election, writing off
the money they had pumped in. The subordinated loan money
enabled the company to keep trading by maintaining the balance
between assets and liabilities, meeting the weekly losses. But once it
had run out the paper would revert to its original position in week
three, and would have to close on the spot. The cost for both partners
would have been substantial, but for the T and G especially, it would
have been cheap at the price.

Oyston was interested in the other option – effectively to buy the
paper by injecting still more money. Barber's job was to see what it
would cost to save the company. Oyston had given him three weeks

to draw up a revised business plan, referred to as the 'RBP'. His instructions were to cut the weekly loss to something sustainable in the short-term while a long-term rescue plan was put together. The target was to get down from the present loss of £130,000 to £40,000.

There was no guarantee that the rescue would be possible. But on the timetable Barber was due to report back just after the election, and Oyston and the T and G would then be able to make an informed decision, with all the financial facts and figures available, about carrying on. Until the election the T and G was over a barrel. The Labour Party was looking to it to prevent the disaster of having *NoS* fold during the campaign, so Oyston, who had taken on his share of the responsibility voluntarily, now had the whip hand. Having committed so much extra money, the union was now in an agonizing position. Although common sense may have told the T and G not to throw good money after bad, the election announcement had given it no choice, and pulled it deeper into the mire. If the paper did close, the union was going to have to explain to furious members how it had now effectively written off nearly £1 million of their money – the original investment of £550,000 plus the extra £400,000 or so committed in subordinated loans.

Oyston too had committed a lot of his own money. But for him there were two bonuses if the paper was kept going – even at a loss. First, for a very small outlay, he would become in practice the owner of a national newspaper, with all the status and media exposure that came with the position. Instead of just being a well-known local figure in Lancashire, he would move out of his small pool on to the national scene. Second, *NoS* was a challenge to him as an entrepreneur. He believed that, with his skill at making money, especially when it was contrasted to the ineptness of the previous management, he could turn it round, as he had the commercial radio stations he had bought. But he wasn't prepared to act on his own, and he needed the T and G to stay in. The union, by matching him pound for pound, doubled the amount of working capital, and at the same time its involvement gave him a core readership of its 1.3 million members. It was already clear that the general Grumbly Brigade as an audience could never be satisfied, and Oyston knew the paper would have to move to a different base support.

From the T and G's point of view, if Oyston made a financial success of the paper the union would not only get its money back, but might even make a large profit at the end of the day by joining in this new Thatcherite approach to the enterprise. It was simply a matter of how deep it was prepared to go in – and a lot of that depended on Barber's figures.

Barber was too shrewd and experienced to make up his mind instantly about *NoS*. He had never worked on a newspaper before, and was highly intrigued by the company, which seemed to be running counter to all his previous experience. But he knew his first job – to stop the financial blood flowing. The rest would be revealed as he went along. The message about 'personal liability' was delivered in writing to all staff the next morning. It instantly froze all action, as it was designed to do. Nobody knew how seriously to take such an ultimatum after months of experience that all ultimatums were movable. But the 'personally liable' was beginning to seep in, so to save face people decided to go through the motions, but treat it all as a bit of a joke. The requests to spend started going in.

Barber acted as he always did in these circumstances. As each person asked for money, whether they wanted to spend £5 or £5,000, he appeared to be listening carefully to the justification. People noticed that he kept a relentless gaze on them and asked very few questions. Many assumed he was some sort of genius, with a prodigious capacity for absorbing information. He seemed to know all about the paper and how it worked. His decisions were not rushed, but they were almost immediate and very simple – either yes or no. There was no arguing. The staff were puzzled and rather overawed. How did he manage to know what to do?

Barber explained afterwards how he worked. The people who thought he had been listening carefully had been wrong – he hadn't tried to take in a word. He could not possibly absorb the complexities of the business to decide whether an item of expenditure was justified or not. Like Horsley, he knew nothing about newspapers. But neither did he need to. Instead of listening to the detail, he used the conversation to assess the person and judge their competence as they talked. Ideally, of course, he would say no to everyone, as his brief was to cut expenditure to the bone, but at the same time the newspaper had to be kept going. There were hundreds of financial decisions to be made every day from the paper clips he had mentioned to that week's print. (The printers were by now demanding payment upfront.) When they had finished speaking, if Barber thought they knew what they were doing he said yes. Otherwise the answer was no.

Barber had commandeered the matching cubicle next to Sutton's – originally intended for Pilger – where he could relax with mugs of coffee and look out across Manchester as he pondered his decisions. The staff's knowledge of events had increased enormously since this room had been used more and more for private meetings. People had discovered that if they borrowed a glass from Jean the tea-lady and placed it against the partition they would hear every word clearly.

Until *NoS* Barber had thought he had seen everything. But he found the company quite extraordinary. Normally when he went in there was a dead-head staff, completely lazy or de-motivated, or both. The place was usually on its last legs. Yet here was a group of dedicated people who worked astonishingly hard, and were obviously passionately committed to their jobs. But, even at a cursory glance, the company was a complete shambles. The more he found out, the odder it became. But meanwhile he had his job to do.

First the staff. It was obvious the wage bill was impossibly high. The RBP would have to contain huge redundancies. He got out the list and examined the different departments, looking for cuts outside the core operation of producing the paper. One department – marketing – stood out like a sore thumb. Walsh's operation was still intact, as he had successfully argued that because the paper had bombed it was needed more than ever. As soon as Oyston came on the scene, Walsh went to see him in his suite in the Ritz with a nine-page 'rescue strategy'. Deeply paranoid after the Wintour report which had recommended canning him, Walsh was now operating above and below the line, and bursting with ideas. Oyston, no stranger to the art of marketing himself, had allowed him to go ahead with some of the plans. In the short term, as part of the election strategy, it had been decided that the issue of 7 June – the last before polling – would be pushed by aggressive radio and TV ads in selected areas with a high concentration of potential Labour voters.

Ben Lowe, still working to get the paper into the hands of the working-class readers, had been evolving various plans to distribute some of the mountains of unsold returned copies free to selected households in marginal constituencies. But Walsh had conceived an even grander strategy for the FA Cup Final between Coventry and Tottenham Hotspur. It was another Walsh brainwave. A total of just over 4,008,900 copies of the first three editions had been printed, of which 2,801,300 had remained unsold and were cluttering up warehouses around the country. The Walsh plan involved taking 50,000 of them to Wembley, where teams of *News on Sunday* Girls would thrust them into fans' hands as they entered the ground. Under the 'strategy', the fans would be so convinced by how wonderful the paper was that, having spent the match reading it rather than watching the game, they would rush out the following day to buy *NoS* and read its match report.

Walsh put Rick 'Rambo' Nelmes in charge of the project. But when Nelmes lit up a fag, furrowed his brow and started thinking about it, he realized it was a non-starter. Apart from its essential absurdity, the logistics of taking tons of old newsprint to the ground were forbidding, and the cost would be horrific. 'Rambo' secured the support of his marketing-department colleagues and mounted a revolt. When the smoke cleared, Walsh knew that he would have to back down. As an alternative, *NoS* paid £28,500 for a banner at the edge of the pitch near the halfway line. Up in Manchester Horsley, detailed by the Board to fob off increasingly hard-edged questions from the staff about the paper's future, used the Wembley banner as evidence of reviving fortunes. The banner, he said, would have been seen by many millions of people on television. The fact that much of the television audience would be outside Britain, which is the reason that the sites command high prices from multinational products, seemed not to have dawned upon either him, Rambo or Walsh.

The following week it was Ben Lowe's turn to go out in a blaze of glory. He popped up with the idea, presented in a convolutedly argued 'paper', of posting 300,000 copies of the colour section – prepared three weeks in advance – to households in selected Labour target marginals. He was steaming ahead with the scheme until stopped in his tracks by Barber.

Under Barber's plan there was going to be practically no money available for marketing. The RBP he was being asked to produce only had the aim of cutting costs, and when Walsh went to see him with the plans for an 'integrated campaign' he said no. By now, like Wintour, he had formed a low opinion of Walsh, and this had been reinforced by other people on the paper who indulged in more than the usual axe-grinding. Walsh's abrasive style and constant inter-ference in other departments had given them plenty of scores to settle. And Barber also felt that while the department was in operation it was committing further money to plans for the future, which he could not allow.

He decided the only answer was the Draconian one of scrapping the entire department. To make sure no more mad schemes were embarked on, they would be instructed to stay at home on full pay, pending dismissal. This would save not just the cost of the phones, but the much greater costs that might be incurred by what was said into them. In real terms, the members of the department were all being fired. Barber rang Oyston to tell him, and the two men spoke for two hours, during which time Oyston opposed the decision, saying that he found Walsh bright and hard-working and thought he had a lot of potential. But Barber was insistent, and, bowing to his chief executive, Oyston reluctantly agreed.

Barber promptly informed the marketing people that under no account must they come to work. They were barred from both buildings. The accounts department, now bustling with yet more Men in Suits, was instructed to prepare the pay-off cheques with the members' notice money – in most cases three months. Barber did not mean to pay the cheques out at that point. But some of the department were too quick for him, and before he knew what had happened, some of the Manchester cheques had been whisked off the desk, specialled through the bank, and their recipients had dis-appeared. Walsh, Hoyland and the London end were left stranded, aghast and furious. Where was their money? Walsh jumped the fence from management to barricades. Before then he had snapped angrily that as a manager he hadn't got time for union meetings. Now amazed members of the SOGAT chapel were joined by a crazed militant who proposed picketing the London office.

The rest of the company quivered with shock. Nobody had ever been sacked from *NoS*, except Matthew Nugent, the Father of the NUJ Chapel, who had been dismissed after another punch-up. (This time the incident had been more ugly. The victim was an innocent sub-editor from the Wigan printworks whom Nugent knocked over in the office, breaking his glasses. He lost any sympathy from the rest of the staff, and was dismissed.) But Barber's action was different. Nobody knew what to do. It had happened so fast that there had not been time for a meeting. As they saw it, nobody seemed to have been consulted. Furthermore, the staff dazedly asked each other, how could Barber do this without appearing to give the department an opportunity to justify its existence? The SOGAT and NUJ Chapels struggled to react. But it was obvious that there was only one answer – Barber must be stopped at Board level.

Barber sacked the marketing department on Monday 1 June, six days after his 'personally liable' speech. The next day, when the Board assembled, he was ready to give his first report on how far he had got in his investigations into the paper.

He took up his usual position at the end of the table opposite Horsley and picked up his notes. 'In all my experience I have never come across such a highly confused and out of control company,' he said. 'It would be right to say I am staggered and absolutely speechless. I am still trying to find out what goes on.' He had been assessing the various people he had met and found that some seemed to have only one objective – producing one or two more issues. He added: 'A lot of other people I can't really understand seem to think that there is some sort of endless supply of funds somewhere.' Barber informed them that he was now putting together his RBP by plotting a 'critical path analysis' of editorial flow. He planned to get rid of peripheral departments which were not contributing as soon as he could.

The Founder-Directors and Worker-Directors who made up half the Board stiffened. There was more to come! In various discussions beforehand they had decided that Barber must be brought to heel, and prevented from making such arbitrary decisions without the consent of the Board. Now the attackers moved in. Why had Barber sacked the marketing department? He replied that in his opinion it was making no effective contribution and was a handicap in the production of the paper. As interim chief executive, he had the authority to close it, and he had consulted the Chair, Horsley, who now confirmed he had approved the decision.

The attack switched. Walsh's lieutenant John Hoyland, who had been allowed in though he was not strictly entitled to be at the meeting, launched an emotional plea for the marketing department. He had already handed out a memo asking the Board 'in the name of common decency' to give the rest of them their cheques. Now he complained that the dismissals by Barber had been 'bizarre and brutal and arbitrary management'. The relationship with the regional groups had been severed. He went even further – the relationship with 'Neil Kinnock, etc.' had been severed. Hoyland was quivering with indignation. The paper had been a very poor-quality product launched to a massively hostile retail trade and the marketing department was being made a scapegoat. It was a shoddy move, and had not been adequately explained.

Hayling's ultimate sympathies were with Hoyland. He himself did not have a job any more, apart from being a Director. With editorial matters firmly in the hands of Sutton, and Oyston in charge of the financial reins, the only part of the paper still being run by anybody from the original group was the marketing department. And Hayling was also convinced, to some extent justifiably, that many of the readers had been produced by Walsh's below-the-line activities. Unaware of how the paper was already changing, Hayling thought that if the marketing department disappeared the paper would lose its direct contact with the committed, and never regain it in the future. He put his argument to the Board in an urgent, concerned voice. He was deeply worried about the political consequences, particularly with the Leader of the Opposition. The marketing department were personally acquainted with large numbers of radical investors. It was a big mistake for the future.

Harry Timpson, the T and G representative, was now in an extremely difficult position. Although the union was in concert with Oyston financially, the way the decision had been made was contrary to accepted trade-union principles. He came down on the side of the protesters and chipped in: 'I request, ask, insist or whatever that the unions must be consulted.'

The real fight came from the Founders, their authority now squarely challenged for the first time. Joan Bohanna, on familiar ground from her experience as a shop steward at Glaxo, took Timpson's demand further. The marketing department should be reinstated until the unions were consulted.

Barber visibly bristled. Speaking directly to Horsley, he said firmly that if his authority was questioned he would resign. In fact, if they really wanted to know, one of the reasons he had acted in this way was because he had not been confident he would get the decision through the Board if it had to be consulted.

There was uproar as the various factions stated their position.

Horsley, who had previously formed a bridge between the camps, had briskened up now that at last he had the sort of chief executive he had been looking for – the 'adjutant' he had previously demanded. The arrival of Oyston and his men had taken the company back to a way of management he understood. Although Northern Foods carried out it Equal Opportunities commitments, it was run first and foremost as a business, and Horsley began now to demonstrate that he too knew about firm management. After all, he had warned them all about the Death Valley Curve and they had taken no notice. Now he was getting more and more exasperated. He had fully accepted the point that Oyston kept making – the company had had its chance, and the party was over. It was no longer a question of saving jobs in the old company – all the jobs had already gone with its effective failure. Now the position had to be looked at through the other end of the telescope. If Oyston and the T and G rescued the company, they would actually be creating jobs, not losing them. Horsley was getting very upset at the Founders' refusal to face up to what he regarded as the reality of the position.

He intervened in a weary voice, as if speaking to small children, saying that if drastic steps were not taken the company would fail. Anthony Everett from Guinness Mahon supported him, emphasizing as well that the consensus party was over. Looking carefully round the table, he said he suspected some people had been in an 'Alice in Wonderland situation'. The sacking of the marketing department might be 'regrettable', but questioning Barber's authority was 'intolerable'. Beber, the accountant from Fisher's, weighed in with more support of the new line.

Hayling tried a last stand. He didn't think the marketing department was damaging the company. Rather some of their functions were going to be needed. Of course the question of job losses was 'rearing its ugly head'. He suggested a last desperate compromise as the uproar began to mount. The marketing department could all be put on notice!

A voice from the corner cut across the hubbub. It expressed softly but firmly how very sad and depressed its owner was to hear these conflicts round the table. Things had clearly got off wrongly, and they must sort out how they were to proceed in the future. Owen Oyston impressed the urgency of the situation. The paper had been within hours of closing the previous week, and it was only after three days' chasing round that he had managed to track down a mystery backer who had agreed after considerable pressure to put in 'substantial sums'. (Oyston was referring to his chase to find Ron Todd of the T and G, an operation complicated as usual by *NoS* input.) 'We have to talk about reality,' he told the Board.

Peter Smith, the lawyer, was then brought on to lay down the realities for all directors. He reminded them of the provisions of the Insolvency Act 1986, and in particular Section 214, relating to wrongful trading. He stressed the 'personal liability' for debt that could arise. The now familiar words caused a shudder round the room. Smith was quite clear. If Barber resigned, and the company therefore had no prospect of rescue, it might have to cease trading on the spot. Everybody looked at each other uneasily, and then at Barber. He sat impassively, looking straight ahead, his arms folded.

It was deadlock. Unless it was resolved, the paper would still close even though it had enough money to keep going, and the terrible prospect of its closure changing the course of the election would reappear. By this stage Labour had survived an early onslaught on the issue of the 'Loony Left', but the Tories were obviously alert to *NoS*. The paper had been featured in Tory press advertisements which mentioned Southwark's £300,000 investment, and asked how many of the council's dustmen actually read it and approved of their pension money being put into it. There had been another nasty moment when a Conservative candidate put out leaflets claiming the paper had gone bankrupt. Peter Smith had used a fine display of legal bluster to have the leaflets withdrawn by threatening a High Court injunction, but it had been a close shave, as the statement was basically true. With the Loony Left issue running out of steam, Labour, recovering from a dip in support over its muddled defence policy, was fighting back with an attack on Mrs Thatcher's personal leadership style. Kinnock was surging ahead in the personality ratings and was emphasizing that it was he, and not the Loony Left, which was in charge of the Labour Party. If the Tories could move the spotlight back to the Loony Left then the T and G, which supported Kinnock, could be castigated to prove that Labour was a bunch of incompetents who could not even run a newspaper.

Harry Timpson, a veteran of crisis meetings with management, knew a problem which needed negotiation when he saw one. And although the rules of the boardroom did not allow for this sort of dilemma, it could be solved if it was treated like a union negotiation. At his suggestion, the Board took a break and he retired with the Founders, as he had before, to find a formula. The consequences for himself, Ron Todd and the Labour Party if the paper closed then did not bear thinking about.

Forty minutes later Timpson came back with the Founder-Directors and a resolution for the Board to vote on. Horsley was deeply shocked. Just like Taylor in his twenty years at the *Guardian*, in thirty years the Board at Northern Foods had never had a vote. It was unheard of. But although he expressed his disgust, he allowed the resolution to go forward. It was a face-saving formula which gave Barber support 'to take all necessary actions in view of the grave financial situation of the company'. In return the Board 'welcomes the forthcoming discussions with the National Officials of the respective Unions'. The resolution was only opposed by one person – the worker-director from the Black Hand Gang, Ivor Hutchinson, who took back his vote against at the next meeting.

Receivership

Oyston's frame of mind was not improved by witnessing these scenes. All the planning he was doing would be useless unless the Founders were prepared to give up the Golden Share. He had talked to them when the question of the subordinated loans first came up, and they had not been prepared to give it up at that stage. But they were prepared to throw Sutton to the wolves. Despite faltering efforts to find a new readership base, at this point the remnants of the Grumbly Brigade were the only readers who could be counted on, and *NoS* was more or less back to where it had started with Ben Lowe. It obviously needed a new editor to match its present upmarket readership, and Sutton had burned his boats with the Founders through SPANKER PROCTOR. So they agreed to suspend their veto over the firing of the editor for three weeks – the same length of time as it would take Barber to prepare his business plan. Sutton had lost the protection which had saved him in the showdown over Pilger.

Now Oyston brought in his second outsider – David Jones. Jones, known as 'Big Dave', was a large, shambling man who walked into the office announcing that he had been made editorial director and was to 'work with the editor'. When journalists asked what the new proprietorial instructions were, he repeated what Michael Connolly, Oyston's lawyer, had already said: 'To make the paper less sad.' Oyston had agreed with pundit Christopher Ward – the 'smile count' needed increasing.

Jones was an odd choice to turn a paper round. He was an experienced independent television producer who had served his time on the Manchester-based *Granada Reports* local news programme. But his newspaper experience was limited to the beginning of his career some twenty years earlier. When he agreed to work for Oyston he was up to his watery eyeballs in a Central Television documentary about the police, and there was great horror at the paper when it was discovered he was not even a current member of the National Union of Journalists.

Jones had met Oyston in the past when he was filming, and the two men had become friends. Oyston had sounded him out about taking the paper 'upmarket', away from the council-estate dwellers, not long after it had launched. He had met Horsley for lunch and agreed to take on the job, but had been unable to get out of a hectic schedule involving the film he was making. He also had the problem of commuting from the Home Counties.

Jones and Sutton produced one paper together, edition six, published on 31 May, and the last but one before the election. There was little sign of Jones's work in it. The front page was pure Sutton. The mindless football chant of HERE WE GO!, the pickets' battle-cry in the miners' strike, was printed in huge type alongside a cut-out picture of Neil and Glenys Kinnock waving triumphantly.

'Neil Kinnock is poised to march into No. 10 as Prime Minister', the 'story' started, eleven days before Labour lost the election by 102 seats. It explained that an 'exclusive computer analysis' of 144 marginals showed Labour had cut the Tory lead to 5 per cent. This heady and wholly erroneous speculation, presented as fact, was based on work by a group of mystery academics whose identity was never publicly revealed. Sutton explained to sceptical reporters that the academics' work had been ignored because the research was 'not user-friendly enough' for the other papers to understand. The story achieved the final insult of being totally ignored in Monday's round-up of the weekend's opinion polls.

The uproar among the reporters at this new inanity was compounded by the story appearing under the byline of Kerry Marcus, the radio journalist who had been hired to set up the Manchester office and recently been promoted to Sutton's personal assistant. A protesting memo from the Manchester reporters – now rapidly wilting, but still enthusiastic enough to want their names on the front page – slammed on to Sutton's desk.

But the next week it was all over, thanks to Gipsy Rose Lee, the clairvoyant on Blackpool promenade. By this point the *NoS* election coverage had virtually collapsed, and Sutton's latest wheeze had been to get Gipsy Rose to predict the outcome. It was another repeat of a *Wapping Post* stunt, where an astrologer had predicted *The Times* would fold by June 1988. Sutton was standing in the newsroom briefing one of the reporters to get the 'story' when a hand descended on his shoulder and he was led away to his office. A long and detailed document, obviously prepared in advance, was brought in within half an hour and plonked in front of him. Examining the clauses suspiciously, he discovered he was being asked to sign away his car. 'What's this?' he demanded. 'It's my car, I own it.' The Men in Suits were baffled. An editor without a company car, when there were thirty-two on the books and he was obviously entitled to one as a perk? There must be some mistake. No, said Sutton, it was his motor. And furthermore the car in question was a 1967 F-registered Volvo, with a street value of about £500. He explained it was a collector's car in Tooting. The Men in Suits took the point and the clause was deleted.

Sutton signed the document, received a cheque for £30,000 for his nine months notice, plus another £1,600 back pay, picked up his few belongings and started to make his way out. As he walked across the office, lugging the Mersey tugboat picture Bohanna had given him, Brian Whitaker called out: 'You might as well take the Charter as well.' Sutton smiled wryly.

The next day he appeared in the London office to say goodbye, and the reporters who had not pinned their colours too firmly to the Pilger-Hayling mast bought him champagne. He regaled them with stories about Oyston, but it was a decidedly flat occasion. Sutton was obviously exhausted, and the London reporters decided he had finally been hit by his own creation and was now totally 'gobsmacked'. He went back to Tooting and slept solidly for five days.

Up in Manchester Jones threw Sutton's pencils and tracing paper in the bin and got on with the job of re-designing the paper for the more upmarket Grumbly Brigade. Jones simply informed the subs that he wanted the paper to look like the *Daily Mail*, which they had worked on for years and with which they were totally familiar. By now the production system had settled down, and chief sub John Whitaker was able to switch the design in a day.

Jones brought out the first *Daily Mail*-style *NoS* on 7 June, the last edition before the election, with a front-page editorial urging readers to vote Labour. The hectoring headline DON'T FALL FOR THE TORIES' CON-TRICK was run over a Steadman cartoon showing Britain splitting across the North–South divide. Inside things had not changed much, but the completely different design, with classic Century Schoolbook serif type, did, as Whitaker had effortlessly organized, look like the *Mail*. The opinion in the office was virtually unanimous. It looked much better, even if it was still dull.

The colour supplement, entitled 'Land of Hope and Glory', was a huge V-sign at the Tories. The dramatic pictures, in black and white, were angry. The front cover showed two policemen expertly throttling a teenage boy. Inside there was a panorama of inner-city destruction. The images were broken glass, scattered rubble, burning buildings, scarred faces. A phalanx of riot police chased a woman carrying a baby. The centre-page spread, in colour, was from the Commonwealth Conference, and showed Thatcher, looking every inch the part, sitting in the middle of a ceremonial line-up of be-medalled heads of state. The Queen was advancing grim-faced across the carpet to get her seat back. But the real thrust of the feature was against Thatcher herself. The pages were led and the pictures captioned by ironic Thatcher quotes.

The Labour Party was so impressed that the publicity department promptly got in touch with *NoS* and used the series of images as the basis for an entire party political broadcast. At last *NoS* was doing something for Labour. And, with the help of the television adver-tising, the seemingly inexorable decline in the circulation, which had now slumped to 200,000, was halted. The paper put on 30,000 copies, giving, as Oyston had intended, a pointer to what might be achieved in the future.

With Jones acting as editor, Oyston now brought in another 'editorial director' in the form of Julian Allitt, former head of journalism studies at Lancashire Polytechnic, Preston. Allitt was a controversial teacher who egged his students on to produce junior versions of the *Sun*, complete with cheesecake pictures of women students. 'Polygirl Julia Adamson puts on a bold front in the student fashion show . . .' was one example of the sort of story he taught them to aim at. Allitt was an obvious candidate for editor as one of the few journalists Oyston knew, but had disbarred himself by standing in the election as SDP candidate for Blackpool, where he was to come last on the night. The T and G could not, of course, accept him, so it was emphasized that he was being employed separately as an outside consultant.

Oyston now started weighing in with wild plans for editorial content and marketing. The department heads were summoned to a 'brain-storming session' at his castle, where they were each encouraged in turn to throw out ideas for the paper. Oyston lost his temper with Karen Needham when she forgot to modify her language for the occasion. 'I will not have that sort of language in my house,' he told her. The 'evening' ended with Henry Stewart finally being the last to be released at 5am, after sitting for two hours in the baronial hall watching Oyston work his way through a huge pile of bills totalling over £80,000, deciding which would or would not be paid. There was nothing unusual about this for Oyston, who describes his workaholic addiction as 'a disease', and who only needs three or four hours sleep a night. But it was not so much Stewart's style, and he staggered distinctly gobsmacked into the dawn.

Down in London, the staff were waking up to the fact that, whatever happened, the office was going to be sold and there were going to be drastic staff cuts. They were enraged that decisions like this could be made without anybody even visiting, and the more pea-brained among them believed that if somebody came down they would change their minds. Eventually Jones grumpily agreed to make the journey. He shambled in and attempted to ingratiate himself with various Right-On sensibilities by giving a silly pep-talk. He said a rumour had gone round that he was a beer-swilling male chauvinist pig, but that this was mistaken. He was a 'beer-swilling feminist'. The joke produced grudging and nervous laughter, and then he told journalists that he would see them for five minutes each privately. They were forced to queue up outside picture editor Colin Jacobson's cubicle, which he had taken over. Jones already knew that under the plan being put together by Barber most of them would have to go, and the names had already been selected, so the exercise was pointless.

The humiliating process was rounded off by the fact that Jones had arrived late and therefore had to rush the process and 'interview' Zoe Picton-Howell, the last in line, in a taxi on the way to Euston to rush back north on proprietor's orders. It was a filthy job, which Jones hated doing, but he was ably assisted by Hayling who, settling some old scores in the process, had provided him with a 'hit-list', outlining who he thought should stay and who could be got rid of. When this list was found later and circulated among the staff, it finished Hayling off. By now he not only had no job, but he had lost practically all support, even from people who had formerly been his friends. There was universal disgust not just that he had constructed such a list, which contained very personal comments, but that it was in parts hopelessly inaccurate. Some people's names had not been spelt correctly, and in some cases Hayling was obviously ignorant of their previous background and the work they had done on the paper.

Two days before election day, 11 June, Barber reported back at the Tuesday Board meeting, which had now become a regular event, that he was making progress with his RBP. He had prepared RBP 2, which cut the losses down to £70,000 a week, and was now progressing to RBP 3, which he hoped would get nearer the target of £40,000. By now the unions had called in their national officers and had expected consultation meetings about the staff cuts, but they had been postponed. Now Barber said everything was being postponed again until Friday 12 June – the day after the election – when he would meet them. He promised that no further action would be taken until then. Meanwhile a resolution was passed which effectively cut out the fringe elements, the worker-directors and the Founders, by establishing a sub-committee of Horsley, Barber, Oyston, Everett and Timpson to plan the reconstruction of the company and the Board, and negotiate with the unions over job losses, and the Founders over their rights.

Although Oyston was present at this meeting, sitting back distanced from the table as usual, he said little except to stress that time was short, and to repeat that one of the problems in the past had been the convoluted decision-making structure in the company. Then, just as the meeting was finishing, he suddenly seemed to lose the patient attitude which had characterized his appearances up to then.

He rounded on the Founder-directors. 'Are the Founders prepared to give up the Golden Share?' he asked sharply. A feeling of shock at this direct question ran round the room, and the answer came back from the Founder-directors that they were not. Horsley commented that they were being 'very childish'. Oyston, apparently very angry, walked out.

On the day after the election, Oyston pounced. He had done his bit for Labour and even organized the sending of a huge bunch of red roses to Neil Kinnock on the night, with an inscription reading: 'Congratulations on the best fight-back since El Alamein'. There was a flurry when the 'propmust' (proprietor says you must) phoned in from the castle to Manchester had passed down to the London office on the mistaken assumption that Kinnock would be at Labour Party headquarters in Walworth Road for the result, rather than his Welsh constituency of Islwyn. The rose instruction was finally dumped on the hapless Welsh circulation rep (based in Birmingham) to sort out.

By now Oyston had lined everything up and a meeting had been arranged on Friday evening at which the Founders expected to meet him to negotiate, as they saw it, the handing over of the Golden Share. He did not come. And now 'walk away' began to replace 'personally liable' in people's minds. Throughout the negotiations with the Founders and the staff which followed, Oyston's tactic was his own absence, while he used appearances on television to make his case to the world, brushing aside interviewers' questions as mere interruptions to his prepared speech. On the ground, he left negotiations in the hands of his Men in Suits – principally Connolly. In a flight of fancy, Alison Macdonald likened him to Mr Pilkington in George Orwell's *Animal Farm*.

Oyston consistently took the stance that he was prepared to 'walk away' if his terms were not acceded to. If that happened, the Receiver would be called in on the spot, since Horsley would put the company into voluntary receivership in the hope that it would pay 100p in the pound to the creditors, which would at least mean an honourable failure. The shareholders would, of course, get nothing. The T and G allowed Oyston a virtually free hand.

The question facing everybody was whether they believed him or not. Oyston obviously now wanted the paper. He was down £250,000, including his original £100,000 investment, and committed to more with the subordinated loans. And although he stressed he did not want to own or control the paper, he had clearly decided to take this once-in-a-lifetime opportunity to be a *de facto* national newspaper magnate. Like other newspaper barons, he expected to have to pay for the privilege, certainly compared to what he could do with the same money in a straight commercial deal. But he wanted the power and the audience, and the platform that would enable him to beat the drum for the north and his own particular brand of capitalist socialism. He was later clumsily to change the masthead to 'Your British Owned Paper' in a xenophobic dig at Murdoch, an Australian turned American, and Maxwell, a Czech turned Briton.

And above all, Oyston wanted the paper as cheaply as possible.

Oyston went back to where he had started with his original letter, when he had demanded total co-operation from everybody involved with the paper. A new thirteen-point letter was sent to 'the representatives of the workforce of News on Sunday', in which he demanded 'immediate and unanimous commitment' to his undisclosed cost-cutting plan. The consultations Barber had promised with the national officers of the unions were scrapped. In effect Oyston was asking everybody to agree to whatever cuts he had in mind, without telling anybody what they were. He cancelled the Friday meeting with the Founders on the grounds that he was working on the business plan, and instead he sent a telex via Conolly's firm of lawyers, Laytons and Ingham, Clegg and Crowther, insisting: 'The Founders Share will have to be transferred today . . . we require tonight a duly executed share transfer form.' The share was to be given to Anthony Everett of Guinness Mahon as a trustee.

Horsley came to talk to the Founders in Oyston's place, and became more and more infuriated as he tried to impress on them the seriousness of Oyston's threat. But the Founders were not impressed by the arguments. Throughout the history of *News on Sunday* they had consistently seen events as a series of conspiracies, plots and factions. Their own body had been rent by bitter and prolonged arguments and violent disagreements, which they made up and laughed about later. But those dealing with them often found themselves in a baffling sea of shifting alliances and convoluted factional viewpoints. As guardians of the purity of the project, theirs was not the nuts-and-bolts concern of getting the paper put together, never mind making it successful. They were the protectors of what was left of the concept of heroic failure, safeguarding the paper for the 'movement'.

The Founders, like everybody else, had to decide whether Oyston was bluffing or would really 'walk away', in which case Horsley and Everett would put the paper into receivership, and they would be set up as the cause. The attraction of receivership from Oyston's point of view was the clean break from the past. There would not even be an obligation to put the Charter in the articles of a new company, as he had promised to do in a reconstructed News on Sunday Publishing plc. He would be free of debts which might come crawling out of the woodwork, of the old Board, the unions, and all the other obligations – including them. But there were disadvantages as well. If the company went into receivership Oyston would have to buy it out as a going concern at a higher price than its break-up value. He would also risk predators coming on the scene and bidding against him to put the price up.

The Founders decided to call his bluff. In a telex sent back to Oyston at his castle, they complained they were being presented with a 'fait accompli', and that they might need time for legal advice. What had happened to the sub-committee set up by the Board, they asked? And, clutching at straws, they even asked what had happened about a meeting of the shareholders – which legally has to be arranged weeks in advance. They wanted more meetings.

Committing the sell-out of giving up the Golden Share presented each of the Founders with an enormous personal, political and psychological trauma. They knew that Oyston had little or no understanding of this, and that he blamed them for much of what had happened. His Men in Suits had disparagingly dubbed them 'the Crazies'. Oyston saw them as unable to face the reality of the situation, and desperately trying to hang on at any cost. He was not prepared to go along with their leisurely terms or to make any attempt to enable them to bow out with dignity. As he saw it, he was guaranteeing the politics of the paper by keeping the Charter. But he trusted them as little as they did him, and was not prepared to start any rescue plan while they still had the power to throw a spanner in the works. Now he decided to junk the whole attempt to get a settlement with them and pull out, which would mean the paper being put straight into receivership.

The midnight deadline came and went, and the Founders had not signed away the Golden Share. An extraordinary, but ultimately futile, poker game was played over the weekend. Marisa Casares-

Roach, acting as a go-between with the T and G, phoned up Timpson just before midnight on Saturday and begged him to act quickly to pull either Oyston or the Founders back from the brink. Timpson phoned Everett to check that the Receiver would come in first thing on Monday morning if nothing changed. Everett confirmed it. With some difficulty Timpson got hold of Oyston at 3am on Sunday morning and pleaded with him to move back. But Oyston had 'walked away' and showed complete indifference. He told Timpson he did not have time to discuss it – he was now busy with expansion plans for his local radio stations.

Casares-Roach had also phoned John Bohanna, the secretary to the Founders who now realized that Oyston had meant what he had said. There was no time to arrange a meeting, so in a series of frantic phone calls over the weekend, the Founders managed to get together a new offer which they and Casares-Roach thought would persuade Oyston to pull back. They put their offer in a telex after Everett and Horsley had been persuaded to stop the Receiver coming in at 9.30am on Monday. They told Oyston it was their duty under the terms of the articles of the company to discuss the business plan first, in order to guard against a takeover which would be contrary to the company's principles. They would hand over the Golden Share, but only after the necessary capital had been raised to put Barber's RBP into operation. And the handover would be subject to a condition – a formal written undertaking that the new Board would negotiate about their role in the new company.

Since this was something less than total surrender, Oyston tore it up. At 10.07am on Monday 15 June the letter that killed News on Sunday Publishing plc was electronically transmitted from Claughton Hall to Horsley at Bridgewater House in Manchester.

'Dear Nicholas,' Oyston wrote, 'I regret to have to tell you that I have no alternative but to resign from the Board of News on Sunday forthwith . . . The powers that the Founders have are a millstone in commercial terms.' As he and Horsley both knew, they rendered any financial rescue package 'futile'.

Oyston justified his decision to have no further dealings with them: 'The Founders have no job risk, no financial involvement, no fiduciary duties as a group on the Board, and no duty of care to employees. In short, they exercise total power without responsibility or accountability. Their own structure is such that they are a self-appointed and self-perpetuating oligarchy. Because I shared the aspirations of those associated with News on Sunday, together we provided a life-support machine for the newspaper while new sources of finance were sought, and my family have provided a fortune in anyone's terms towards this end. I do not regret spending the money but I am saddened that I have been prevented by the Founders from taking the paper as a commercial proposition to other investors – because no-one will invest in the enterprise with the controls and vetoes exercised by a force outside the Board.'

The Board meeting the following evening started on the dot for the first time. Horsley was brusque and businesslike. He read out Oyston's letter. The company now had no hope of rescue and would have to go directly into receivership. The Receiver had been alerted and was standing by, and it was just a question of the Board agreeing. Horsley stressed that the receivership was voluntary, and that it was hoped the company would be folding honourably. The rest of the Board had no choice but to agree. Just as the resolution was being passed, the unfortunate Founder-director Steve Riley from Ford Dagenham, used to meetings started at *NoS*-time, crashed into the room. He was told he might as well not have bothered to come.

Growfar

Receivership – the final failure – brought the submerged bitterness to the surface. As they went to the lift Horsley and John Bohanna, the secretary of the Founders, found themselves standing side by side. Bohanna, appalled by the way the Board had folded the company, looked at Horsley and said: 'Nick, you are a coward.'

Horsley stared back at him, reflecting the gulf between the two that would never be resolved. 'And you, John, are a fool,' he replied. 'And that makes us 30-all.'

The staff, who had been struggling to comprehend the baffling new turn of events, went off to drown their sorrows at the pub. The next day they drifted in to work and watched the Receiver, Mr Cyril Nield of Cork Gully, move in with yet more Men in Suits. But the pace soon speeded up. For the next ten days, as they tried to ape the Founders and fight against the inevitable, the staff were to find themselves in a peculiar nightmare of rapid-fire events in which Oyston seemed to win hands down at every turn.

Now that News on Sunday Publishing plc was officially dead and transferred into the hands of the Receiver, it could continue to trade but only on the same basis as before – it must not spend any money. The Receiver's job in turn was to sell it to the highest bidder, preferably as a going concern, with the money being used to pay off the creditors. And the Receiver was in the same position as the Board had been – the company's only real asset was its continuing publication.

Oyston's men, led by Connolly, now reappeared under the new name of Growfar, a £100 off-the-shelf company bought in Bootle that morning. Growfar now moved to purchase a licence from the Receiver to publish the paper on a week-by-week basis, meeting all the bills involved.

The receivership meant that the staff, like the other creditors, were plunged into the normal nightmare that accompanies these events. Their outstanding wages for three weeks (the company had never organized the weekly payments promised by Horsley), expenses and any other money due would now not be paid out until the liquidation of the company – which was expected to take between eighteen months and two years. And even then there was no guarantee they would be paid in full. The staff would get their notice period as part of the settlement, but for the moment they were broke, and the prospect of being paid notice money to leave now had vanished.

In theory at this moment the staff, unlike the Founders, really did have the whip hand. If they refused to produce the paper, the break in publication might well kill it off. Readership was shaky, and any disruption might cause the whole distribution chain to fold. Oyston had sweetened the newsagents by upping the percentage arranged by Liz Cooper, adding on a little extra to win back the 'goodwill' they had withdrawn. Peter Smith, the lawyer, had also demonstrated entrepreneurial flair by examining the small print and swiftly extricating *NoS* from the print contracts arranged by Hayling, which it had been feared would cost a fortune in loss-of-profit compensation.

Now he offered the workers a carrot. If they produced the next issue they would be paid their back wages for the month, and any expenses that were due. Some of the more dim-witted, who hadn't moved fast enough, were owed more than £1,000. Oyston also promised to pay contributions due to regular freelances, many of whom had been hassling unsuccessfully for payment for weeks, and were also owed large sums of money. The offer plunged the staff into chaos. By now many of them were completely disorientated, and matters had not been helped by a dearth of information from the top. Wild rumours ran round, and there were warnings that a 'headless chicken situation' would soon develop. Journalists seeking guidance from the editor, David Jones, would go into the cubicle to find only a massive dog-chewed pair of training shoes parked under the desk. But one thing they did grasp was that receivership had made them all redundant – a prospect not unwelcome to those with good employment prospects. And whether they had another job or not, they now insisted that Oyston honour their contracts with the now-defunct News on Sunday Publishing plc and pay them the one or three months salary they were owed in lieu of notice. Otherwise, they said, they would not work.

Now it was their turn to be treated to the Oyston brinkmanship. The lines between the Manchester office and Oyston, sitting in his suite on the twelfth floor of the London Hilton, crackled with bizarre conversations, threats and counter-threats. Oyston, in a long and emotional outburst, told the staff how he had not had a holiday for twenty-eight years, and berated them for not being able to see that he was creating jobs, not destroying them. Ron Todd of the T and G was dug out and rushed round to the Hilton, and the journalists asked Roy Hattersley to apply some leverage. But Oyston was adamant. He was still fuming from his tussle with the Founders, and threatened that unless everyone joined with him in helping the new venture, he would 'walk away'. At one point he decided to do just that, after being needled on the telephone in an open-line conversation with the union representatives. He wearily and angrily announced that he had had enough, that there was a TV crew waiting in the hotel, and that he was going out to announce that it was all over. He was only stopped by chance when another of the many participants in the drama caught him as he was leaving the room and managed to calm him down.

But underneath Oyston knew he had the winning cards. The less confident people in the company, who could not face the prospect of unemployment in the same way as the more senior journalists, forced them to buckle. The incentive of paying the freelances, whom they felt they had let down, and the thought of the wages for the rest of the staff, had piled on the pressure. They gave in, the computer screens went back on, and the office began to hum with life.

Meanwhile Oyston's people started negotiating with the Receiver to extend the licence for week-by-week publication to put off the point at which they had to buy the assets. Growfar, or 'Growbag' as it had now sneeringly been christened, was a wholly separate company, and therefore had none of the obligations of the old News on Sunday Publishing plc. But Oyston promised it would have the Charter written into its articles of association. The shareholding in the new company was split between Oyston, with a 37.5 per cent share, and the same share for the T and G. The remainder – 25 per cent – was given to the old shareholders of News on Sunday Publishing plc.

The left-wing councils and unions had begun to wake up to the fate of their investment, and hurriedly started work on excuses and explanations. It was not even as if the paper had 'had a go' – even worse, it had come and gone and hardly been noticed. By any standards there was a lot of explaining to do. But the 25 per cent Oyston was giving them served as a financial fig-leaf to hide their embarrassment. Although the shares were only worth a fraction of their original value, it was possible to fend off questions by instead pointing to a bright future with Growfar. And the move also stifled any criticism of Oyston in the shareholders' ranks, even though – apart from the Charter – the paper was no longer the one they had originally invested in.

Supported by the T and G, Michael Connolly finally revealed Barber's RBP 3 short-term plan for the new company. It was a decimation. Total staffing level was to be cut from 181 to seventy-two. The journalists were to be reduced from sixty, way down past the fifty recommended by Charles Wintour, to a minute twenty-three. *NoS* was unleashing another unfortunate new precedent for its trade-union backers – a staffing level lower than on any other national newspaper, and so low that the National Union of Journalists initially said that it could not ratify the arrangement, because it would give other proprietors licence to cut their own staffs rights down. Here was a supposedly Labour paper planning to run the whole operation on less than seventy-five employees. The editorial staff alone of the *News of the World* was that many. The colour section was to shut down, and the London operation be cut right back, with the building being sold off. With these cuts, Barber calculated the paper would lose £34,000 a week on an average circulation of 240,000 (that week's issue had sold 220,000), but would break even on a circulation of 400,000.

The first Growfar edition was published with an editorial claiming the paper's future was secure and – as though to underline the support of the Labour establishment for Oyston's plan – a major article by Neil Kinnock. The staff, having done their duty to themselves and others by producing it, went to get paid off. Then they found the catch in the Growfar offer. To receive the money, each employee had to sign a loan agreement with the company, assigning it the right to collect the wages back from the liquidator on their behalf at the end of the day. Few people realized the significance of the arrangement. But at the top level of the company Horsley had been informed by Henry Stewart that £275,000 of the subordinated loan money offered by Oyston and the T and G to keep the old company afloat had not been used. Worse still, it had not even been paid in before the company went into receivership. And it was this money that Oyston was now using to pay the staff wages.

The result made Horsley gasp. What had previously been a subordinated loan, and last in the queue for payment, had suddenly become a first-line credit as wages owed. Horsley was appalled by what he considered to be sharp business practice, but there was nothing illegal about it. One of the few people to realize what was going on was Chris Walsh – ever alert – who began proposing legal action against Oyston. After a flurry of activity, nothing happened.

Now there followed the last, and most seedy, scene of all. David Jones had assembled a list of the new journalistic staff, and put names against each of the jobs. Nobody except him knew who was on it. He appeared on the editorial floor, angry and clearly upset at the rigours of his job under his new master, and announced that he had to go to Hull as part of his filming commitments. He left the list with the union representatives and announced that they should organize applications from any of the original staff who wanted to work. Then he disappeared.

Whatever could be said about the entire staff of *News on Sunday*, they had all worked tremendously hard in difficult circumstances.

Now they had to volunteeer for work like dockers at the gates. The union reps sat at the desk in Manchester collecting names of volunteers, and the others were phoned up from London. The journalists had ninety minutes to make up their minds. It was a bizarre position for the union reps. On the one hand they were receiving the names of those who wanted to work, and at the same time they now had the list of those being offered jobs. The two obviously did not coincide. Some of the professionals, including the two authors, had decided they had had enough and were not interested in working for Growfar. Sports editor Bob Edwell, features editor Polly Pattullo and her deputy Alison Macdonald, picture editor Colin Jacobson and systems editor Eugenie Verney did not reapply. Anna Coote had already left after clashing with Jones about her column. Sutton had been sacked, and the marketing department had gone. Yet, most weird of all, nearly all the people who had been involved before capitalization wanted to join Growfar, seemingly unconcerned at the way the nature of the company had changed. Although Oyston was promising to keep the Labour Party line, the consensus way of managing the company, the involvement of staff in decision-making, the safeguard of the Founders and the commitment to positive discrimination were being swept away.

The Founders themselves joined in the lame rationalization. In a last message to the workforce, they said they hoped the majority of the workers were now aware that 'we carried out the role entrusted to us the only way possible – straight'.

'It became patently obvious to us that whatever we did, or offered, would be refused . . . It's difficult to negotiate when the side holding all the cards (aka cash) have no interest in reaching a jointly agreed settlement . . . Although we believe that the new paper can never achieve the original aims of those involved right from the beginning we hope that it will go some way to meeting the founding objectives,' they concluded. 'To those who are staying – keep struggling – and the best of luck.'

Even though many of the paper's most experienced journalists had walked away, enough staff stayed to make sure ink kept hitting paper, and Oyston made one of his increasingly frequent television appearances. He announced he would run the paper lightly through the summer, and bring it back with a bang in the autumn after he had raised another £8 million to finance a re-launch. He talked confidently of 'soon selling a million'.

The Great Dream was over. And as always at *News on Sunday*, there was no ceremony to mark the occasion, as there had been no Christmas party in London in 1986 and no speeches at the launch. People gathered their belongings in a desultory fashion and the last CVs rolled off the photocopier. Aspiring freelances staggered out with reams of computer print-out from the information unit. Those staying and those going hung about cracking embarrassed jokes about life under Growbag. But most of the remarks were close to the bone. Many of the journalists staying felt ashamed, explaining they would leave as soon as they got another job. Most of the redundant ones were going back to London, their strange adventure in this northern outpost over. None of them voiced regrets about joining the paper.

But for those outside the relatively cosy world of journalism it was more serious. The Black Hand Gang, whose trade had been abolished even if they were still given jobs, had hundreds of unemployed on its local books. And dozens of straightforward office jobs, which are hard to come by in the north, had gone in the cuts. Many of these people desperately wanted to stay. Some were trying to rationalize Growfar as a continuation of *News on Sunday*, while others had by now lost all principles and were just desperate for a job. More than half were not on the list for re-employment, and instead had to go to Christine Jackson's office, where she handed them a sheet of paper formally dismissing them. Outside Jackson's office sat Jane Shepherd, an ebullient disabled person and former social worker who was personnel-department secretary. She had been out of a job for nine months when she joined the paper, and had been so delighted with her first paycheck that she had kissed it, leaving a perfect lipstick bow above the signature.

Shepherd was staying, but one of the people who went past her to get his cards was David Collier, another disadvantaged person. Collier was deaf and dumb, or profoundly deaf in Right-On-speak. He was twenty-two, and had been thrilled and enormously grateful to be given a job in the postroom, one of the positive results of the outreach programme. Because he came with grants, he only cost the company £40 a week. But Collier had no slot in R B P 3, and, unable to talk to anyone, he filed out miserably, caught up in the rush of events and almost unnoticed. It was four months to the day since the staff of the paper had been invited to attend a day of 'deafness awareness training', designed to help them identify and sympathize with the problems of deaf people.

10 · Who killed *News on Sunday*?

In the dying days of the paper, to pass the time while they were waiting for Oyston, the journalists played a game called 'Who Killed News on Sunday?', loosely based on Cluedo. The rest of the staff were mightily impressed that 'the writers', as they were known, were at last showing the intelligence for which they had been hired.

The game had various 'murderers' – the Men in Suits, Attila the Stockbroker, Horsley, Hayling, the present/last/next editor, Walsh, Oyston, the hacks, spooks, the Black Hand Gang, the punters, Jean the tea-lady and the Founders. The weapons varied – the Steadman cartoons, market research, Hoyland's pop concerts, the VAT returns, Equal Opportunities, the Golden Share, Barbara Altounyan's clocks, a certain person's cocaine habit, the newsagents, the Norsk Data computer, and the advertising campaign. The third element was a choice of various locations. The answer, for what it was worth, was Chris Walsh, at the picture desk, with the VAT returns.

In such a revolving disaster as *News on Sunday*, the game was not as facile as it seems. After the paper collapsed, the stream of 'It wasn't my fault' articles led off with Hoyland in the *New Statesman* explaining the project had been hijacked by professionals who had taken it away from its original aims. Sutton chose the *UK Press Gazette* to explain that in the old days they used to teach archers to aim for the moon. The paper had 'aimed for the moon in Manchester, the lunar left', was how he put it. He was halfway through replying to Hoyland when there was a hot spell, and he went sunbathing in Tooting Lido instead. Sylvia Collier replied to Sutton petulantly on behalf of Hayling, who in turn dumped a pile of memos on *City Limits* to 'prove' it wasn't his fault. Later fall-out brought in Horsley, who explained in the *Guardian* that the original investment was justified and that the paper had failed because there was not a market.

Brian Whitaker wrote a bizarre piece, again for the *Guardian*, ending with a weak joke about a cactus with its roots in the air. Each of the pleaders had some justification when they cast their stone. What they forgot was that they were writing from inside a greenhouse. The result was the sound of more breaking glass.

The chain of events which led to the disaster was inexorable. The original thesis for the paper would have been sound, provided the project was in other hands. There was no justification in the pleading of the amateurs that it was the RSGB market research which persuaded them to make the disastrous error of aiming the paper at a split market. It emerged from their own faction fighting. Just as basic a flaw was the inability of *NoS* to face the realities of that market to achieve its sales. The setting up of headquarters in Manchester was a terminal mistake in journalist terms; those who supported it showed their ignorance of the newspaper business. Then the company was launched on too small a budget ever to be able to succeed, with no slack to allow for error. On top of this was loaded an unworkable management structure run by people with little or no experience in many cases. The original workers were unable to relate to the professionals they chose, who will almost universally admit that they operated much below par in the circumstances and were very unhappy with their work. And so it went on – right down to the last compounding error of the dust-up with the newsagents at the end of the line.

It sounds like simplistic nonsense to say that the paper failed simply on the basis of the old cliché that the left cannot get its act together. But unfortunately, it is basically true. In so far as there was a central cause, it was the one stated by Roy Barber, a professional with vast experience. His conclusion was quite definite – it was the structure of the company which killed *News on Sunday*. Barber was full of praise for the workforce, which he described as extremely highly motivated, dedicated and hard-working. But he believed that with its lack of clear decision-making structure, the company never stood a chance.

The inherent flaws in the structure were compounded by a mixture of incompetence and inexperience at the higher levels of manage-ment, which was largely the result of the theory of 'gifted amateurs'. This, refined into the theory of '1960s talent which has now matured', postulates that there are people who have never followed conven-tional careers, but who would be brilliant if they had ever bothered. Although superficially attractive, the argument misses out the factor of experience, the major one in successful management, and the one for which there is no substitute.

The reply of the amateurs is that when they employed professionals the project was subverted by people who did not understand it. This overlooks two things. First, they were so intensely suspicious of professionals, especially journalists – whom many of them actively hate – that the idea of employing straightforward cheerful hacks who will do whatever they are told is beyond most of them. And second, the determination to recruit people who were ideologically pure not only drove away a lot of talent, but freed the amateurs of the responsibility of explaining to people arriving what they were required to do. They were somehow supposed to know. And as the advertising agency BBH found out, when the amateurs had to lay down what they were doing, they hadn't even thought it out enough to know themselves.

The sad fact about *News on Sunday* is that from the beginning it was a closed circle of the original people, who kept the project very close to their chests, even as they tore each other apart. Professionals who arrived later were often pawns in a factional game. The Men in Suits naïvely went through the same experience – a couple of weeks thinking how clever these people were, as it was impossible to see how the place worked, followed by the sickening realization that there was a simple answer – it didn't. And because there was so little communication between the amateurs and the professionals, there arose huge misunderstandings which could never be resolved.

Into this structure was thrown an extraordinary collection of individuals, who complicated matters further with bitter internecine warfare, ruthlessly and relentlessly conducted without any thought of the overall aim of the exercise, which was to produce a successful popular newspaper and run the company at a profit. Many of the people at the paper never thought about this side of it, and instead ground their own axes obsessionally, blithely ignoring the wider consequences. And because nobody at the top of the company could defeat the structure and 'bang their heads together', as many people put it, they were allowed to go their own way unrestrained. And that way, for all that *News on Sunday* masqueraded as the 'People's Paper', was essentially the concerned and middle-class approach – the earnest and deeply held belief that 'the people' (who invariably only appeared as dots on market-research charts) were crying out for a paper like theirs.

Alan Hayling's muddled brief for *News on Sunday* said: 'Today too many people despair of the popular press . . .' They do, but the despairers tend to be the middle classes who don't read the pops, and yet at the same time arrogantly believe that pop readers are morons who believe all the rubbish served up to them. But *Sun* readers call their paper 'The Comic'. Some *News of the World* readers in the market-research groups expected their paper to be all lies, and the old adage that people do not believe what they read in the papers has not changed. *News on Sunday* itself was not without fault. Like the other papers, it carried articles and stories which were sometimes sloppy, biased or embellished.

On top of this attitude towards its readers, *NoS* tried to run before it could walk. With no experience, the gifted amateurs thought that with the help of a few cheap professionals they could go straight on to the centre of the stage with such a morally correct brief that people would automatically flock to them. There was little feeling that the paper had to earn respect, or enlist more solid grass-roots support, and there was absolutely no margin for error.

But, of course, *News on Sunday* was hopelessly flawed by going for its twin markets and effectively trying to wrap the *News of the World* and the *Observer* into one package. It also suffered from an element of simplistic thinking that just because it was downmarket it could treat its readers like idiots. The argument of John Pilger and others is that just because a paper is a tabloid, it should not underestimate the intelligence of its readers. Instead the duty is to communicate intelligent coverage in a way which they can understand, and not to browbeat them with crude propaganda about various pet causes.

There is certainly an audience for a paper similar to *News on Sunday* – if it is done properly. Contrary to what Horsley says, the authors believe that an upmarket 'caring professionals' Sunday tabloid, properly produced, would have weekly sales of at least 250,000. But the paper that was produced was too poor to give the concept a fair testing, which in turn pointed up the arrogance of those who started the project in believing that a quality product could be produced in so short a period and with so little money. For all that most people have complaints about their regular newspaper, *News on*

Sunday went a long way to proving that newspapers are complicated things which need a great deal of skill and experience to get right. They don't happen overnight.

Hilarious and crass though many of the events in the paper's history may have been, a quick look at launches of other newspapers, such as *Today* and *London Daily News*, shows paths strewn with unforeseen pitfalls and hazards which can trap even the most experienced professionals.

But there is a horrible example for the left and others who say that it can't be done. While *News on Sunday* was getting on the road, another paper was starting up, designed to be 'irreverent . . . young . . . witty . . . with picture power . . . campaigning . . . investigative . . . etc.' It too was aimed at a small but dedicated core readership, and, unlike *News on Sunday*, it has proved to be a howling commercial success.

That paper is the tits-and-bums *Sunday Sport*, started by soft-porn king David Sullivan, publisher of the mag *Whitehouse*. Its target audience was badly educated young males in the lowest socio-economic brackets, and it worked on the premiss that it could go further than Sundays like the *News of the World*, which thought they had already scraped the bottom of the barrel in terms of acceptable popular taste. *Sunday Sport* is known in the trade as 'the rude one'; some of its notable scoops have been pictures of a woman Buddhist monk in California with ninety-two-inch breasts; Cynthia Small, who has eighty-four-inch breasts, and sold successfully as a poster; the revival of seventy-four-inch 'Chesty' Morgan; and a girlie pic of a woman with three breasts.

The lesson is not in the content, which is obvious enough for the target audience of wankers, but in the way Sullivan went about the operation. Instead of taking the grand *News on Sunday* road, *Sunday Sport* was started on a tiny budget of £150,000, with another £2 million set by for the TV ads. But this money was never needed. The ads were banned by the IBA – giving the paper masses of free publicity instead.

On the editorial side, it had only had eleven journalists, and a total staff of thirty, which was so small that the NUJ refused to recognize it as a national newspaper.

The paper took full advantage of the new technology and negotiated deals with the NGA (the Black Hand Gang) and contract printing. And in contrast to *NoS* there was no research, no sales target, and only one dummy edition. The launch, on 14 September 1986, was in London and the south-east only, and issue one contained pictures of more than fifty nipples. By December the paper was expanding rapidly and had launched in the north. Sales had increased to 230,000 and by May the paper was selling more than 500,000, and was well into profit.

News on Sunday wasn't all bad. The paper did counter the usual right-wing bias in the press, it did have some good stories, and although it was hopelessly gloomy, it was refreshing to have a tabloid without tits, cheesecake and a lot of the rubbish that fills its rivals. And with a longer run in its original form, it would undoubtedly have got better. The paper did pick up readers at the bottom end of the market who genuinely had given up newspapers in disgust and were cheered by its appearance. The desire for something 'decent' for the masses appealed at least to a few of them.

Whatever excuses or justifications are offered, in the end the fact has to be faced that *News on Sunday* was a Right-On roadshow, and like most other gifts from the Right-Ons, it has left few friends behind. One of the worst things about the paper was the way it careered from one disaster to another, sucking up thousands of people along its way and then letting them down. Many were messed about, and some were not paid. Supporters were misled with promises of editorial excellence which were not fulfilled. In simple human relationships, the failure of *News on Sunday* was ignominious and complete. And that is the point, the most shattering thing for the Founders and the others who struggled to keep the concept pure to accept. This is where they feel the professionals let them down. BBH produced a slogan which they could not stomach and which was universally adjudged to be naff. Sutton produced a paper whose design and content got the same verdict. Both were sincere, if slightly muddled, attempts to follow the brief of a million-selling pop newspaper.

It is said that most of the people who set the paper up never entertained for a moment the idea that it might fail. But *News on Sunday* was obsessed with failure. It was, in truth, never meant to succeed in the world as it is, because the thinking behind it wants to sweep that world away and replace it with a new one. This was no search to find a slightly less heartless niche in a heartless world. Compromise was never on the agenda. The plan was that either the world would change to make way for *News on Sunday* or the paper would bow out in glorious heroic failure.

And it couldn't even do that.

Postscript

The attempt by Owen Oyston to make *News on Sunday* a commercial success turned out to be doomed to failure.

Oyston, feeling his way as newspaper owner, made a celebrated trip to a motorway service station in his Rolls-Royce to observe punters buying the paper, and came to the conclusion that *NoS* was an impulse purchase. Trying to boost sales, he reverted to the original plan of an aggressive pop tabloid approach, and told his editor, David Jones, to move the paper back downmarket again. Jones, who had been editor for just six unhappy weeks, had had enough and left.

The paper veered about in search of a readership, with the first mild girlie cheesecake pictures appearing. But nothing too outrageous was printed for fear of upsetting the remnants of the Grumbly Brigade, some of whom were still buying *NoS*, unaware even of the ownership change. Jones was replaced by another cumbersome two-man editorial structure, reminiscent of the original Pilger–Sutton arrangement. Brian Whitaker was elevated to acting editor, but with power effectively in the hands of a newcomer to the scene – Bill Nutting, a competent, if uninspired, Fleet Street veteran.

But the paper's circulation continued to slide, and it became obvious that editorially it was a zombie, effectively dead, but still tottering on to the news-stands every Sunday. It did show one flicker of life at the beginning of August, when, in a naked publicity stunt, it printed extracts from Peter Wright's banned book *Spycatcher*, with a provocative promise that there would be more next week. There wasn't. Instead the paper, which was promptly told by the Attorney General that it would be proceeded against for criminal contempt of court, lost its nerve and appeared with an extraordinary front page featuring Winston Churchill giving a V-sign, with the headline OUR

MESSAGE TO THE LAW LORDS and a strapline of NEWS ON SUNDAY FIGHT FOR FREEDOM.

This event gave Oyston a taste of the expensive and hazardous legal environment into which papers were being forced, and led to an immediate flap about who was responsible. It also resulted in the demise of Whitaker, who, as Pilger had done, demanded to know who exactly was running what. Whitaker presented his demand as an ultimatum to Oyston, who ignored it, leaving him no choice but to resign. Nutting took over full editorial control, and the paper staggered on through the summer with no discernible direction, except for the sales graph, which went inexorably down.

By the Labour Party conference in October 1987 the paper was selling just over 130,000 and losing £85,000 a week – more than £4 million a year. The ambitious plans for a huge autumn re-launch to bring it up to its profit figure of 400,000 copies a week were ditched. Oyston, who had possibly got more of a challenge than he expected, laid on a lavish soirée at the conference, and his Rolls-Royce beat Robert Maxwell's similar machine to the prime parking spot outside the conference hall. But even his extrovert personality and various 'brain-storming' sessions to throw up new ideas made no impression on the actual product, which was rapidly sinking out of sight.

On 20 November Oyston finally pulled the plug, after the failure of a plan to keep the paper alive by selling bulk subscriptions based on union membership. By then circulation was down to 115,000. The staff got a month's notice money.

But meanwhile Oyston had not been idle. He fulfilled an ambition of many years by buying Blackpool Football Club, and his burgeoning cable-TV interests grew to include Sir Alastair Burnett, whom he signed up as Chairman of Oyston Productions Ltd, an independent film, cable and television production company. Burnett also joined the Board of the Oyston Family Group Ltd.

Oyston announced that Growfar, which had bought *News on Sunday* from the Receiver, would continue. The company, which still carried the original Labour movement and council investors as holders of 25 per cent of the shareholding, would be going on to investigate business opportunities based on trade-union membership. Oyston had already talked of ideas involving some sort of trade-union credit card. He had seen it in operation in America, and was fully aware of the potential of trade unionists as a market. The prospects for Growfar were, of course, immensely brighter without the drain of what had once been 'the paper for the people'.

*

The original Founders, people involved before capitalization, and the hired professionals went their separate ways.

Gerry Taylor took over as chief executive for the *New Statesman*; BBH got the account for the *Independent*; and John Pilger continued working for Central Television.

Of those not invited to join Growfar, Alan Hayling and Sylvia Collier started work on a film for Channel 4 about nuclear dumping in the Pacific, the story at the heart of Hayling's dummy edition in November 1985. Polly Pattullo and Anna Coote joined up to write a book on women in politics; Chris Walsh claimed to be writing his own book on *NoS*, concentrating on practical fund-raising advice; Keith Sutton took a job re-designing the local paper at Barrow-in-Furness in Cumbria; Barbara Altounyan went freelancing, mainly for the *Observer*; John Hoyland got a job 'in the arts' whose nature he refused to disclose to the authors.

Many of the people who joined Growfar had left before Oyston finally closed the paper. Nick Horsley joined the Board of the new company, but resigned after a couple of months; Christine Jackson left to try life without work for a change; Ben Lowe left the paper in October and started organizing a conference on anti-Imperialism; Henry Stewart was promoted by Oyston and ended up effectively running the financial side of the paper, before leaving at the same time as Lowe. Liz Cooper and Karen Needham both resigned. David Collier, the deaf and dumb postroom worker, was taken on again by Growfar, but, like the rest, ended up back on the street in November.

One of the Founders, Mike Power, went to the City University in London for a training course in journalism. The Founders as a group continued to hold meetings.

Index

Note: Please refer to the entry for *News on Sunday* for specific details

APPENDIX

News on Sunday plc Shareholder List, 20 August 1987, giving name and address followed by number of shares

Alexander Kenneth John Wilson Sir
9 West Shore, Pittenweem, Fife KT10 2NV
1250

Aubrey John Nicholas Crispin Esq
Hockpitt Farm, Nether Stowey,
Bridgwater, Somerset TA5 1EX
1000

Bakers Food & Allied Workers Union
Stanborough House, Great North Road,
Stanborough, Welwyn Garden City,
Herts AL8 7TA
1500

Balfe Richard A Esq
147 Powis Street, London SE18 6JN
1000

Barclays Nominees, KWS Limited 55 a/c
Goodenough House, 33 Old Broad Street,
London EC2P 2JE
250000

Barclays Nominees, Thames Limited 1175 a/c
Ebbgate House, 2 Swan Lane,
London EC4R 3TS
100000

Barnes Michael John Esq
15 Woodstock Road, London W4 1DS
2000

Bartlett Dennis George Esq
Sogat House, 274/288 London Road, Hadleigh,
Benfleet, Essex SS7 2DE
10000

Bohanna John Henry Esq
12 Honister Walk, Woodlands Estate,
Netherley, Liverpool L27 5RY
1000

Brown Michael Barratt- Esq
Robin Hood Farm, Baslow, Bakewell,
Derbyshire DE4 1PQ
1000

Christie Julie Frances Ms
c/o Heald & Nickinson, 48 Bedford Square,
London WC1
1000

**City Financial Administration Nominees
Limited KEA a/c**
Regis House, King William Street,
London EC2R 9AR
5000

**Clapham Sydney Frank Esq/Comerford
Herbert Esq/Litchfield Charles Henry Esq**
9 Parsons Road, Irchester,
Wellingborough, Northants NN9 7EA
5000

Cleveland County Council
PO Box 100, Municipal Buildings,
Middlesbrough, Cleveland TS1 2QH
250000

Cliffe Lionel Ronald Esq/Cliffe Doris Mrs
70 Edgedale Road, Sheffield, S7 2BR
1000

Condon Judith Ms/Flynn Laurie Esq
52 Old Park Road, Palmers Green,
London N13 4RE
1000

**Confederation of Health Service
Employees, The**
Glen House, High Street,
Banstead, Surrey SM7 2LH
15000

**Cook Anthony William Frazer Esq/
Cook Christine Mary Mrs**
The Old Rutland, Hoby,
Melton Mowbray, Leics LE14 3DU
6000

Crosswall Nominees Limited
8 Montague Close, London SE1
50000

Derbyshire County Council
PO Box 2, County Offices,
Matlock, Derbyshire DE4 3AH
305000

Devonald Bryn Clive Esq
4 Hampstead Walk, Michaelston-Super-Ely,
Cardiff, South Glam
1000

**Dodds Julian Robert Esq/Perkins Michael
Francis Esq/Palmer Peter Esq, SCPS**
124/130 Southwark Street, London SE1 0TU
50000

Durham Colliery Mechanics Association, NUM
26 The Avenue, Durham City DH1 4ED
5000

**Eagle Place Trustees,
Boyd Phillip Duckett Esq/
Howard William Esq**
211 Piccadilly, London W1A 4SA
5000

Educational Institute of Scotland, The
46 Moray Place, Edinburgh EH3 6BH
10000

**Edwards Harry Esq/Coomer Terry Esq/
Bailey Peter Esq**
Hillcrest House, Garth Street, Hanley,
Stoke on Trent, Staffs
50000

Ellman Michael Peter David Esq
114 Cranley Gardens, London N10 3AH
1000

Elson Christine Janet Esq
10 Cecilia Road, London E8 2EP
10000

Erith C Esq/Pole E Esq/Roe J Esq/Baker A Esq
c/o Sogat, 82 Westminster Chambers,
2 Calton Road, Sneinton, Nottingham NG3 2AN
1000

Everett Anthony Charles Esq
5 Spring Terrace, Paradise Road,
Richmond, Surrey
3000

Fenchurch Nominees Limited
The Lawn, Bath Road,
Newbury, Berks RG13 1QN
200000

Fife Regional Council SF a/c
Fife House, North Street,
Glenrothes, Fife KY7 5LT
100000

Fire Brigades Union
Bradley House, 68 Coombe Road,
Kingston-upon-Thames, Surrey KT2 7AE
50000

Follett Kenneth Martin Esq/
Follet Daphne Barbara Ms
92 Cheyne Walk, London SW10 0DQ
10000

Ford James Glyn Esq
149 Old Road, Ashton-under-Lyne,
Lancs DL6 9DA
1000

Forman Adam Dr
43 Montgomery Road, Sheffield S7 1LN
2000

Forman John Denis Sir
The Mill House, Howe Street,
Chelmsford CM3 1BG
5000

Franklin Andrew Cecil Esq
27 Ingham Road, London NW6 1DG
1000

Franklin Norman Albert Jessel Esq
78 Lawn Road, London NW3 2XB
1000

Franklin Samuel Alexander Esq
23 Camborne Road, Sheffield S6 1HN
1000

Gardiner Margaret Emilia Ms OBE
35 Downshire Hill, London NW3 1NU
3000

GLEB Investments Limited
63/67 Newington Causeway, London SE1 6BD
115000

GMG Nominees Limited LDCF a/c
32 St May at Hill, London EC3P 3AJ
150000

Gosling Paul Esq
20 Filbert Street East, Leicester LE2 7JJ
1000

Gray Ronald Esq/Gray Anita Claire Mrs
3 Princes Way, London SW19 6QF
1000

**Greater Manchester Economic Development
Corporation Limited**
Bernard House, Piccadilly Gardens,
Manchester M1 4UD
30000

**Greater Manchester Passenger
Transport Executive**
PO Box 429, 9 Portland Street,
Manchester M60 1HX
175000

Guinness Mahon Nominees Limited
32 St Mary at Hill, London EC3P 3AP
260750

Hall Mark Anthony Esq
24 Woodstock Road, Redland, Bristol
5000

Hart Anthony Bernard Esq
3 Ennerdale Road, Kew,
Richmond, Surrey TW9 3PG
1500

Haskins Gilda Susan Mrs/
Haskins Christopher Robin Esq
Quarryside Farm, Skidby,
Cottingham, East Yorkshire HU16 5TG
10000

Henderson Nominees Limited, NFS a/c
26 Finsbury Square, London EC2A 1DA
30000

Hopper David Esq/Guy David Esq
NUM, Durham Area, PO Box 6,
Redhill, Durham
8000

Horsley Alec Stewart Esq
Talbot Lodge, Woodfield Lane,
Hessle, East Yorkshire HU13 0EW
7000

Horsley George Nicholas Seward Esq
2 Dale Road, Welton,
Brough, North Humberside
10000

Horsley Ida Seward Mrs
Talbot Lodge, Hessle, Hull, North Humberside
5000

Invicta Cooperative Society Limited
19/33 Spital Street, Dartford, Kent DA1 2AL
2000

Kaldor Nicholas Prof Lord/
Kaldor Clarissa Elizabeth Lady
2 Adams Road, Cambridge CB3 9AD
5000

Lewenstein Silvion Oscar Esq
11 Western Esplanade, Portslade,
Brighton, East Sussex BN4 1WE
1000

Lothian Regional Council
12 St Giles Street, Edinburgh EH1 1PT
200000

Masters and Officers Trustees Company Limited
Oceanair House, 750/760 High Road,
Leytonstone, London E11 3BB
10000

Matlock John Esq/Charles David Arthur Esq/Kelly John Esq
55 New Walk, Leicester LE1 7EB
5000

Mayor and Burgesses of London Borough of Brent
Brent Town Hall, Forty Lane, Wembley, Middx
250000

Mayor and Burgesses of the London Borough of Camden, SF a/c
Town Hall, Euston Road, London NW1 2RU
100000

Mayor and Burgesses of the London Borough of Hammersmith and Fulham
Town Hall, King Street, London W6 9JU
150000

Mayor and Burgesses of the London Borough of Haringey
PO Box 264, Civic Centre,
Wood Green, London N22 4LE
250000

Mayor and Burgesses of the London Borough of Hounslow, SF a/c
Civic Centre, Lampton Road,
Hounslow, Middx TW3 4DN
100000

Mayor and Burgesses of the London Borough of Lambeth, 5 a/c
18 Brixton Hill, London SW2 1RL
250000

Mayor and Burgesses of the London Borough of Lewisham
Town Hall, Lewisham, London SE6 4RX
50000

Mayor and Burgesses of the London Borough of Newham
Town Hall, East Ham, London E6
175000

Mid Glamorgan County Council, SFA a/c
Treasurers Department, County Hall,
Cathays Park, Cardiff CF1 3NJ
25000

Morgan Nominees Limited, NNT a/c
23 Great Winchester Street,
London EC2P 2AX
250000

National Union of Mineworkers
Miners Offices, Derbyshire Area, Salgate,
Chesterfield, Derbyshire
5000

National Union of Seamen
Maritime House, Old Town, Clapham,
London SW4 0JP
50000

Nominees Limited
c/o 45 Beech Street, London EC2P 2LX
5000

Nominees Limited
100 Wood Street, London EC2P 2AJ
250000

Norwest Holst Group Limited
60 Whitworth Street, Manchester
75000

NUM Northumberland Area
Burt Hall, Northumberland Road,
Newcastle upon Tyne NE1 8LD
5000

Nutraco Nominees Limited
33 King William Street, London EC4R 9AS
300000

Openshaw Keith Esq
16 Devonshire Road,
Salford, Greater Manchester M6 8HY
1000

Osborn George Charles Esq/Clynch Richard Ernest Esq/Hanchard William Henry Esq
195 Upper Selsdon Road,
South Croydon, Surrey CR2 0DY
1000

Oyston Owen John Esq
Claughton Hall, Claughton, Lancaster LA2 9LA
100000

Robertson Bruce Alan Esq/ Robertson Wlodzimiera Mrs
38 Thorpewood Avenue, London SE26 4BX
1000

Roland Joffe Directors Pension Scheme
Kingsmead House, 250 Kings Road,
Chelsea, London SW3
1000

Roodhill Nominees Limited, 69 a/c
78/80 Cornhill, London EC3V 3NJ
2000

Roodhill Nominees Limited, 70 a/c
78/80 Cornhill, London EC3V 3NJ
5000

Samuels Albert Esq/ Hunter Joseph Edmund Esq
12 Mornington House, Station Road,
Westcliffe on Sea
550000

Sebestyen Amanda Miss
60 Finsbury Park Road, London N4
10000

Sebestyen Juliet Mary Ms
191 North Sherwood Street,
Nottingham NG1 4EH
17500

Sheffield Branch of NALGO
48/62 Pinstone Street, Sheffield S1 2HU
500

Sheffield City Council
Town Hall, Sheffield S1 2HH
10000

Smith Alexander Richard Esq/
Rubner Ben Esq/Priestley Granville Esq
General Confederation of Trade Unions,
Central House, Upper Woburn Place,
London WC1H 0HY
1000

Society of Graphical and Allied Trades
Bristol and West of England Branch,
Sogat House, 4 Emery Road,
Brislington, Bristol BS4 5PF
1000

Society of Graphical and Allied Trades
Greater Manchester Branch
4/8 Great George Street, Salford M3 6FH
2000

Society of Telecom Executives
102/104 Sheen Road,
Richmond, Surrey TW9 1UF
10000

Sogat 82
119 Jesmond Road,
Newcastle upon Tyne NE2 1NL
1000

Sogat 82 Manchester Central Branch
10 Swan Street, Manchester M4 5JR
20000

Stewart Henry Angus James Esq/
Cooper Elizabeth Stanley Ms
38 Brighton Grove,
Newcastle upon Tyne NE4 5NS
1000

TASS
Park House, 64/66 Wandsworth Common
North Side, London SW18 2SH
10000

Trafford Commercial Investments Limited
Trafford Town Hall, Talbot Road,
Stretford, Greater Manchester M32 0TH
25000

Tuffin Alan David Esq/Clarke Anthony
James Esq/Binks Frederic John Esq
UCW House, Crescent Lane,
Clapham, London SW4 9RN
75000

Unity House Holdings Limited
Unity House, Euston Road, London NW1 2BL
50000

Unity House Holdings Limited, PSF a/c
Unity House, Euston Road, London NW1 2BL
150000

Wainwright Hilary Anne Mrs/
Bhaskar Ram Roy Esq
11 Balfern Street, London SW11
2000

Wainwright Martin Scurrah Esq
67 Burlington Lane, London W4 3ET
1000

Walsh Michael Christopher Esq
92 Brooke Road, London N16
1000

West Glamorgan County Council
County Treasurer, County Hall,
Swansea SA1 3SN
25000

West Midlands Enterprise Board
Investments Limited
Wellington House, 31/34 Waterloo Street,
Birmingham B2 5TJ
25000

Williams John Esq
6 St Albans Road, London NW5 1RD
5000

Wolverhampton Borough Council, SF a/c
Finance Department, Civic Centre,
St Peters Square,
Wolverhampton, West Midlands WV1 1RL
300000

Wood David McKinnon Esq/
Wood Jocelyne Louisa Ms
3 Wharf Lane,
Radcliffe-on-Trent, Nottingham NG12 2AN
10000

Woodhead Edward Esq/Ramsay Harry Esq
21 Oakdene Avenue, Chislehurst, Kent
250000

With acknowledgement to the Companies Registration Office.

A selection of bestsellers from Sphere

FICTION

INFIDELITIES	Freda Bright	£3.99 ☐
THE GREAT ALONE	Janet Dailey	£3.99 ☐
THE PANIC OF '89	Paul Erdman	£3.50 ☐
WHITE SUN, RED STAR	Robert Elegant	£3.50 ☐
A TASTE FOR DEATH	P. D. James	£3.50 ☐

FILM AND TV TIE-IN

BLACK FOREST CLINIC	Peter Heim	£2.99 ☐
INTIMATE CONTACT	Jacqueline Osborne	£2.50 ☐
BEST OF BRITISH	Maurice Sellar	£8.95 ☐
SEX WITH PAULA YATES	Paula Yates	£2.95 ☐
RAW DEAL	Walter Wager	£2.50 ☐

NON-FICTION

THE DARKNESS IS LIGHT ENOUGH	Chris Ferris	£4.50 ☐
TREVOR HOWARD: A GENTLEMAN AND A PLAYER	Vivienne Knight	£3.50 ☐
INVISIBLE ARMIES	Stephen Segaller	£4.99 ☐
ALEX THROUGH THE LOOKING GLASS	Alex Higgins and Tony Francis	£2.99 ☐
NEXT TO A LETTER FROM HOME: THE GLENN MILLER STORY	Geoffrey Butcher	£4.99 ☐

All Sphere books are available at your local bookshop or newsagent, or can be ordered direct from the publisher. Just tick the titles you want and fill in the form below.

Name_____

Address_____

_____

Write to Sphere Books, Cash Sales Department, P.O. Box 11, Falmouth, Cornwall TR10 9EN

Please enclose a cheque or postal order to the value of the cover price plus:

UK: 60p for the first book, 25p for the second book and 15p for each additional book ordered to a maximum charge of £1.90.

OVERSEAS & EIRE: £1.25 for the first book, 75p for the second book and 28p for each subsequent title ordered.

BFPO: 60p for the first book, 25p for the second book plus 15p per copy for the next 7 books, thereafter 9p per book.

Sphere Books reserve the right to show new retail prices on covers which may differ from those previously advertised in the text elsewhere, and to increase postal rates in accordance with the P.O.

A BETTER ◄WAY TO► MANAGE

MALCOLM BIRD

ARE YOU "A BORN LEADER"?
DID ANYONE EVER TEACH YOU HOW
TO MANAGE?
DO YOU BELIEVE THAT MANAGERS ARE
BORN NOT MADE?

Most people become managers because they are
good at what they do and are therefore promoted to
supervise other people doing the same thing without
being given any training about how to manage
people, systems and money.

Malcolm Bird examines the many common mistakes
made by "born managers" and comes to the
conclusion that there is a better way to manage.
A BETTER WAY TO MANAGE is entertaining
and amusing and is illustrated with wonderfully
appropriate cartoons by Ken Pyne but at the same
time it is practical and informative and should prove
a useful book for all aspiring managers and many
established managers.

0 7474 0098 9   MANAGEMENT   £3.50

FROM THE SUPERSELLING AUTHOR OF THE CRASH OF '79

THE PANIC OF '89

Paul Erdman

It's a world where sleep is wasted time, where digital screens are constantly flashing the latest prices and only the quickest lock into the lucrative main chance with a predatory instinct as deadly as the eagle's eye on a silver dollar. It's the whizz-kid world of international high finance where profit and power are the only principles . . . and with the money market on the brink of a massive collapse, the heat is really on!

The Swiss, the Russians and the Latin Americans are conspiring to bring the United States' economy to its knees. A combination of ruthless financial machination, searing political power-play and suicidal terrorism is threatening to trigger the greatest economic catastrophe the world has ever known. Across the globe the PANIC OF '89 is about to begin . . .

0 7221 3355 3   ADVENTURE THRILLER   £2.99

FROM THE WINNER OF
THE WORLD FANTASY AWARD

THE DAMNATION GAME

CLIVE BARKER

**A CHILLINGLY BRILLIANT NOVEL FROM THE NEW
STEPHEN KING OF HORROR**

'I have seen the future of horror . . . and his name is Clive
Barker'
STEPHEN KING

'I think Clive Barker is so good that I am almost literally
tongue-tied'
STEPHEN KING

'Clive Barker writes about horrors most of us would
scarcely dare imagine'
RAMSEY CAMPBELL

'The most impressive first novel I've read for a long, long
time. Touches of sheer brilliance throughout'
JAMES HERBERT

0 7221 1416 8 HORROR £3.50

**Also by Clive Barker in Sphere Books:
BOOKS OF BLOOD Volumes 1–6**